MW00812158

African
Interiors

PHOTOS BY DEIDI VON SCHAEWEN
TEXT BY FREDERIC COUDERC & LAURENCE DOUGIER

African Interiors

EDITED BY ANGELIKA TASCHEN

TASCHEN

HONG KONG KÖLN LONDON LOS ANGELES MADRID PARIS TOKYO

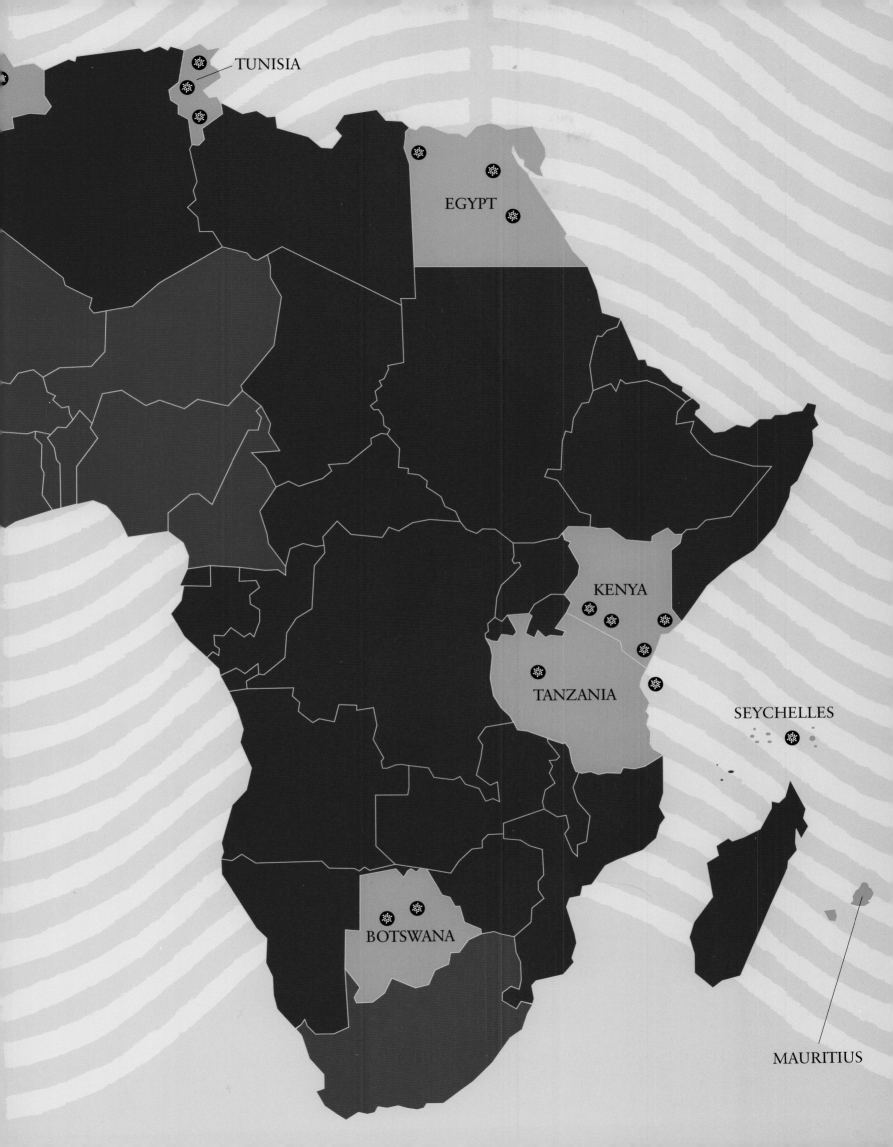

TUNISIA

EGYPT

KENYA

TANZANIA

SEYCHELLES

BOTSWANA

MAURITIUS

MAURITANIA

SENEGAL

IVORY COAST

BURKINA FASO

MALI

NIGER

NIGERIA

BENIN

TOGO

GHANA

CAMEROON

SOUTH AFRICA

Interview with Deidi von Schaewen

by Michèle Champenois, Paris

After four years of travelling across the continent of Africa, four years of discoveries and encounters from north to south and east to west, what is the African landscape or memory that most immediately springs to your mind?

Oddly enough, I think of the very last evening I spent there, in Agadez, Niger. There was a full moon; the night was magical, seeming to sum up all the marvels and surprises of my many trips to the continent. The job was done; I had visited no fewer than 20 countries, to complete a book which had far outstripped our early expectations. There was a party in progress, in the house of the Swiss artist Not Vital. The walls of the broad courtyard were crowned with cattle horns, standing out against the night sky. Our Tuareg friends were busy preparing a heavily-spiced dish to be served on fresh bread straight from an oven dug in the sand, a real desert oven. As they cooked, they sang to the beat of improvised drums.

Whether you're talking about modern houses or traditional methods of construction, the book seems to have two distinct and alternating lines of approach. Each in its way expresses a quest for harmony, for a way to demonstrate hospitality. The memory you have just mentioned expresses that.

Yes, the moment in Agadez was a unique and rare one. Like so many other people I met in the course of my travels, the people there showed apparently inexhaustible reserves of generosity and kindness. In Africa, peoples' houses resemble them: the ones photographed for the book all spring from the traditions and the natural richness of Africa's landscapes, though so many are threatened. In Agadez, looking back, I felt a sudden spurt of admiration for the countless ingenious ways there are of building, which have allowed African men and women to live in such widely different climates and under so many different conditions.

The book would never have come into existence were it not for my passionate desire to travel, to see, and to understand ever more about this source of harmony. The unexpected and impromptu things that happen to you indicate good fortune; they are the traveller's most cherished companions, and I've had my full share of them.

You've travelled in India. On five continents, you've assembled the most extraordinary examples of art brut and landscapes imagined and laid out by builders, many of whom lay no claim to the status of artist. How does Africa fit into this pattern?

This book has been a crazy enterprise – but it's also a link in the chain. I had just finished Indian Interiors for TASCHEN, a book on a civilization and a group of peoples that I know well. In Africa I was able to use that book time and again to show exactly what I was up to with this next project. South Africa, where I had already spent a lot of time preparing my book Fantasy Worlds (also published by TASCHEN), served as my point of departure. By the time I was finished, four and a half years later, I had made over 50 trips by air, in small private planes, helicopters and once even in a military aircraft. I also travelled in buses, boats, on foot, by bush taxi, and on motorbikes. Above all, I rode on the wings of friendship; and I will always be grateful for the way in which friends, old and new, have contributed to the success of my collection of reportages.

Where did you start?

I decided in 1999 to begin the adventure in Cape Town and Johannesburg. In South Africa I knew I could find magnificent modern architecture, observe the life of the townships, and visit the painted houses of the Ndebele, who continue to draw their geometrical frescoes in different shapes and brighter colours than ever before. The whole span of the book was right there in SA – brand new ultra-modern buildings, the painted earth homes of the Ndebele, and the hard struggle in the townships to salvage and use every particle of discarded building material.

Where does contemporary architecture stand in all of this?

There are plenty of fine contemporary buildings throughout Africa; in Morocco you'll see magnificent contemporary interiors, in Mauritius too; also in the hotel sector, in South Africa, in the Ivory Coast and even in Ghana. The more modern and handsome it is, the more it seems to me that recent African architecture looks to be inspired by the age-old rules – whose aim, of course, is secret harmony.

Which was the longest and most complex stage of your journey?

The core of my work awaited me in the heartland of West Africa. In Paris I had obtained nine visas for nine different countries, itself something of a feat; thereafter I flew out to Abidjan to join my friend Pauline, who had been living in Africa for many years. She helped me move through Burkina Faso, Ghana and Togo, visiting the territories of the Lobi, the Kassena and the Tamberma peoples. I learned to sleep on the roofs of houses and to wash with the minimum of water. At night I went to neighbourhood parties and met the women who, at the close of the rainy season, were busy redecorating and painting their homes, contributing in their own way to the fight against ubiquitous concrete building materials. Sometimes I was allowed to enter rooms specially reserved for religious ceremonies, where I was asked not to take any pictures: this side of my travels, unphotographed, was one more way of gaining a more intimate knowledge of these communities. For two months after this, I continued alone through Ghana, Benin, Nigeria, Cameroon and Mali.

You prepare your journeys with infinitely careful research, working with large numbers of contacts. To what extent did you leave room for improvisation, always such a vital ingredient ?

It would take another whole book to describe the frequently chaotic nature of my travels, and the unexpected opportunities that constantly presented themselves to my greedy eyes and ears. For example, at one point I found myself at an astonishing funeral in a village in Ghana, because in a neighbouring town I had happened to notice a carpenter making a coffin in the shape of an elephant. Another time, to get an audience with the king of Abomey, in Benin, I needed the formal introduction of an archaeologist friend in Paris to an orthodox priest, who happened to be a member of the ruling family. The king himself finally received me surrounded by his wives and courtiers, graciously accepting the royal gifts of fruit and live fowls that I brought him.

Were there any other landmark encounters?

Tons. In Nigeria, I at last met with Susanne

Wenger, an Austrian by birth who became a priestess among the Yoruba and has dedicated the last fifty years of her life to the preservation of a sacred grove by the expedient of building temples and altars among the trees. I entered the Yoruba country under full diplomatic and musical protection, in the company of a touring percussion band whose members I had met at the French Cultural Centre in Lome (Togo).

New Year's Day of 2001 found me all alone on a beach in Cameroon, with no festivities whatever in the offing; though before long, travelling in the new millenium, I was invited in Mali by Aminata Traore, an old friend who had become her country's minister of culture. There I sailed down the Niger from Mopti to Timbuktu, with a troop of artists and musicians who had come from other countries to celebrate the culture of Black Africa.

Your predominant theme is the African habitat and the architecture of places where people live. The forms and materials of Africa are used in accordance with widely different codes; they're adapted to their landscapes and molded by tradition. But still uniformity is a growing threat, specifically the uniformity of industrial building products…

Of course all these ways of life are threatened with extinction. Yet a single example will serve to show how modern materials – and even corrugated iron, which is used abundantly throughout the world because it is so practical and cheap – can yield highly interesting shapes and lines. Consider the multiple conical roofs of the chiefs' compounds in the west of Cameroon. The number of roofs expresses the power of the chief; they sparkle and glitter in the landscape, but because they're kept perfectly proportioned, they manage also to reproduce the ancestral outlines governing such constructions. When I crossed Mauritania, I was intrigued by the many and various clever uses made of scrap metal: an example being the tin cabin, as used for shops and storage facilities by the semi-nomadic people who build them. These constructions are of infinite variety, yet they are all basically the by-product of salvaged diesel and oil barrels.

The value of these strange constructions is the value of creativity in its most immediate form, expressed by the use of salvaged materials. *But the greatest sculptural works, the greatest African traditions, seem to be expressed within the landscape by the use of earth and clay as basic materials.*

Indeed. I found myself increasingly fascinated by the purity of earth architecture, and by its perfect adaptation to the environment. Throughout the length and breadth of Africa, I was to observe these qualities time and again, in all their endlessly-renewable formal diversity. In Tunisia there are the cave dwellings in the south and the fortified granaries, or ghorfas, on the edge of the Sahara desert. In Cameroon I paid a visit to the northern region and its *obu cases*. These are made of earth, with reinforced walls that make it possible to clamber right up to their tops to carry out repairs. They are a majestic addition to a landscape that is already breathtaking enough.

In the territory of the Dogon in Mali, I remember the ridge road along which every village was a poignant memorial to a great architectural tradition. There we had three punctures in a single day, and all of them were fixed with makeshift tools by men who materialized out of nowhere – another proof of Africa's unfailing zest for improvisation. Other things awaited me, farther up the mountain; a meeting with a spiritual master, and the sight of a great palaver house with its low ceiling to prevent disputes from degenerating into stand-up violence. In this construction everyone has his turn to express himself before a decision is made. This was a building I knew, having admired it many years earlier; I was happy to find its venerable painter still alive and there to greet me.

Then it was the director of another French institute – this time in Kano, Nigeria – who tactfully guided me into the presence of the local emir and made it possible for me to photograph his palace, a superb building entirely constructed of clay. Alas, money from Saudi Arabia has been flooding in of late, that has permitted the construction nearby of a brand new concrete meeting-house.

The simplicity of earth construction is really admirable, but one of the customs best represented in Africa today is that of painted decoration.

Among the Kassena tribes of Burkina Faso, the old style of red and brown painted décor is still used, only the colours have changed to black and white, now that tar is available in the country. The Ndebele still have their geometrical motifs, only nowadays they include portrayals of scenes and objects from daily life. In Mauritania, a thousand kilometers from Nouakshott on the Road of Hope which cuts straight across the desert, I saw the painted houses of Oualata, whose doors and windows are framed with lime-washed motifs. But above all it was in the Soniké villages on the Senegal River, that I and my friend Mucky Wachter found the most beautiful mural paintings imaginable.

If I'm not mistaken, men aren't the only odd creatures that inhabit the African continent. I'm told there are extraordinary animals too …

When you think of African wildlife, you think of elephants and lions and such. They're really extraordinary, it's true, and not just in photographs! But my strangest experience was on the shores of Lake Naivasha, where I saw a large colony of hippos moving from one lake to another in the night. Their huge shapes glided past our silent group in the semi-darkness, while we goggled at them through infra-red binoculars. Hippos are frightening creatures, not to be treated lightly. I thought of them again in Zanzibar, when I was lucky enough to find myself swimming offshore alongside a school of forty dolphins; I was as free in my movements among them, as they were in their demonstrations of friendship.

You're a passionate lover of Africa. What kind of future would you hope to see there?

We're drawn to Africa and intrigued by it. At the same time we know it to be fragile in the extreme, and we've seen how gravely the patterns and imperatives of the industrial West can threaten the ways of life and the ways of building sanctioned by centuries of African experience. Many of the African interiors shown in this book may vanish forever in the next few years. I have tried to do my best to show the boundless beauty and diversity of African houses and interiors, in the broader hope that a better understanding of the continent's heritage – and particularly of this heritage – will give its cultures the strength to regenerate.

Interview mit Deidi von Schaewen

Das Gespräch führte Michèle Champenois, Paris

Sie sind vier Jahre lang von Süden nach Norden, von Osten nach Westen quer durch Afrika gereist. Welche Landschaft haben Sie vor Augen, woran erinnern Sie sich spontan bei all den Entdeckungen und Begegnungen?

Eigenartigerweise an den letzten Abend in Agades, Niger. Es war Vollmond. Diese magische Nacht schien alle Entdeckungen, Überraschungen und Wunder meiner 15 Reisen in sich vereinigen zu wollen. Und ich habe 20 Länder des afrikanischen Kontinents bereist, um dieses Buch zu realisieren. Wir feierten bei dem Schweizer Künstler Not Vital. Die mit Stierhörnern geschmückten Mauern des weitläufigen Innenhofs zeichneten sich gegen den Himmel ab. Im Hof bereiteten Tuareg-Freunde ein scharfes Gericht zu. Es wird auf Brot serviert, frisch gebacken in einem in den Sand gegrabenen Ofen, einem richtigen „Wüstenofen". Der Gesang der Tuareg erfüllte die Nacht, begleitet von rhythmischem Getrommel auf improvisierten Instrumenten.

Das Buch spielt mit unterschiedlichen Auffassungen, wenn sowohl moderne Häuser als auch Zeugnisse traditioneller Bauweisen vorgestellt werden. Und jede zeugt auf ihre Weise von Harmonie und auch Gastfreundschaft, so wie die Erinnerung, die Sie gerade beschrieben haben.

Ja, es war ein unvergesslicher Moment. Wie bei so vielen Menschen, die mir auf meinen vielen Reisen in der ganzen Welt begegnet sind, begegnete mir in Afrika eine große Herzlichkeit und Gastfreundschaft. Die für dieses Buch fotografierten Häuser spiegeln das wider: Sie schöpfen ihre Schönheit aus dem natürlichen Reichtum der Landschaften dieses Kontinents und aus den Traditionen, von denen aber viele bedroht sind. Das Buch zeigt die unzähligen, überaus erfinderischen Bauweisen, die den Menschen das Leben in diesen extrem unterschiedlichen Klimaverhältnissen erst möglich machen. Ohne meine große Reiselust, ohne den Wunsch, mehr zu sehen und zu lernen, hätte dieses Projekt nicht verwirklicht werden können. Unvorhergesehene Ereignisse und der Zufall waren aber immer wertvolle Reisebegleiter.

Sie haben intensiv Indien bereist, und Sie haben auf allen fünf Kontinenten außergewöhnliche Beispiele der Art brut dokumentiert. Diese Bau- und Kunstwerke der Fantasie wurden nach den Vorstellungen ihrer Schöpfer von Baumeistern errichtet, die sich keineswegs immer als Künstler verstanden. Welche Rolle spielt Afrika in diesem Zusammenhang?

Auch wenn das Buch „Fantasy Worlds" (ebenso bei TASCHEN erschienen), auf das Sie hier anspielen, ein verrücktes Unterfangen war, ist es dennoch ein Glied in einer Kette. Ich hatte bei TASCHEN bereits den Band „Indien Interieurs" veröffentlicht, ein Buch über Kultur und Bevölkerung eines Landes, das ich sehr gut kenne und das mir für das Afrika-Projekt viele Türen geöffnet hat. Während der Arbeit an „Fantasy Worlds" hatte ich bereits einige Zeit in Südafrika verbracht, deshalb wählte ich dieses Land auch als Ausgangspunkt für dieses Buchprojekt. In den über viereinhalb Jahren meiner Reisen bin ich etwa 50 Mal geflogen, auch mit kleinen Maschinen, Helikoptern, sogar in einem Militärflugzeug. Ich habe aber auch Busse und Schiffe benutzt, musste zu Fuß gehen, mich mit Buschtaxis oder Mopeds fortbewegen … Doch mehr als alle Transportmittel hat mich die Freundschaft weitergebracht … die Freunde, alte oder neue, haben unendlich zum Erfolg dieser Reportagen beigetragen.

Wo hat alles begonnen?

Anfang 1999 habe ich mich unter anderem von Kapstadt und Johannesburg aus auf dieses Abenteuer eingelassen. In Südafrika gibt es nicht nur eine großartige moderne Architektur, ich konnte auch das Leben in den Townships und die bemalten Häuser der Ndebele erkunden. Die Künstler dieses Volkes erneuern ständig die überlieferten geometrischen Wandmalereien mit neuen Mustern und lebhafteren, haltbareren Farben. In Südafrika eröffnete sich mir die ganze Bandbreite des Buches: vom hoch modernen Haus über die bemalten Lehmhäuser der Ndebele bis zur „Recycelmanie" in den Townships.

Welche Rolle spielt bei all dem die zeitgenössische Architektur?

Schöne Beispiele finden sich im Norden ebenso wie im Süden: in Marokko, wo die Interieurs sehr modern sind, auch in verschiedenen Hotelbauten auf der Insel Mauritius, in Südafrika, an der Elfenbeinküste und sogar in Ghana.

Je moderner und gelungener die zeitgenössischen Interieurs sind, umso mehr orientieren sie sich an alten Regeln und Traditionen, vielleicht auf der Suche nach einer verborgenen Harmonie.

Welches war der längste und komplexeste Abschnitt der Reise?

Der wichtigste Teil meiner Arbeit wartete im Zentrum Westafrikas. Es war mir gelungen, in Paris Visa für neun Länder zu ergattern, was an sich schon eine ganze Reise war. Anschließend traf ich mich in Abidjan mit meiner Freundin Pauline, die selbst in Afrika lebt. Sie half mir auf der Reise durch Burkina Faso, Ghana und Togo in den Gebieten der Lobi, Kassena und Tamberma, wo wir auf Dächern schliefen und lernten, uns mit möglichst wenig Wasser zu waschen. Wir nahmen an nächtlichen Festen teil, trafen Frauen, die nach der Regenzeit ihre Häuser neu schmücken und bemalen und so auf ihre Weise gegen das Vordringen der Betonbauweise kämpfen. Man gab mir hier und da die Erlaubnis, Räume zu betreten, die sonst nur Zeremonien vorbehalten sind, in denen ich allerdings nicht fotografieren durfte. Dieser undokumentierte Teil meiner Reise verhalf mir zu einem tieferen Verständnis für die Einwohner dieser Gegend. Dann bereiste ich in den darauf folgenden beiden Monaten alleine die Länder Ghana, Benin, Nigeria, Kamerun und Mali.

Sie bereiten Ihre Reisen durch ausgiebige Recherche und zahlreiche Kontakte sehr gründlich vor. Welche Bedeutung hat da noch die Improvisation, die unersetzliche Freiheit des Reisenden?

Es ist nicht möglich, in wenigen Worten die zeitweise chaotischen Reisebedingungen zu beschreiben. Doch dem aufmerksamen Beobachter bieten sich immer wieder Gelegenheiten, Unerwartetes zu entdecken. Wie etwa das feierliche Begräbnis in Ghana, an dem ich teilnehmen konnte, weil ich zufällig bei einem Schreiner der Nachbarstadt einen Sarg in Form eines Elefanten entdeckt hatte. Für die Begegnung mit dem König von Abomey in Benin hingegen bedurfte es der formellen Einführung durch einen befreundeten Pariser Archäologen bei einem orthodoxen Priester, der zur königlichen Familie gehörte. Der Herrscher empfing uns im Kreise seiner Frauen und Höflinge und akzeptierte gnädig unser Geschenk, arrangiert aus Früchten und piepsendem Geflügel.

Gab es weitere herausragende Begegnungen?

Ja, sicher. In Nigeria traf ich endlich die gebürtige Österreicherin Susanne Wenger, was schon seit langem mein Wunsch war. Sie wurde dort Priesterin der

Yoruba und widmet sich seit 50 Jahren der Rettung des heiligen Hains, indem sie dort Tempel und Altäre baut. Ich war im Schutz von Diplomatie und Musik nach Nigeria eingereist, zusammen mit einem Orchester tourender Percussionisten, die ich im französischen Kulturzentrum von Lomé in Togo getroffen hatte.

Dann begrüßte ich das Jahr 2001, fern aller Festivitäten, alleine an einem Strand in Kamerun. Unterwegs im neuen Jahrtausend wurde ich in Mali von meiner langjährigen Freundin Aminata Traoré, der ehemaligen Ministerin für Kultur, eingeladen, mit einem Schiff den Niger von Mopti nach Timbuktu hinunterzufahren, und zwar in Begleitung von Künstlern und Musikern aus verschiedenen Ländern, die ihre schwarzafrikanische Kultur feierten.

Ihr Hauptthema ist das Wohnen, die Architektur von Lebensräumen. In Afrika folgt der Umgang mit Formen und Materialien unterschiedlichen Gesetzmäßigkeiten, er passt sich der Umgebung an und ist durch Traditionen geprägt. Und doch lässt sich eine Uniformität nicht aufhalten, insbesondere durch den Rückgriff auf industrielle Produkte.

All diese Lebensformen drohten in der Tat zu verschwinden. Jedoch auch neuere Materialien, ja sogar Blech, das auf allen fünf Kontinenten sehr oft verwendet wird, weil es praktisch und preisgünstig ist, kann zu interessanten Formen inspirieren. Ich habe es im Westen Kameruns gesehen, als ich die vielen konischen Dächer der Chefferien (die Macht des Chefs ist an der Zahl der Dächer abzulesen) fotografiert habe. Das glänzende Wellblech leuchtet in der Landschaft, es ist gut proportioniert und wahrt die traditionelle Form dieser Bauwerke. Ein anderer Gebrauch von Metall hat mich auf der Durchreise durch Mauretanien sehr beeindruckt: Die Blechhütten, die die halbnomadischen Völker in praller Sonne errichtet haben und die entweder als Läden oder als Vorratshütten dienen. Diese Ansammlungen von wieder verwertbarem Material sind äußerst erfindungsreich, abhängig von den zufälligen Funden der Diesel- oder Benzinkanister.

Die Bedeutung dieser ungewöhnlichen Konstruktionen liegt ohne Zweifel in der spontanen Kreativität bei der Verwendung von Recyclingmaterial. Aber nehmen die großen skulpturalen Werke, die großen Traditionen nicht eher in Form von Lehm und Ton Gestalt an?

Ja, das ist wahr. Besonders fasziniert mich immer wieder die Architektur aus Lehm, die sich auf so bemerkenswerte Weise an ihre Umgebung anpasst. Ihre perfekten Proportionen, ihre eleganten, klaren Linien findet man in vielerlei Variationen auf dem gesamten Kontinent. Im Süden Tunesiens sind es die Höhlenwohnungen und die *ghorfas* (befestigte Speicher) am Rande der Sahara. Im Norden Kameruns besuchte ich die Gegend der *obu*-Hütten. Sie sind aus Lehm gebaut, die Wände durch Rippen verstärkt, damit man bei nötigen Reparaturen bis zur Spitze hochsteigen kann. Sie fügen sich auf majestätische Weise in die an sich bereits erstaunliche Landschaft.

Ich erinnere mich an einen Weg auf dem Bergkamm in Mali, im Land der Dogon, wo jedes Dorf wie ein lebendes Monument wirkt, wie ein eindringliches architektonisches Zeugnis. Nur am Rande erwähnt: Damals gaben an einem einzigen Tag drei Autoreifen den Geist auf. Und jedes Mal wurden sie sofort und fast ohne Werkzeug von Männern repariert, die aus dem Nichts aufgetaucht waren – ein weiterer Beweis für die unerschöpfliche Kreativität der Menschen dieses Kontinents. Andere bewegende Ereignisse standen mir noch bevor. So die Begegnung mit einem Hohepriester hoch oben auf den Klippen und der erneute Besuch einer Palaverstätte mit ihrem Versammlungsraum, dessen niedrig angelegte Decke jeden Streit im Keim ersticken soll und wo Entscheidungen erst dann gefällt werden, wenn alle Anwesenden einmal zu Wort gekommen sind. Ich hatte diesen Ort bereits vor Jahren bewundert und freute mich sehr, auch den alten Maler dort wiederzutreffen, dessen Werke die Außenwände schmücken.

Der tatkräftigen Unterstützung des Direktors einer anderen französischen Institution in Kano im Norden Nigerias habe ich es zu verdanken, dass ich bereits nach einer knappen Woche Kontakt zum ortsansässigen Emir herstellen konnte. Dieser erlaubte mir, seinen Palast zu fotografieren, ein einmalig schönes Bauwerk aus Lehm, ebenso eindrucksvoll wie bedroht. Mit saudiarabischen Fonds wurde schon in unmittelbarer Nähe ein Versammlungssaal gebaut ... aus Beton.

Die Schlichtheit der Lehmbauten ist zweifelsohne bewundernswert, doch einer der verbreitetsten Bräuche in Afrika ist die farbige Wandbemalung.

Bei den Stämmen der Kassena in Burkina Faso wurden die Wände ursprünglich rot-braun bemalt.

Diese Tradition wird seit der Einführung von Teer mit schwarzen Mustern auf weißen Wänden fortgesetzt. Bei den Ndebele findet man bunte geometrische Motive wie eh und je, in die sie heute jedoch alltägliche Szenen und Objekte integrieren. In Mauretanien fuhr ich, 1000 Kilometer von Nouakchott entfernt, auf der „Straße der Hoffnung" durch bis nach Oualata, um die berühmten bemalten Häuser zu sehen, deren Türen und Fenster von Ornamenten aus einer Mischung aus Sand und Kalk eingerahmt sind. Doch die schönsten Wandmalereien, die ich je gesehen habe, entdeckte ich mit meiner Freundin Mucky Wachter in den Dörfern der Soninke im Gebiet des Flusses Senegal.

Soweit ich weiß, leben auf dem afrikanischen Kontinent nicht nur Menschen. Man sagt, dass auch die Tiere außergewöhnlich sind ...

Bei den Tieren Afrikas denkt man sofort an Elefanten, Löwen, Nashörner. Sie sind wirklich außergewöhnlich und in der Natur viel beeindruckender als auf einem Foto. Mein unvergesslichstes Erlebnis aber hatte ich am Ufer des Sees Naivasha in Kenia, wo eine große Population von Flusspferden jeden Tag von einem See zum anderen wandert. Bei Einbruch der Dunkelheit zogen diese Tiere mit ihren unheimlichen Körpermassen an unserer kleinen Gruppe vorbei. Wir verhielten uns absolut ruhig, ausgestattet mit Nachtsichtgeräten, denn Flusspferde gehören zu den gefährlichsten Tieren überhaupt. An dieses Erlebnis musste ich auch denken, als ich auf hoher See vor Sansibar das unglaubliche Glück hatte, frei und unbeschwert in einer Gruppe von 40 freundlich gesonnenen Delfinen zu schwimmen.

Sie haben eine große Leidenschaft für Afrika. Was wünschen Sie diesem Kontinent?

Afrika ist ohne Zweifel gleichermaßen anziehend wie beunruhigend, unter anderem, weil es so verletzlich ist. Wir wissen nur zu gut, dass die Modelle des industriellen Westens, mit den aus ihnen resultierenden Zwängen, die über Jahrhunderte erprobten Lebens- und Bauweisen Afrikas bedrohen. Viele der in diesen beiden Bänden enthüllten Intérieurs könnten im Laufe der nächsten Jahre verschwinden. Ich wollte in dieser Publikation die umwerfende Schönheit des schwarzen Kontinents in all seiner Vielfalt zeigen – nicht zuletzt in der Hoffnung, dass eine bessere Kenntnis dieses Kulturerbes hilft, es zu bewahren.

Entretien avec Deidi von Schaewen

Propos recueillis par Michèle Champenois, Paris

Au terme de ces quatre années de voyages à travers le continent africain, de découvertes et de rencontres, du sud au nord et d'est en ouest, quel paysage, quel souvenir vous vient immédiatement à l'esprit?

Curieusement, c'est le dernier soir passé en Afrique, à Agadez, au Niger. Une nuit de pleine lune, magique comme si elle devait résumer les merveilles et les surprises des 15 reportages entrepris dans 20 pays différents pour réaliser ce livre qui a dépassé les espérances initiales. C'est un soir de fête, chez l'artiste suisse Not Vital. Dans la cour immense dont les hauts murs surmontés de cornes de bovins se découpent sur le ciel sombre, ses amis touareg préparent un plat très épicé qui sera servi sur les pains sortis d'un four creusé à même le sable, véritable fourneau du désert. Des rythmes frappés sur des instruments improvisés accompagnent un chant qui monte dans la nuit.

Maisons modernes ou témoignages de traditions constructives, votre ouvrage fait alterner deux approches. On devine qu'elles répondent, de manière différente, à une recherche d'harmonie, à une manière d'exprimer l'hospitalité, comme le souvenir que vous évoquez.

Oui, c'est un moment singulier, à l'image des rencontres faites au long de ces voyages et des ressources inépuisables de l'hospitalité et de la gentillesse des habitants. Les maisons photographiées pour ce livre puisent leur beauté dans la richesse naturelle des paysages du continent et dans les traditions dont beaucoup sont menacées. Ce livre se veut un hommage aux mille manières de construire, tellement inventives, qui ont permis aux hommes de vivre sous tous les climats. Il n'existerait pas sans la passion que suscite un tel voyage, le désir d'en voir et d'en savoir plus. Solutions imprévues, départs impromptus, la chance est toujours le bagage essentiel du voyageur.

Vous avez parcouru l'Inde, mais aussi rassemblé sur les cinq continents des exemples extraordinaires d'art brut, de paysages construits sous la dictée de leur imaginaire par des bâtisseurs qui n'ont pas toujours le titre d'artistes. Comment se situe l'Afrique sur ce parcours?

Si ce livre est une entreprise un peu folle, il est aussi un maillon. J'avais terminé les «Intérieurs de l'Inde» (publié par TASCHEN), une civilisation et des peuples que je connais bien, et le livre sur l'Inde a souvent été mon ambassadeur pour expliquer le projet. L'Afrique du Sud, où j'avais déjà passé beaucoup de temps pour préparer «Fantasy Worlds» (TASCHEN), m'a servi de point de départ. En quatre ans et demi, j'ai pris l'avion une cinquantaine de fois, des petits coucous, des hélicoptères et même un avion militaire, mais je me suis aussi déplacée en bus, en bateau, à pied, en taxi-brousse, en mobylette. Et surtout sur les ailes de l'amitié... Je ne dirai jamais assez à quel point les amis, anciens ou nouveaux, ont contribué à la réussite de ces reportages.

Par où commencer?

J'ai choisi, dès 1999, Cape Town, Johannesburg et l'Afrique du Sud pour engager cette aventure, un pays où je pouvais trouver de magnifiques architectures modernes, autant qu'observer la vie des townships et m'approcher des maisons peintes des Ndebele qui continuent à tracer leurs fresques géométriques en renouvelant les trames et les couleurs, désormais beaucoup plus vives. Déjà, tout le thème du livre était là: de la maison la plus moderne aux maisons de terre peintes des Ndebele, jusqu'à la frénésie de récupération dans les bidonvilles.

Quelle est la place de l'architecture contemporaine?

On en trouve de beaux exemples, du Nord au Sud: au Maroc avec des intérieurs très contemporains, à l'Île Maurice, dans l'hôtellerie, en Afrique du Sud, en Côte-d'Ivoire et même au Ghana. Plus elles sont modernes et réussies, plus les créations récentes s'inspirent de règles anciennes, à la recherche d'une harmonie secrète.

Quel a été votre périple le plus long, le plus complexe?

Il me fallait aborder le vif du sujet, le centre de l'Afrique occidentale. Ayant décroché neuf visas pour neuf pays à Paris, une sorte d'épopée en soi, j'ai rejoint à Abidjan Pauline, une amie installée en Afrique et qui allait m'aider à parcourir, au Burkina Faso, au Ghana et au Togo, les territoires des Lobis, des Kassenas et des Tambermas. Cela signifiait dormir sur le toit des maisons, apprendre à se laver avec très peu d'eau, assister à des fêtes nocturnes, rencontrer ces femmes qui, après la saison des pluies, redécorent et peignent leurs maisons et luttent ainsi à leur manière contre l'avancée universelle du parpaing de béton. Être admise, parfois, dans des pièces réservées aux cérémonies où l'on me demandait de ne pas faire de photos. Ce périple, entre deux prises de vues, était aussi une manière d'avancer dans la connaissance intime de ces communautés. Pendant deux mois, j'ai continué, seule, vers le Ghana, le Bénin, le Nigeria, le Cameroun, et le Mali.

Vous préparez vos déplacements par un travail intense de documentation et de nombreux contacts. Quelle est la part de l'improvisation, cette irremplaçable liberté du voyageur?

Impossible de détailler en quelques lignes les conditions parfois chaotiques des déplacements. Mais, bien sûr, si on prête l'oreille, les occasions inattendues de découvrir autre chose sont fréquentes. Je me souviens de ces funérailles solennelles, dans un village du Ghana, auxquelles j'ai pu assister parce que, chez le menuisier de la ville voisine, la préparation d'un cercueil en forme d'éléphant m'avait intriguée et que j'avais interrogé l'artisan.

En revanche, pour rencontrer le roi d'Abomey, au Benin, il m'a fallu une introduction officielle, celle qu'un ami archéologue parisien m'avait proposée, auprès d'un prêtre orthodoxe, membre de la famille régnante. Le roi, entouré de ses femmes et de sa cour, nous a reçus et a accepté les fruits et les volailles piaillantes que nous lui apportions.

D'autres rencontres marquantes?

Bien sûr. Au Nigeria, j'ai pu enfin rencontrer Susanne Wenger. Cette Autrichienne, devenue prêtresse chez les Yoruba, consacre sa vie, depuis 50 ans, au sauvetage de la forêt sacrée en y bâtissant des temples et des autels. Une autre fois, c'est en compagnie d'un orchestre de percussionnistes en tournée, rencontrés au centre culturel français de Lomé, au Togo, que je suis entrée dans le pays, sous protection diplomatique... et musicale.

Seule sur une plage du Cameroun, j'ai franchi, loin de toutes festivités, le passage à l'an 2001. En route vers un nouveau millénaire, j'ai aussi été invitée au Mali par Aminata Traoré, une amie de longue date

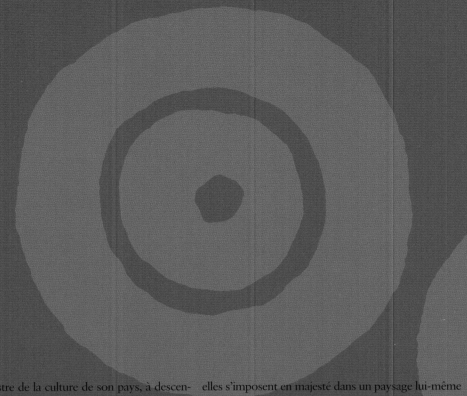

devenue ministre de la culture de son pays, à descendre le fleuve Niger de Mopti à Tombouctou, avec des artistes et des musiciens venus de plusieurs pays célébrer les cultures de l'Afrique noire.

Votre thème central, c'est l'habitat, l'architecture des lieux de vie. Les formes, les matériaux sont travaillés selon des codes très variés, adaptés aux paysages et forgés par les traditions. Mais l'uniformisation guette, notamment à cause du recours à des produits industriels …

Evidemment, tous ces modes de vie sont menacés… de disparition. Pourtant, même un matériau récent, comme la tôle, utilisée couramment sur les cinq continents parce qu'elle est pratique et peu coûteuse, peut se prêter à des lignes intéressantes. Je l'ai vu, dans l'ouest du Cameroun, où j'ai photographié des chefferies avec leurs toits coniques multiples (la puissance du chef est fonction de leur nombre), auxquels la tôle confère une brillance remarquable dans le paysage mais qui, parce qu'ils restent bien proportionnés, respectent les silhouettes ancestrales de ces constructions.

En traversant la Mauritanie, j'ai été aussi vivement intéressée par l'usage qui y est fait du métal: des cabanes en tôle, dressées en plein soleil, servent soit de boutiques soit d'entrepôts à des populations seminomades. Ces assemblages de récupération sont des plus inventifs, au hasard des trouvailles de barils de gasoil ou de pétrole.

Ce qui fait la valeur de ces étrangetés, c'est sans doute la créativité dans son expression la plus immédiate, à partir des matériaux de récupération. Mais les grandes œuvres sculpturales, les grandes traditions, c'est plutôt en terre qu'elles prennent forme dans le paysage.

Oui, l'architecture en terre me fascine pour sa pureté, son équilibre et son adaptation remarquable à l'environnement. J'ai eu souvent l'occasion, du nord au sud du continent, de vérifier ces qualités, toujours renouvelées dans leur diversité. En Tunisie, ce sont les maisons troglodytes, dans le sud, et les *ghorfas*, ces greniers fortifiés, aux portes du Sahara. Au Cameroun, j'ai arpenté, au nord, la région des cases-obus. Façonnées en terre, dotées de parois renforcées qui permettent d'accéder au sommet pour les réparations,

elles s'imposent en majesté dans un paysage lui-même étonnant.

Au Mali, dans le pays Dogon, je me souviens de ce chemin de crête, où chaque village est un monument vivant, un témoignage poignant d'architecture. Juste pour l'anecdote, trois pneus crevés dans la même journée, ont été réparés sur place sans outillage par des hommes apparus de nulle part, nouvelle preuve d'inventivité sans limite … Mais j'ai aussi connu d'autres émotions dans cette région: la rencontre d'un grand féticheur, sur la falaise; et les retrouvailles avec une maison de palabre, cette grande structure basse de plafond pour décourager toute dispute où l'on discute chaque décision en donnant la parole à chacun. Je l'avais admirée il y a des années. Le vieux peintre que j'avais vu était toujours là lui aussi …

Au nord du Nigeria, avec l'aide du directeur de l'institut français de Kano, j'ai pu entrer en contact, au bout d'une petite semaine, avec l'émir du lieu afin que celui-ci m'autorise à photographier son palais, un superbe édifice en terre, aussi remarquable que menacé. C'est que déjà, hélas, des fonds provenant d'Arabie saoudite ont servi à financer la construction, toute proche, d'une salle de réunion … toute en béton.

La simplicité de la terre est admirable, certainement, mais l'une des coutumes les mieux représentées en Afrique est le décor peint.

Dans les tribus Kassenas, au Burkina Faso, les anciennes peintures rouge et brun se perpétuent, mais en noir et blanc, avec l'arrivée du goudron. Chez les Ndebele, on trouve toujours des motifs à base géométrique dans lesquels ils insèrent aujourd'hui des scènes ou des objets de la vie quotidienne. En Mauritanie, à 1000 kilomètres de Nouakchott, sur la «route de l'Espoir», qui part tout droit à travers le désert, je suis allée sans hésiter jusqu'aux maisons peintes de Oualata, où les portes et les fenêtres sont bordées de motifs à la chaux. Mais c'est surtout dans les villages Soninke, dans la région du fleuve Sénégal, que nous avons trouvé, avec mon amie Mucky Wachter, les peintures murales les plus belles que j'aie jamais vues.

Si j'ai bien compris, les hommes ne sont pas seuls à habiter le continent africain. On dit qu'il y a des animaux extraordinaires …

Quand on pense aux animaux d'Afrique, on songe tout de suite aux éléphants, aux lions, aux rhinocéros. Ils sont extraordinaires, c'est vrai, et beaucoup plus qu'en photo! Quant à moi, j'ai vécu le moment le plus inouï au bord du lac Naivasha, où une importante colonie d'hippopotames se déplace chaque jour d'un plan d'eau à l'autre. À la tombée de la nuit, les bêtes ont frôlé de leur masse inquiétante notre petit groupe d'individus silencieux et armés de jumelles à infrarouges. Pas question d'approcher ces animaux parmi les plus redoutables. J'y ai repensé plus tard, lorsqu'au large de Zanzibar, j'ai eu la chance de nager au milieu d'une quarantaine de dauphins, libre de mes mouvements comme eux de leurs démonstrations d'affection.

On comprend que vous êtes une amie passionnée de l'Afrique. Que lui souhaitez-vous?

Si l'Afrique attire et intrigue à juste titre, c'est aussi parce qu'elle est fragile. Nous savons combien les modèles et les impératifs de l'Occident industriel menacent les modes de vie et les manières de bâtir consacrés par des siècles d'expérience. Beaucoup des intérieurs d'Afrique dévoilés dans cet ouvrage risquent de disparaître dans les prochaines années. Ce livre vise à faire découvrir l'immense beauté du continent noir dans sa diversité. En espérant qu'une meilleure connaissance du patrimoine aidera ces cultures à se perpétuer.

Dar Moulay Boubker

Carla & Franca Sozzani

Dar Badi

MOROCCO

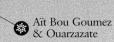

Dar El Hanna

Aït Bou Goumez
& Ouarzazate

CARLA & FRANCA SOZZANI

MARRAKESH

The Casa Sozzani, decorated by an American artist,
offers a new brand of orientalism in the heart of the medina.

A 12th century mosque with Spanish-Moorish minaret marks the entrance to Marrakesh's medina. Here, in the maze of alleys and *souks*, a pair of Italian sisters have made their home. Carla Sozzani is the founder of the Corso Como boutique in Milan, and her sister Franca is a top editor with Condé Nast Italy.

Drawing on the combined experience of their two careers, they have transformed two Marrakesh *riyads*, turning old ruined patios into pools and gardens filled with banana trees. It took three years of dedicated restoration work, with Kris Ruh, an American artist who lives between Marrakesh and Italy, putting together the various elements of the décor. From the door and window frames, whose columns are entwined with metal foliage, to the curtain rods, radiator grilles and wrought iron bed heads, right through to the metal tube chandeliers picked up at the city dump, every element was something for Ruh to use creatively and differently. The spaces are extraordinary, as are the fabrics and the colours. You're about to be overwhelmed completely when someone quietly takes you by the hand. There's mint tea waiting on the terrace, which is one of the highest in the medina. You can see as far as the Atlas mountains from here. "This isn't quite reality," murmurs Franca Sozzani. But *chi lo sa?*

Hinter der Moschee aus dem 12. Jahrhundert beginnt das Labyrinth der Gassen, in dem sich zwei italienische Schwestern niedergelassen haben. Während Carla Sozzani eine Galerie am Corso Como in Mailand betreibt, betreut ihre Schwester Franca im Verlag Condé Nast verschiedene Magazine.

Im Bewusstsein ihrer langjährigen Berufserfahrungen schufen sie innerhalb von drei Jahren aus zwei miteinander verbundenen *riyads* ein neues Anwesen. Intensive Restaurationsarbeiten waren vonnöten; so wurde ein Patio in einen Pool und der andere in einen Garten voller Bananenstauden verwandelt. Kris Ruh, ein amerikanischer Künstler, der zwischen Italien und Marrakesch pendelt, übernahm die Ausstattung. Ziel seiner Kreativität waren ebenso die Tür- und Fensterrahmen wie die verkleideten Heizkörper, Gardinenstangen und das Kopfteil eines Bettes mit schmiedeeisernen Schlangen. Der Künstler verwandelte das Gebäude in all seinen Bestandteilen, sodass sich der Betrachter heute nicht satt sehen kann am allgegenwärtigen Farbenspiel, an der Vielfalt der Einrichtungsgegenstände, der Stoffe und Gewebe. Doch schon bald werden wir weitergeführt, denn auf der Terrasse – einer der höchst gelegenen in der ganzen Stadt – erwartet uns bereits der Pfefferminztee. Von hier aus kann man sogar das Atlasgebirge erkennen. »Zu schön, um wahr zu sein«, bekräftigt Franca Sozzani.

La mosquée du 12e siècle et son minaret hispano-mauresque signalent l'entrée du labyrinthe. Ici, dans l'écheveau des ruelles et le lacis des souks, deux sœurs italiennes ont établi leur résidence. Carla Sozzani est la fondatrice de la boutique Corso Como à Milan, sa sœur Franca cumule les responsabilités éditoriales chez Condé Nast Italie.

Déroulant le fil des mérites glanés au cours de leur carrière, elles ont transfiguré deux riyads en trois années de restauration. Les patios sont devenus piscine et jardins agrémentés de bananiers. Kris Ruh, artiste américain partagé entre Marrakech et l'Italie, a conçu les éléments du décor. Des encadrements de portes et fenêtres aux colonnes habillées de feuillage en métal, des tringles à rideaux, cache radiateur ou tête de lit à serpent en fer forgé, aux lustres en tubes de métal dénichés à la décharge de la ville, tout élément fut, pour l'artiste, matière à détournement et création. Volumes des pièces, jeu de couleurs, étoffes en pagaille, l'œil ne sait plus où s'attarder. Mais vite, on vous prend par la main. Le thé à la menthe est servi sur la terrasse, l'une des plus élevées de la médina. Le regard porte jusqu'à l'Atlas. «Ce n'est pas la réalité», admet Franca Sozzani. Mais, *Chi lo sa?*

✳ **ABOVE** In the dining room, a sari serves as a tablecloth and a painted tree flickers with candles. **FACING PAGE** The salon on the second floor, with its wrought iron chandelier and, at the centre of the room, a black ottoman. ✳ **OBEN** Ein Sari dient Carla und Franca Sozzani in ihrem Speisezimmer als Tischtuch. Mildes Kerzenlicht beleuchtet das Wandbild eines Baumes. **RECHTS** Der Salon im zweiten Stock mit dem schmiedeeisernen Lüster und der schwarzen Ottomane in der Mitte. ✳ **CI-DESSUS** Dans la salle à manger, un sari tient lieu de nappe. Face aux convives, un arbre peint scintille à la lueur des bougies. **PAGE DE DROITE** Le salon du deuxième étage avec son lustre en fer forgé et l'ottomane noire au milieu de la pièce.

✳ **FACING PAGE** The entrance to Franca's bedroom, with carpets. **ABOVE** Star chandeliers from the souks of Marrakesh combine with the yellowed glass of the windows to flood this bathroom in golden light. **FOLLOWING PAGES** Meals are prepared under the starlit kitchen ceiling and served by staff wearing traditional clothes. ✳ **LINKS** Der mit Teppichen verzierte Eingang zu Francas Zimmer. **OBEN** Die Lichter der Souks von Marrakesch fallen durch die gelb getönten Scheiben und tauchen das Bad in goldenen Glanz. **FOLGENDE DOPPELSEITE** Das traditionell gekleidete Personal serviert die Mahlzeiten, die in der mit Sternenlampen geschmückten Küche zubereitet werden. ✳ **PAGE DE GAUCHE** Entrée de la chambre de Franca bordée de tapis. **CI-DESSUS** Les étoiles des souks de Marrakech et les verres jaunis des fenêtres distillent une lumière dorée dans cette salle de bains. **DOUBLE PAGE SUIVANTE** Préparés sous le ciel étoilé de la cuisine, les plats sont servis par un personnel en habit traditionnel.

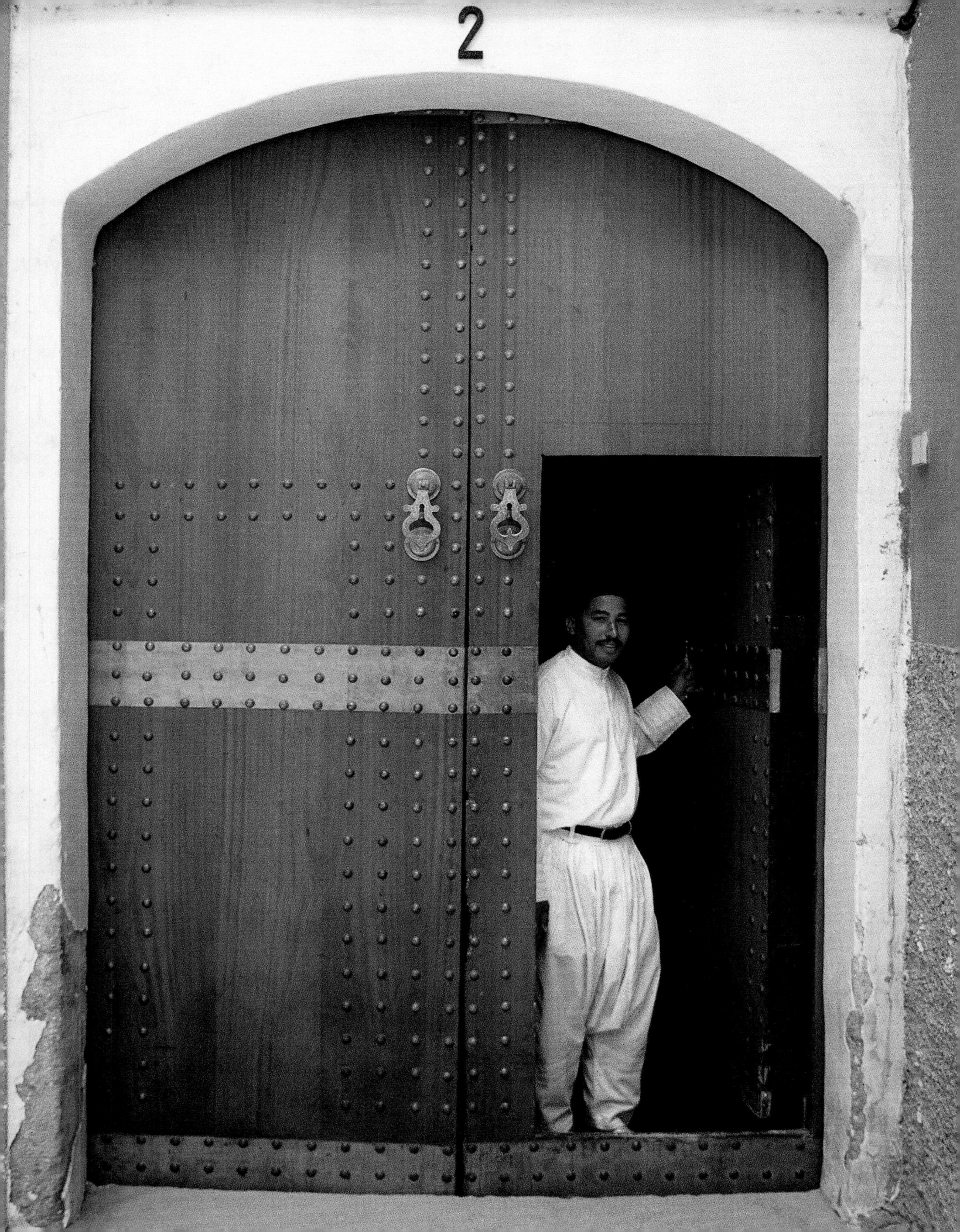
2

Dar MOULAY BOUBKER MARRAKESH

The restoration of this Moroccan palace expresses one man's passion for a magical city.

There may be a hidden meaning to the swimming pool, at the bottom of which the Greek god Hermes, guide to travellers, contemplates the tree of life.

Xavier Guerrand-Hermès, fit descendant of a family that has always loved Marrakesh, has restored a palace here that is typical of the stately buildings of 17th century Morocco. In the old days, Dar Moulay Boubker – the name of the palace – formed a complex of harem, patio, reception rooms on the ground floor and private apartments on the first floor. It is hard to imagine that only recently the floors here were still of beaten earth, and the beams and plasterwork in the last stages of decay. Authenticity applies, as in seats encrusted with mother-of-pearl, furniture from Baghdad, and a noble Persian tapestry shot with gold thread. A final detail: the palace is very close to the Sidi-Bel-Abbès mosque. Not by chance, perhaps, since Xavier Guerrand-Hermès is an acknowledged specialist in comparative religion. *Mektoub*, it is written, as they say in Arabic.

Koketterie oder sanfter Spott? Am Grund des Swimmingpools beherrscht der griechische Gott Hermes, der Begleiter der Wanderer und Reisenden, einen Baum des Lebens.

Was Xavier Guerrand-Hermès mit diesem Bild auch im Sinn gehabt haben mag – als treuer Nachfahre einer Familie, die der Stadt Marrakesch seit langem verbunden ist, ließ er einen Palast restaurieren, der die marokkanischen Herrschaftsresidenzen des 17. Jahrhunderts beispielhaft repräsentiert. Zuvor bestand der Palast Dar Moulay Boubker aus einem Harem, einem Patio, Empfangsräumen im Parterre und Privatgemächern auf der ersten Etage. Man kann sich kaum vorstellen, dass diese Böden noch bis vor kurzem aus gestampftem Lehm bestanden und störendes Gebälk oder Stuck in diesen Räumen zu verfallen drohten. Die Einrichtung ist hingegen authentisch, wie die syrischen Stühle mit ihren Perlmuttintarsien, die Möbel aus Bagdad und der mit Goldfäden gearbeitete persische Wandteppich aus dem 17. Jahrhundert. Ein letztes Detail: Der Palast liegt in unmittelbarer Nähe der Sidi-Bel-Abbès-Moschee. Reiner Zufall? Xavier Guerrand-Hermès ist ein anerkannter Experte auf dem Gebiet der Vergleichenden Religionswissenschaft. *Mektoub*, sagt man auf Arabisch: »So steht es geschrieben«.

Coquetterie ou sens de la dérision? C'est au fond de la piscine que le dieu grec Hermès, guide des voyageurs, domine un arbre de vie.

N'importe ce sens caché, c'est en fidèle descendant d'une famille attachée à Marrakech depuis longtemps que Xavier Guerrand-Hermès a restauré un palais typique des nobles bâtiments marocains du 17e siècle. Autrefois, Dar Moulay Boubker, c'est le nom du palais, formait un ensemble partagé entre le harem, le patio, les pièces de réception au rez-de-chaussée et les appartements privés à l'étage. Difficile d'imaginer que les sols étaient récemment encore en terre battue; impossible d'envisager que les poutres, ou les plâtres, agonisaient ici. L'authenticité s'applique encore au mobilier avec ces chaises syriennes incrustées de nacre, ces meubles de Bagdad, ou encore cette tapisserie perse du 17e siècle, cousue de fils d'or. Dernier détail: le palais est situé tout près de la mosquée Sidi-Bel-Abbès. Hasard des destinées? Xavier Guerrand-Hermès est un spécialiste reconnu de l'histoire comparée des religions. *Mektoub*, c'était écrit, dit-on en arabe.

❋ **FACING PAGE AND ABOVE** A low table with a mosaic top and marble armchairs from India match the nobility of the 17th century patio. ❋ **LINKE SEITE UND OBEN** Dieser niedrige Tisch mit der Mosaikplatte sowie die indischen Marmorsessel tragen zur edlen Wirkung des Patios aus dem 17. Jahrhundert bei. ❋ **PAGE DE GAUCHE ET CI-DESSUS** Table basse au plateau en mosaïque et fauteuils indiens en marbre s'accordent à la noblesse du patio du 17ᵉ siècle.

✳ **FACING PAGE** The first floor salon opens on the swimming pool, through the door to the left. A panorama by Dufour lit by 19th century Moroccan lanterns. **ABOVE** Syrian mother-of-pearl encrusted furniture is a feature throughout the house. On the commode with its Bedouin clock, Moroccan jewelry. ✳ **LINKE SEITE** Die rechte Tür im Salon auf der ersten Etage führt zum Swimmingpool. Marokkanische Lampen aus dem 19. Jahrhundert beleuchten eine Panorama-tapete von Dufour. **OBEN** Exemplare dieses mit Perlmuttintarsien verzierten syrischen Mobiliars sind über das ganze Gebäude verteilt. Auf der Kommode eine beduinische Standuhr und marokkanischer Schmuck. ✳ **PAGE DE GAUCHE** Le salon de l'étage s'ouvre sur la piscine par la porte de droite. Un papier panora-mique de Dufour est éclairci par des lanternes marocaines du 19ᵉ siècle. **CI-DESSUS** Le mobilier syrien incrusté de nacre est une constante dans la maison. Sur la commode dotée d'une horloge à la bédouine, des bijoux marocains.

✣ **ABOVE** The work of Marrakesh artisans – *zelliges* on the walls and floors, painted and carved wood – is stunningly beautiful. **PAGES 88–95** Abdelghani Benkirane, a specialist in restoration, oversaw the work for three years. ✣ **OBEN** Die Handwerksarbeiten von Marrakesch – *zelliges* an Wänden und Böden, Holzmalerei und -schnitzerei – sind überwältigend in ihrer Pracht. **SEITE 88–95** Abdelghani Benkirane, ein Restaurationsexperte, überwachte drei Jahre lang die Arbeiten. ✣ **CI-DESSUS** Le travail des artisans de Marrakech – *zelliges* qui habillent murs ou sols, bois peints ou sculptés –, est étourdissant de beauté. **PAGES 88–95** Un spécialiste de la restauration, Abdelghani Benkirane, a veillé pendant trois années aux travaux.

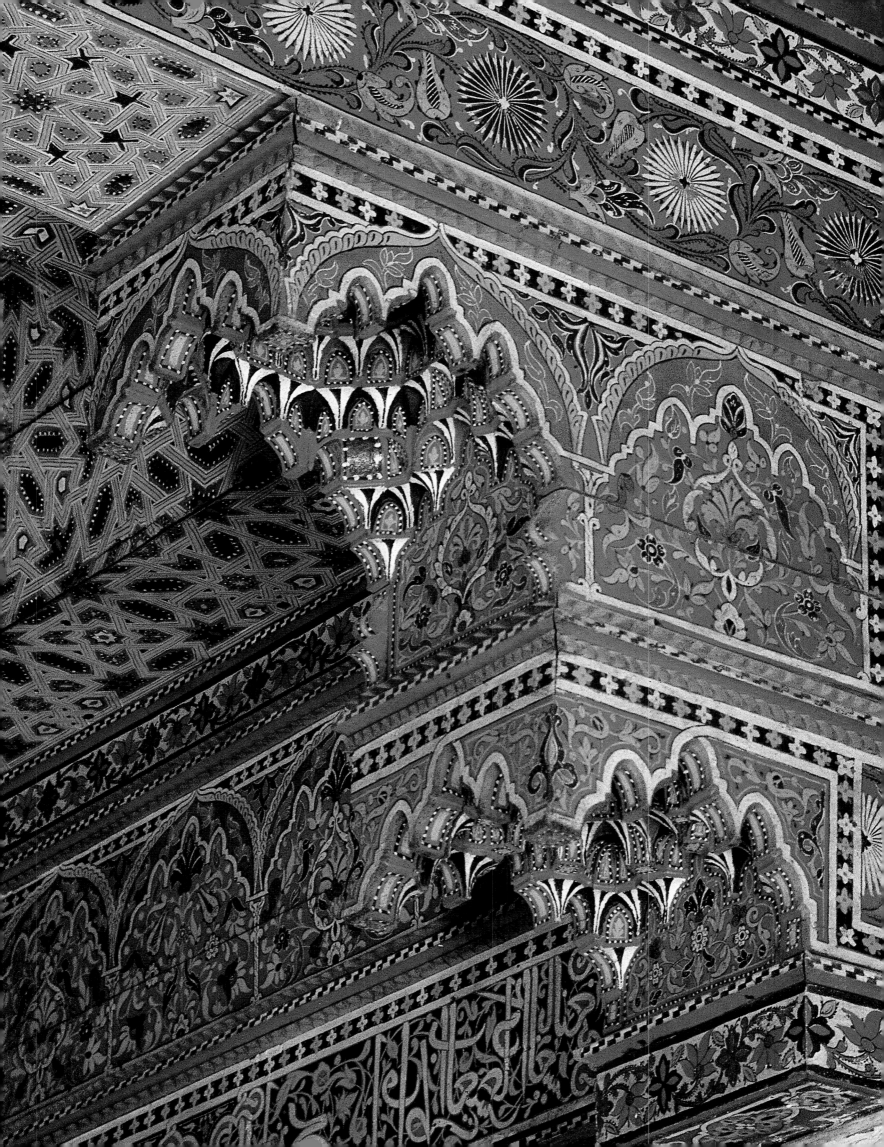

※ **ABOVE** The terrace surrounding the patio offers a superb view of the medina and minaret of the Sidi-Bel-Abbès mosque. And – luxury of luxuries – the tower has an elevator. ※ **OBEN** Die Terrasse, die den Patio einfasst, bietet eine herrliche Aussicht auf die Medina und das Minarett der Sidi-Bel-Abbès-Moschee. Außerordentlich luxuriös ist auch der Aufzug im ehemaligen Wehrturm. ※ **CI-DESSUS** La terrasse entourant le patio offre une vue splendide sur la médina et le minaret de la mosquée Sidi-Bel-Abbès. Comble de luxe, la tour de guet abrite désormais un ascenseur.

Dar Badi
ASILAH

The view of the Atlantic from this house on the rampart is as good as it gets.

Confronted with the elements, sometimes furious and sometimes at peace, the owners of this former fisherman's house have banished all trace of clutter which might interfere with the view. Limpidity can be a deliberate decorative choice.

The pure white walls will only bear the thinnest of coloured stripes; the furniture is pared to a minimum, with nothing but banquettes and sofas made by local craftsmen for collapsing on when it's too hot outside. The overwhelming décor here is the sea. The owners are specialists, and they know nothing can upstage nature. The architect Charles Chauliaguet raised this house to its present height, given that it was partly built inside the 6 foot thick medina walls. Organized around a patio with a hundred-year-old fig tree, the original low construction was nothing more than a single large and lightless room. Today, with two floors atop along with plenty of window apertures and terraces linked by walkways, the house has a contemporary air without belying its origins. This is Northern Morocco inspired by the Mediterranean of antiquity. Here even Ithacan Ulysses might have come to approve the sunset over the wine-dark Atlantic.

Die Besitzer dieses Fischerhauses haben angesichts der mal harmlosen, mal entfesselten Elemente alles Überflüssige, jeden Blickfang in ihren Räumen vermieden. Das Haus ist durchgehend klar und nüchtern gestaltet und wirkt beinahe keusch.

Das strahlende Weiß der Wände wird nur an den Durchgängen durch ganz schmale Farbstreifen gebrochen. Die Möblierung ist entsprechend sparsam, doch laden mehrere Sofas und Bänke, die von den Handwerkern der Umgebung gefertigt wurden, zu Ruhepausen während der heißen Tage ein. Der eigentliche Schmuck des Hauses ist das Meer, denn die Besitzer sind der Überzeugung, dass die Natur als Dekoration nicht zu überbieten sei. Der Architekt Charles Chauliaguet hat das Haus, das zum Teil in die 1,80 m starken Befestigungsmauern der Medina gebaut war, nach allen Regeln der Kunst aufgestockt. Das vorhandene untere Bauwerk, das um einen Patio und einen hundertjährigen Feigenbaum angelegt war, war kaum mehr als ein großer, stets schattiger Raum. Nun, nachdem es mit zwei weiteren lichtdurchfluteten Stockwerken überbaut worden ist, mit Terrassen, die durch Stege miteinander verbunden sind, weht ein Hauch von Zeitgeist durch das Haus, ohne dass es seinen Ursprung verleugnete. Angeblich ist der marokkanische Norden von der mediterranen Antike inspiriert. Hier aber genießen Penelope und Odysseus allabendlich gemeinsam den Sonnenuntergang auf den silbergesäumten Fluten des Atlantiks.

Face aux éléments, tantôt apaisés, tantôt déchaînés, les propriétaires de cette maison de pêcheurs ont banni le fouillis où pourrait se perdre le regard. La limpidité est un choix en décoration, un vœu de chasteté en somme.

Les murs, d'une blancheur immaculée, ne tolèrent que de fines rayures posées sur les passages. Point trop de mobilier, juste des banquettes et des canapés réalisés par les artisans des environs et où l'on peut s'alanguir les jours de grande chaleur. Au fond, le vrai décor, c'est la mer. Les propriétaires, en spécialistes, savent bien qu'il n'y a pas plus décoratif que la nature elle-même. L'architecte Charles Chauliaguet a surélevé dans les règles de l'art une maison en partie édifiée à l'intérieur des remparts de la médina (dont l'épaisseur est de 1,80 m!). Organisée autour d'un patio et du figuier centenaire, cette construction basse n'était qu'une grande pièce plongée dans la pénombre. Surélevée de deux étages, percée de part en part d'ouvertures, ses terrasses reliées par des passerelles, elle est traversée par un souffle contemporain sans renier ses origines. On se dit ainsi que le Nord marocain s'inspire de la Méditerranée antique. Mais ici Pénélope et Ulysse jouissent ensemble, chaque soir, d'un soleil qui se couche sur des flots ourlés d'argent de l'Atlantique.

❊ **PREVIOUS PAGES** As the waves break against the ramparts below, the owners savor the success of their project. **ABOVE** The world is blue, seen from this fisherman's house where meals are taken under a white awning. Every evening the sun sets directly in front. You can view it from terrace or walkway – the choice is yours. ❊ **VORHERGEHENDE DOPPELSEITE** Wenn die Wellen sich unterhalb der Befestigungsanlage brechen, genießen die Hausbewohner ihr Meisterwerk. **OBEN** Von diesem Fischerhaus aus, unter dem Sonnenschutz aus Segeltuch, scheint die ganze Welt in Blau getaucht. Allabendlich bietet sich hier das Schauspiel des Sonnenuntergangs, das man nach Belieben von der Terrasse oder vom Steg aus beobachten kann. ❊ **DOUBLE PAGE PRÉCÉDENTE** Tandis que les vagues se brisent sous les remparts, les propriétaires de la maison savourent la réussite de leur projet. **CI-DESSUS** Le monde est bleu depuis cette maison de pêcheurs où l'on se restaure à l'abri d'un taud blanc. Chaque soir, le soleil se couche juste en face. En terrasse ou sur la passerelle, c'est au choix pour le spectateur.

✳ **ABOVE** The owners reject the Pierre Loti style as "neo-colonist orientalism", preferring to show nothing but furniture and objects made in the Rif region. "We've done our best to fit in", they say. ✳ **OBEN** Die Eigentümer halten nichts vom »Pierre-Loti-Stil«, von neokolonialistischem Orientalismus. Sie dekorieren ihr Haus lieber mit Möbeln und Produkten aus der Umgebung des Rifgebirges. »Wir haben uns alle Mühe gegeben, uns zu integrieren«, lautet vielmehr ihre Philosophie. ✳ **CI-DESSUS** Les propriétaires rejettent «le style Pierre Loti», «cet orientalisme néocolonialiste», pour n'exposer dans la maison que des meubles ou objets fabriqués dans la région du Rif. «Nous avons fait de notre mieux pour nous intégrer», philosophent-ils.

❊ **BELOW** In the starkly decorated bedrooms, simple furniture in harmony with the holiday atmosphere. Thus the Moroccan North acquires a dash of the Mediterranean. ❊ **UNTEN** In den mönchisch kargen Zimmern passt sich die schlichte Möblierung dem Stil eines Ferienortes an. Der marokkanische Norden gibt sich hier mediterran. ❊ **CI-DESSOUS** Dans les chambres monacales, un mobilier simple s'harmonise au décor balnéaire. Le Nord marocain prend ainsi des allures méditerranéennes.

❊ **ABOVE** The green bedroom has a toilet area with a basin and a looking glass fashioned from *zelliges*. **BELOW** In the big blue bedroom, the masonry banquettes (*doukana*) are covered with fabrics of the kind worn by women of the Rif (*fouta*) and thin woolen blankets (*haïk*). ❊ **OBEN** Im grünen Zimmer gibt es eine Waschgelegenheit mit einem Waschbecken und einem mit *zelliges* verkleideten Spiegel. **UNTEN** Im weiträumigen blauen Zimmer bedecken Gewebe (*fouta*), die auch die Frauen des Rif tragen, und Decken aus feinem Leinen (*haïk*) die gemauerten Bänke (*doukana*). ❊ **CI-DESSUS** La chambre verte dispose d'un coin toilette avec un lavabo et un miroir façonnés de *zelliges*. **CI-DESSOUS** Dans la grande chambre bleue, les banquettes en maçonnerie (*doukana*) sont recouvertes d'étoffes portées par les femmes du Rif (*fouta*) et de couvertures de laine fine (*haïk*).

Dar EL Hanna

Essaouira

The owner of this house has made the utmost of a limited space filled with secret corners.

A hippie rendezvous in the early 1970s and Orson Welles' playground when he was filming "Othello", Essaouira has long attracted artists, writers and fashion people.

Without directly belonging to this tribe, Geneviève Canet and Joël Martial discovered the region in the early 1990s. They were enchanted by the hospitality of the local people and the magnificence of the landscapes, and a year later they bought a village house nearby. It was a ruin, and anyway much too small, everybody said. But what a surprise for the begrudgers! The place has metamorphosed into a charming retreat. Ever since the beaten earth of the patio gave way to checkerboard slabs and the terrace walls were covered in pinkish lime wash to go with its cement tiles, the visitors have stopped sneering. In essence, the house has lost nothing of its original structure. Facing the patio, a kitchen-living room leads through to a bedroom. Upstairs, the terrace opens onto two small bedrooms. The argan wood furniture, designed by Joël Martial, is the work of a local carpenter.

Essaouira, Anfang der 1970er Jahre ein berühmter Hippie-Ort, wo sich Orson Welles zur Zeit seines Othello-Erfolges vergnügte, zieht seit vielen Jahren Künstler, Schriftsteller und Modemacher an.

Geneviève Canet und Joël Martial gehören zwar nicht direkt zu dieser Szene, als sie die Gegend jedoch Anfang der 1990er Jahre entdeckten, waren sie von der Gastfreundschaft der Einheimischen und der großartigen Landschaft so begeistert, dass sie ein Jahr später in der Umgebung ein Haus kauften. Mit seiner bescheidenen Fassade in einem kleinen Dorf war es zunächst kein Prunkstück. Zweifler, die es kritisch als Ruine oder Zwergenhäuschen bezeichnet hatten, wurden spätestens eines Besseren belehrt, als der schlichte Lehmboden im Patio sich in ein schwarzweißes Schachbrett verwandelt hatte. Die gekalkten Mauern, die auf der Terrasse rosa getüncht sind, überzeugen ebenso wie der Fliesenbelag aus Zement. Trotzdem ist die ursprüngliche Bauweise noch zu erkennen. Vor dem Patio liegt ein großes Wohnzimmer, eine Kombination aus Salon und Küche, das in einen weiteren Raum führt. Im ersten Stock grenzt eine Terrasse an zwei kleine Zimmer. Die Möbel aus Arganholz wurden nach einem Entwurf von Joël Martial in einer Schreinerei vor Ort angefertigt.

Cité hippie au début des années 1970, terrain de jeu d'Orson Welles à l'époque de son Othello, Essaouira attire depuis longtemps artistes, écrivains et gens de mode.

Sans directement appartenir à la tribu, Geneviève Canet et Joël Martial découvrent la région au début des années 1990. Séduits par l'hospitalité du cru et la magnificence des paysages, ils achètent une année plus tard une maison des environs. À l'origine modeste façade au cœur d'un humble village, l'endroit se mue en refuge de charme. Quelle surprise pour ses contempteurs! Une ruine, disaient les uns, un mouchoir de poche, prétendaient les autres. Mais, depuis que la terre battue qui couvrait le patio a été reléguée aux oubliettes, qu'à la place un damier noir et blanc joue à la marelle, que les murs passés à la chaux, teintés en rose sur la terrasse, amusent des carrelages de ciment, eh bien, les visiteurs ne badinent plus. Fondamentalement, la maison n'a pas perdu sa structure originelle. Devant le patio, une salle de séjour à la fois salon et cuisine borde une chambre; à l'étage, une terrasse s'ouvre sur deux petites chambres. Le mobilier en bois d'argan, dessiné par Joël Martial, est l'œuvre d'un menuisier local.

❉ **ABOVE AND FACING PAGE** After the black and white of the entrance came colours and cement tiles, from the corridors to the lime washed terrace area. The wainscoting of the corridor leading to the living room is made with cement tiles. ❉ **OBEN UND RECHTE SEITE** Auf das Schwarzweiß im Eingang folgen die Zementfliesen und die gekalkten Mauergänge der Terrasse. Auf dem Boden und im unteren Bereich der Wände im Gang zum Salon liegen Zementkacheln. ❉ **CI-DESSUS ET PAGE DE DROITE** Après le noir et blanc de l'entrée, la couleur et les carreaux de ciment prennent le relais, des couloirs aux murs de la terrasse passés à la chaux. Le soubassement du couloir qui mène au salon est fait de carreaux de ciment.

※ **FACING PAGE AND ABOVE** The masonry banquettes (*doukana*) of the ground floor living room are covered with Indian cushions. The furniture, like this lantern and ironwork table, was made by a local craftsman from sketches by Joël Martial. ※ **LINKE SEITE UND OBEN** Auf den gemauerten Bänken (*doukana*) im Salon im Erdgeschoss liegen indische Kissen. Die Möbel, wie die Laterne und der Eisentisch, wurden nach Entwürfen von Joël Martial vor Ort produziert. ※ **PAGE DE GAUCHE ET CI-DESSUS** Les banquettes en maçonnerie (*doukana*) du salon du rez-de-chaussée sont recouvertes de coussins indiens. Le mobilier, comme cette lanterne et cette table en fer, a été fabriqué par un artisan local d'après les croquis de Joël Martial.

❋ **ABOVE** Behind a narrow doorway, the round shower in a bathroom pared to essentials. **BELOW** In the bedroom by the terrace, local objects supply the decoration; for example, this large piece of pottery in its niche painted in the local colours. **FACING PAGE** The bed stands on a plinth behind a linen curtain. Light and shade make subtle play in this soberly-decorated space.
❋ **OBEN** Hinter einer schmalen Tür liegt ein einfaches Bad mit runder Dusche. **UNTEN** Die orientalische Atmosphäre in dem Zimmer vor der Terrasse entsteht durch die Ansammlung von Produkten des einheimischen Kunsthandwerks. Auch das Tongeschirr in der mit marokkanischen Farben bemalten Nische trägt dazu bei. **RECHTE SEITE** Das Bett liegt etwas erhöht, ein Leinenvorhang schützt es vor neugierigen Blicken. Licht und Schatten treiben in diesem schlicht dekorierten Raum ein subtiles Spiel. ❋ **CI-DESSUS** Derrière une porte étroite, la douche ronde d'une salle de bains dépouillée. **CI-DESSOUS** Dans la chambre située près de la terrasse, des objets locaux assurent la décoration à l'image de la monumentale poterie placée dans la niche peinte aux couleurs locales. **PAGE DE DROITE** Le lit est placé sur une estrade voilée par un rideau en lin. Ombre et lumière jouent à cache-cache dans cet espace décoré sobrement.

Aït BOU GOUMEZ
& Ouarzazate

The Berber buildings in this fortified village have stood for centuries
at the foot of the mountain range.

On either side of the High Atlas, villages built of *pisé* melt into the same background of arid earth dotted with low bushes. The time of *razzias* (raids) is long past, but the defensive architecture so characteristic of the Berbers still remains.

At the first sign of trouble, people, animals and provisions were piled up together in these houses, which were like strongboxes against thieves and bandits. Around Ouarzazate they have several floors, with the ground one reserved for mules, goats and sheep, the first for fodder, the second for the family and the third for an open terrace. The towers on their corners have no windows, only a hole or two just big enough for a gun barrel to poke through. Life was and still is lived in the courtyards below, where there is plenty of light and fresh air. These *pisé* houses, constantly gouged by rain and eternally under reconstruction, radiate a sense of both strength and fragility. The spirit of the people here is still wedded to the soil. Time has left deep marks on their faces, and they've stood up to so much harsh weather they can defy the world. Only the mention of djinns, the evil spirits of their legends, can make them shudder – but not for long. A shrug, a prayer…and they go back to their fields again.

Auf beiden Seiten des Hohen Atlas verschmelzen die Lehmdörfer mit der trockenen, überall von Buschwerk durchsetzten Landschaft. Die Zeiten kriegerischer Auseinandersetzungen und Razzien sind vorbei, doch die wehrhafte Architektur der Berber blieb erhalten.

In den Behausungen drängen sich Menschen und Vieh; auch die Vorräte sind dort untergebracht. In der Gegend um Ouarzazate stehen mehrstöckige Bauten, deren Erdgeschoss den Maultieren, Ziegen und Schafen vorbehalten ist. Die erste Etage dient als Speicher, auf der zweiten wohnt die Familie, während das dritte Stockwerk die Terrasse bildet. Die schlanken Ecktürme haben keine Fenster sondern nur Schießscharten, durch die gerade ein Gewehrlauf passt. Das Leben spielt sich im lichten, luftigen Hof ab. Diese Lehmbauten, die ständig vom Regen ausgewaschen und genauso oft wieder aufgebaut werden, wirken fragil und robust zugleich. Die Menschen, die bereits so viele Unbilden erlitten haben, bieten der Welt trotzig die Stirn. Die Zeit hinterlässt tiefe Spuren in den Gesichtern. Es ist nicht leicht, den Dorfbewohnern Furcht einzujagen, es sei denn, man erwähnt einen Dschinn, einen bösen Geist aus alten Geschichten. Aber auch das hält nicht lange vor – schon zucken sie mit den Schultern, sprechen ein Gebet … und kehren aufs Feld zurück.

Des deux côtés du Haut Atlas, les villages en pisé se confondent avec la terre aride parsemée de buissons. Le temps des rixes et des razzias est loin, mais l'architecture défensive, caractéristique des constructions berbères, demeure.

Les hommes, le bétail et les provisions s'entassent dans les habitations, sorte de coffre-fort à la mode tribale. Autour de Ouarzazate, elles disposent de plusieurs niveaux avec un rez-de-chaussée réservé aux mulets, chèvres et moutons; un premier étage qui fait office de grenier, un deuxième réservé à la famille, et un dernier niveau en guise de terrasse. Sur les tours élancées qui ornent les angles, pas de fenêtres, juste une ouverture pour laisser passer le canon d'un fusil. La vie se passe dans la cour qui apporte air et lumière. De ces maisons en pisé, ravinées par la pluie, éternellement rebâties, émane un sentiment de fragilité et de puissance à la fois. L'âme des habitants est restée près de la terre. Les corps ont résisté à tant d'intempéries qu'ils peuvent bien défier le monde. Sur les visages, le temps a laissé des traces profondes. Seule l'évocation des djinns, ces esprits malins des contes, peut effrayer les villageois. Mais pas longtemps. Un haussement d'épaule, quelques prières … et ils repartent aux champs.

✻ **ABOVE AND FACING PAGE** The common room in a house in the valley of Aït Bou Goumez. Coloured motifs characterize a space which changes constantly all through the day. The colours also have a way of warming the place in winter, which is otherwise icy cold. ✻ **OBEN UND RECHTE SEITE** Gemeinschaftsraum eines Hauses im Tal von Aït Bou Goumez. Bunte Muster zieren den Raum, der sich im Laufe des Tages ständig verändert. Die Farben bringen Wärme an diesen im Winter eisigen Ort. ✻ **CI-DESSOUS ET PAGE DE DROITE** Pièce commune d'une maison de la vallée de Aït Bou Goumez. Des motifs colorés habillent un espace qui se transforme tout au long de la journée. Les couleurs réchauffent un habitat glacial en hiver.

Dar En Nadour

Dar Djellouli

TUNISIA

Dar En Nadour

Sidi Bou Saïd

To visit this house with the blue Mediterranean spread before it,
is to follow in the footsteps of Henri Matisse.

From the terrace, the view offers an inexhaustible source of Mediterranean nuance, dominated by a subtle shifting quality of blue that lingers in the memory.

The owners of Dar en Nadour still remember Henri Matisse sitting on their terrace, painting. It's a place of deep serenity. For generations the vine-clad house behind has been giving of itself to all comers. With a décor veering from the West to the Orient and back again, it is filled with sofas, poufs and cushions, along with a collection registered as part of Tunisia's national heritage with the ministry of culture. Among the masterpieces here are a couple of large Roman mosaics, sculptures of animals, and numerous busts and statues from antiquity. Corridors and walls of enamelled tiles (14th century Spanish-Moorish *zelliges*) lead through to cool, often windowless rooms; in the heat of the day, shade is more to be valued than any panorama, no matter how unique. At sunset, a light breeze caresses the fronds of the palm tree.

Von der Terrasse aus bietet sich eine umwerfende Aussicht auf die stets wechselnden Farbnuancen des Mittelmeers mit seinem feinen changierenden Blauton.

Die Eigentümer können sich noch daran erinnern, wie Henri Matisse auf eben dieser Terrasse gemalt hat. Allein, dass der Maler hier residierte, spricht für die heitere Ausstrahlung des Ortes. Das mit Weinreben berankte Haus beherbergt seit Generationen Gäste. Wie eine sinnliche Verbindung von Orient und Okzident quillt es über vor Sofas, Kissen und gepolsterten Hockern, damit es niemandem an einer Sitzgelegenheit mangele. Hier findet sich auch eine beeindruckende Sammlung, die beim tunesischen Kultusministerium verzeichnet ist. Eine kleine Auswahl: zwei echte große römische Mosaiken, außerdem antike Tierskulpturen, Statuen und Büsten. Über Fliesen aus *zelliges* im spanisch-maurischen Stil des 14. Jahrhunderts gleitet man in die angrenzenden kühlen fensterlosen Räume. Wenn es richtig heiß ist, siegt die Sehnsucht nach Schatten über die Freude am Panoramablick, auch wenn dieser einmalig ist. Abends streicht eine sanfte Brise durch die Palmblätter.

Depuis la terrasse, la vue est une source inépuisable de nuances méditerranéennes où domine un bleu subtil et changeant. Reflet de la mer dans le ciel, la couleur éblouit et se fixe dans les mémoires.

Les propriétaires se souviennent encore du peintre Henri Matisse peignant ici. La présence du maître suffit à attester la force sereine de l'endroit. Recouverte de vigne, la maison reçoit, donne, et ce depuis des générations. Dédale sensuel entre Orient et Occident, elle déborde de sofas, poufs et coussins pour accueillir son monde. On ne peut manquer une collection impressionnante inscrite au patrimoine du ministère tunisien de la Culture. Pièces de choix: deux grandes mosaïques authentiquement romaines, des sculptures d'animaux, des statues et des bustes antiques. Parmi les carreaux peints, ces *zelliges* de style hispano-mauresque du 14ᵉ siècle, on se glisse dans les pièces fraîches parfois sans fenêtres. C'est qu'aux heures chaudes, l'ombre a plus de valeur qu'un panorama, même si il est unique. En fin de journée, un vent léger caresse les feuilles de palmier.

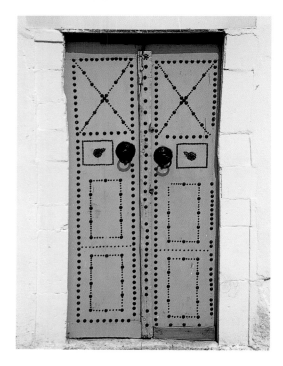

❊ **PAGE 64** The black nails driven into the front door are typical of Tunisia. **PREVIOUS PAGE** The luxuriant gardens, the mosaics and the Roman columns on the Bay of Carthage offered an image of Paradise that Matisse came to paint just before his death. **BELOW** The patio and its lemon tree. **FOLLOWING PAGES** A former café adjoining the house has now been integrated into it.
❊ **SEITE 64** Die mit schwarzen Nägeln beschlagene Tür ist charakteristisch für Tunesien. **VORHERGEHENDE SEITE** Die üppigen Gärten, die Mosaiken und die römischen Säulen der Bucht von Karthago zeichnen ein Bild vom Paradies, das Matisse als Motiv besonders schätzte. **UNTEN** Der Zitronenbaum im Patio. **FOLGENDE DOPPELSEITE** Zum Haus gehört auch ein altes Café. ❊
PAGE 64 Le cloutage noir de la porte d'entrée est un travail propre à la Tunisie. **PAGE PRÉCÉDENTE** Les jardins luxuriants, les mosaïques et les colonnes romaines sur la baie de Carthage sont une image de paradis que Matisse aima peindre avant sa disparition. **CI-DESSOUS** Le patio et son citronnier. **DOUBLE PAGE SUIVANTE** Un ancien café attenant à la maison est intégré à l'espace.

※ **FACING PAGE** A collection of valuable glasses and decanters. **ABOVE** After the patio, the long vestibule contains a collection of opalines, glass, and old Arab perfume bottles against a background of earthenware tiles. ※ **LINKE SEITE** Eine bemerkenswerte Sammlung wertvoller Gläser und Karaffen. **OBEN** Der Vorraum hinter dem Patio beherbergt eine Opalglas-Sammlung, Glaswaren und alte Flakons mit arabischem Parfüm vor Fayencehintergrund. ※ **PAGE DE GAUCHE** Une collection de verres précieux et des carafes retiennent l'attention. **CI-DESSUS** Après le patio, le long vestibule abrite une collection d'opalines, de verreries et de vieux flacons de parfum arabe sur fond de faïence.

✳ **FACING PAGE AND BELOW** The *zliss* (enamelled earthenware tiles) of the small salon and dining room are of the same type as those at the Alhambra in Granada. On the bed of the Dey (governor), the kilims echo the geometry of the tiles. This is a cool place, often used for siestas. **FOLLOWING PAGES** Turquoise wooden panels and *zliss* floors in the magnificent bathroom with its traditional taps and fixtures. ✳ **LINKE SEITE UND UNTEN** Die *zliss* (glasierte Fayencefliesen) im kleinen Salon und im Esszimmer sind in dem gleichen spanisch-maurischen Stil gehalten wie in der Alhambra von Granada. Die Kelims auf dem Bett des Dey, des Gouverneurs, nehmen das geometrische Muster der Fliesen auf. Hier im Kühlen wird Siesta gehalten. **FOLGENDE DOPPELSEITE** Türkisfarbene Täfelung und mit *zliss* verkleidete Böden schmücken das prächtige Bad mit den traditionell angehauchten Armaturen. ✳ **PAGE DE GAUCHE ET CI-DESSOUS** Les *zliss* (carreaux de faïence émaillée) du petit salon et de la salle à manger témoignent du style hispano-mauresque tel qu'on peut l'admirer à l'Alhambra de Grenade. Sur le lit du Dey (gouverneur), les kilims répondent à la géométrie des carrelages. C'est ici qu'on fait la sieste, à la fraîche. **DOUBLE PAGE SUIVANTE** Boiseries turquoise et sols de *zliss* pour la splendide salle de bains avec sa robinetterie d'inspiration traditionnelle.

Dar Djellouli
Tunis

Dar Djellouli in Tunis, a labyrinthine palace at the heart of the mediaeval medina.

At Dar Djellouli, it's hard to resist the cracked white walls, the mosaics, the mysterious light and the marble floors polished and worn by generations of *babooshes*. This palace is a perfect example of the kind of household kept by the old Mediterranean families of Tunis.

An ancestor here was governor of Sfax; his descendants, notables and ministers all, have done him honour, right down to the present incumbent, Ahmed Djellouli. A patriarch of splendid bearing, he comes to the heavy studded door in person to show us around. Beyond the archway is his private world, a mixture of styles around a broad patio paved with marble, with four columns and a melodious fountain. The space includes the kitchen, dining room and Arab and European salons with finely wrought plaster in the manner of Granada. Italian chandeliers hang from painted ceilings; flower motifs and gold leaf abound, in an evocation of Venetian baroque. The neo-Louis XV furniture adds a rococo touch; and for convenience the Djellouli family likes to leave a number of other rooms swathed in sheets and mothballs while the sands of time run on. We can only guess at the treasures they conceal.

Der Anblick der strahlend weißen rissigen Mauern, des Farbenspiels der Mosaiken, des Lichterzaubers oder mehr noch der glänzenden Marmorböden ist sehr beeindruckend. Dar Djellouli ist ein vollkommenes Beispiel für die Paläste der alten mediterranen Familien in Tunis.

In diesem Fall war der Vorfahre kein Geringerer als der Gouverneur von Sfax. Seine Nachkommen waren als Notabeln oder Minister nicht weniger erfolgreich, ebenso wie sein heutiger Nachfahre Ahmed Djellouli. Der Patriarch mit der stolzen Haltung führt persönlich durch die Räume hinter der schweren beschlagenen Tür im maurischen Stil. Jenseits des Spitzbogens beginnt sein privater Bereich, eine Mischung verschiedener Stile um den weiträumigen mit Marmor ausgelegten Patio, der mit vier Säulen und einem freundlich murmelnden Brunnen aufwartet. Der Palast umfasst darüber hinaus eine Küche, ein Esszimmer, arabisch und europäisch gestaltete Salons, die jeweils mit prunkvollen Arabesken aus Stuck im Stil von Granada dekoriert sind. An den bemalten Decken hängen Kronleuchter im italienischen Stil. Die Blumenmuster und die Vergoldungen gipfeln in einer Beschwörung des venezianischen Barock, während die Möbel einen Hauch von Neorokoko beisteuern. Aus Bequemlichkeit überlässt die Familie Djellouli weitere Räume ihrem Schicksal und dem Geruch von Mottenkugeln. Träumen wir weiter von ihren verborgenen Schätzen.

Difficile de ne pas succomber à la blancheur des murs fissurés, aux jeux des mosaïques, aux sortilèges de la lumière ou, encore, aux sols de marbre polis par le glissement des babouches. Dar Djellouli représente parfaitement les palais tenus par les vieilles familles méditerranéennes de Tunis la douce.

Ici, l'ancêtre était gouverneur de Sfax; sa lignée de notables et de ministres ne l'a pas trahi, jusqu'à l'actuel descendant, Ahmed Djellouli. Patriarche au port altier, c'est lui le guide au-delà de la porte lourdement cloutée de style mauresque. Passée l'arche ogivale, voici son monde privé, mélange de styles autour d'un vaste patio dallé de marbre, aux quatre colonnes, et à la fontaine mélodieuse. L'espace abrite la cuisine, la salle à manger, les salons arabes et européens ornés chacun de somptueuses arabesques de plâtre ciselé comme à Grenade. Des lustres à l'italienne ornent des plafonds peints. Les motifs de fleurs et les dorures abondent dans une évocation du baroque vénitien. Le mobilier néo-Louis XV achève la touche rococo. La famille Djellouli, par commodité, laisse sommeiller d'autres pièces dans leurs boules de naphtaline et laisse couler le sablier du temps. Imaginons leurs trésors.

❋ **FACING PAGE** The hall, where the master of the palace used to receive his tradesmen. **ABOVE AND FOLLOWING PAGES** Beyond this room, only important visitors were admitted to the patio, with its green and blue mosaics. Marble floors, ceilings covered in gold paint and arabesques, *zliss* (enamelled faience tiles). ❋ **LINKE SEITE** Der Eingangsbereich, wo der Herr des Palastes die Kaufleute empfing. **OBEN UND FOLGENDE DOPPELSEITE** Von diesem Raum aus wurden nur bedeutende Besucher weiter in den Patio mit seinen grünen und blauen Mosaiken geführt. Marmorböden, Decken, die durch vergoldete Malerei und Arabesken hervorgehoben werden sowie *zliss* (glasierte Fayencefliesen). ❋ **PAGE DE GAUCHE** L'entrée où le maître du palais recevait ses marchands. **CI-DESSUS ET DOUBLE PAGE SUIVANTE** Depuis cette pièce, seuls les visiteurs importants étaient introduits dans le patio aux mosaïques vertes et bleues. Sols en marbre, plafonds rehaussés de peintures dorées et d'arabesques, *zliss* (carreaux de faïence émaillée).

❋ **ABOVE** A bedroom with the traditinal wooden alcove and 18th century motifs. On the side table, a Louis XV clock. **FACING PAGE** The Louis XV mirrors overlooking the Arab salon reflect the light shed by a Venetian chandelier. Chiselled plaster arabesques and a three-part banquette. ❋ **OBEN** Ein traditioneller hölzerner Alkoven mit Motiven aus dem 18. Jahrhundert schmückt dieses Zimmer. Auf dem hochbeinigen Tisch steht eine Standuhr im Louis-XV-Stil. **RECHTE SEITE** Spiegel im Louis-XV-Stil beherrschen den arabischen Salon und reflektieren das Licht des venezianischen Lüsters. Arabesken aus Stuck und eine dreiteilige Bank. ❋ **CI-DESSUS** Une chambre ornée de la traditionnelle alcôve en bois aux motifs 18e. Sur la commode, une pendule Louis XV. **PAGE DE DROITE** Des miroirs Louis XV dominent le salon arabe et reflètent les lumières du lustre vénitien. Arabesques de plâtre ciselé et banquette en trois pièces.

✳ **ABOVE AND FACING PAGE** In the salon, which is completely encircled by stucco, are photographs and decorations presented by the state to Ahmed Djellouli's distinguished forebears (photo facing page), who have been prominent Tunisian citizens and ministers for three centuries past. ✳ **OBEN UND RECHTE SEITE** In dem stuckverzierten Salon hängen Fotos und die gesammelten Auszeichnungen der Großeltern von Ahmed Djellouli (auf dem Foto auf der rechten Seite), Notabeln und Minister der letzten drei Jahrhunderte. ✳ **CI-DESSUS ET PAGE DE DROITE** Dans le salon cerclé de stuc, photos et récompenses glanées par les aïeuls d'Ahmed Djellouli (en photo page de droite), notables et ministres depuis trois siècles.

Pierre Pes

Hammamet

Hidden behind the high walls of Tunisia's Saint-Tropez are a number
of traditionally-designed, originally-decorated villas like this one.

You're lost in a maze of streets, with something new and amazing round every corner. Carved and studded doorways of varnished wood open to show clusters of pink and mauve flowers cascading over the immaculate walls beyond.

At the end of a narrow alley, a chink offers a glimpse of a patio in which the interplay of plants and stones echoes the geometry of tiles and arches. Tropical scents float around you as you push open the door with its fish and hand motifs. Welcome to the home of Pierre Pes, a traveller and aesthete who, following the example of Violette and Jean Henson, the Americans who launched Hammamet in the 1930s, has given orientalism fresh impetus with a style all in white. You may well ask, what exactly is a foreign-based aesthete looking for? A moment's hesitation, and the reply comes back: confrontation, influences that might enrich, a clean break, and above all, the illusion of controlling the passage of time. By cheerfully straddling the centuries and surrounding himself with objects passed down by the civilisation of the Moors in Spain, Pierre Pes makes a mockery of the years.

In diesem Wirrwarr der Gassen, das an jeder Ecke neue Überraschungen bereithält, kann man sich hoffnungslos verirren. Die Portale aus lackiertem Holz, mit Nägeln beschlagen und mit Reliefs verziert, erlauben einen Blick auf rosa- und malvenfarbene Blütenstände, die sich über strahlend weiße Mauern ergießen.

Am Ende einer Gasse erspäht man durch einen Türspalt einen Patio, in dem Pflanzen und Steine passend zur Geometrie der Bodenfliesen und Rundbögen arrangiert sind. Ihr tropischer Duft weht auf die Gasse hinaus. Die traditionell mit Nägeln beschlagene Tür zeigt die Fetischmotive Fisch und Hand. Willkommen bei Pierre Pes, dem reisenden Ästheten, der einen rein weißen, orientalisch anmutenden Stil bevorzugt – wie bereits die beiden mondänen Amerikaner Violette und Jean Henson, die Hammamet in den 1930er Jahren zum Aufschwung verhalfen. Die Frage, was dieser anerkannte Schöngeist im Ausland sucht, ist durchaus berechtigt. Ein kurzes Zögern, dann sprudelt die Antwort nur so aus ihm heraus: Konfrontation, bereichernde Einflüsse, Brüche, vor allem aber die Illusion, die Zeit anhalten zu können. Pierre Pes überwindet die Epochengrenzen, indem er sich fröhlich in verschiedenen Jahrhunderten bedient und mit ererbten Gegenständen der spanisch-maurischen Zeit umgibt.

Vous êtes perdu dans un dédale de venelles qui offre à chaque tour et détour son lot d'étonnement. Les portails en bois verni, sculptés et cloutés, laissent transparaître des grappes de fleurs roses, mauves, retombant sur des murs immaculés.

Au bout d'une ruelle, une porte presque close laisse entrevoir l'intérieur d'un patio où l'enchevêtrement des plantes et des pierres répond à la géométrie des carrelages et des arches. Des essences tropicales déferlent jusqu'à vous. Poussez la porte traditionnellement cloutée des motifs fétiches du poisson et de la main. Bienvenue chez Pierre Pes, esthète voyageur qui, à l'instar des très mondains Violette et Jean Henson, ce couple d'Américains qui lança Hammamet dans les années 1930, prolonge l'orientalisme en un style tout de blancheur. Légitimement, vous vous interrogez: que cherche un esthète établi en terre étrangère? Un temps d'hésitation, puis la réponse jaillit: une confrontation, des influences qui pourraient l'enrichir, une rupture et, surtout, l'illusion de maîtriser la fuite du temps. En franchissant allègrement les siècles, en s'entourant d'objets hérités de la civilisation hispano-mauresque, Pierre Pes se rit des époques.

※ **ABOVE, BELOW, FACING PAGE AND FOLLOWING PAGES** Hammamet, which not so long ago was a small village with a shop and a mosque, is now Tunisia's Saint-Tropez. In its small palaces, like the one owned by Pierre Pes shown here, the style is predominantly white, with an antique purity in a place filled with archaeological vestiges left by Carthaginians, Greeks, Romans and Christians. ※ **OBEN, UNTEN, RECHTE SEITE UND FOLGENDE DOPPELSEITEN** Hammamet, das früher nur aus einer Moschee und wenigen Hütten bestand, entwickelte sich zum tunesischen Saint-Tropez. In den kleinen Villen, wie etwa der von Pierre Pes, dominiert die Farbe Weiß in einer antik anmutenden Reinheit – in einer Gegend, die reich ist an archäologischen Funden aus der punischen, griechischen, römischen und christlichen Epoche. ※ **CI-DESSOUS, CI-DESSOUS, PAGE DE DROITE ET DOUBLE PAGES SUIVANTES** Hammamet, qui n'était qu'un petit village avec quelques cases et une mosquée, est devenu le Saint-Tropez de la Tunisie. À l'intérieur des petits palais, comme ici chez Pierre Pes, domine un style tout de blancheur, une pureté antique sur un sol qui recèle des vestiges archéologiques des époques punique, grecque, romaine et chrétienne.

GHORFAS & TROGLODYTES

Matmata

A visit to a Saharan fortress that continues to hold out against time and a hostile environment.

On the mountains, the *ksour* (fortified village) overlooks the stoney plains of the great Tunisian south. Like giant beehives, its fortified grain stores (*ghorfas* in the Berber language) form complexes of rooms on several levels which are accessible from the outside by stairways.

Ever since the Middle Ages, people in these parts have had to protect themselves from a hostile outside world. For centuries, they were victims of *razzias* (raids); threatened by war, they had no other choice but to protect their precious staples. In this way one of North Africa's greatest architectural curiosities was born of a constant need for security. With its mosque and its school, Matmata has long been a village of cave-dwellers, numbering about a hundred families. In the middle of the last century, the younger generation began to move away to Tunis or migrate to Europe. Today, only a few people are living in the troglodytes, obstinately keeping their distance from the modern world. But they're no longer alone, and far from hostile – because now the troglodyte village has given a brand new possibility to its young. At last they are opening their heavy palm-wood doors to strangers, in the form of tourists, and treating them as friends.

Der *ksour* (eine befestigte Ortschaft) am Berghang thront über den steinigen Ebenen im weiträumigen tunesischen Süden. Die befestigten Speicher (*ghorfas* in der Berbersprache) gleichen riesigen Bienenstöcken und enthalten auf mehreren Etagen ein Geflecht von Räumen, die von außen über Treppen zugänglich sind.

Seit dem Mittelalter schützen sich die hier ansässigen Menschen vor der lebensfeindlichen Außenwelt. Lange Zeit wurden regelmäßig Razzien durchgeführt. Die vom Krieg bedrohten Stämme waren gezwungen, die zum Leben notwendigen Güter zu schützen. Aus dieser allgegenwärtigen Sorge um ihre Sicherheit entstand eine der seltsamsten Architekturformen Nordafrikas. In Matmata, das auch über eine Moschee und eine Schule verfügt, wohnten damals Hunderte von Familien in Höhlen. Mitte des letzten Jahrhunderts wanderten die Jungen nach Tunis und bis nach Europa aus. Die wenigen Familien, die hier noch unterirdisch am Rande der Zivilisation ausharren, leben allerdings inzwischen nicht mehr so einsiedlerisch, auch ihr Misstrauen gegenüber der Außenwelt ist gesunken. Heutzutage eröffnen sich den Höhlenbewohnern neue Möglichkeiten der Zukunftssicherung: Zunehmend werden freundlich gesonnene Touristen an den stabilen Türen aus Palmholz willkommen geheißen.

À flanc de montagne, le *ksour* (village fortifié) domine les plaines caillouteuses du grand Sud tunisien. Telle des ruches géantes, des greniers fortifiés (*ghorfas*, en langue berbère) sont un entrelacs de pièces sur plusieurs étages accessibles de l'extérieur par des escaliers.

Depuis le Moyen-Âge, on se protège ici d'un monde extérieur hostile. L'époque a longtemps été aux razzias. Menacées par la guerre, les tribus n'avaient pas d'autre choix que de protéger leurs produits de première nécessité. Une des plus grandes curiosités architecturales d'Afrique du Nord est ainsi née de ce souci permanent de sécurité. Avec sa mosquée et son école, Matmata a longtemps été un vrai village troglodyte où vivaient une centaine de familles. Au milieu du siècle dernier, la jeunesse s'est exilée à Tunis et jusqu'en Europe. Aujourd'hui, quelques familles s'obstinent encore à vivre à l'écart du monde moderne dans des cavernes. Mais elles ne sont plus seules et encore moins hostiles. Ainsi le village troglodyte s'invente un nouveau destin pour l'avenir de ses enfants: l'étranger, en la personne du touriste, peut franchir en ami les solides portes en bois de palmier.

❋ **FACING PAGE** At the foot of their fortified granaries, *ghorfas* in the Berber language, the men go about the ceremony of serving tea. **ABOVE** Considered impregnable, these arched cells overlook the mountains and withstand the heaviest rains. ❋ **LINKE SEITE** Vor den befestigten Speichern, die in der Berbersprache *ghorfas* genannt werden, zelebrieren die Männer die Teezeremonie. **OBEN** Die wabenförmigen Gewölbe, die jedem Angriff standhalten sollen, thronen über den Bergen und trotzen selbst sintflutartigen Regenfällen. ❋ **PAGE DE GAUCHE** Au pied des greniers fortifiés, *ghorfas* en langue berbère, les hommes procèdent à la cérémonie du thé. **CI-DESSUS** Jugées imprenables en cas d'attaque, les cellules voûtées dominent les montagnes et résistent aux pluies diluviennes.

✻ **ABOVE** The troglodyte abodes of Matmata have always resisted attacks by hostile tribes. **PAGES 106–109** There is very little furniture in these homes: nature supplies nearly every need. ✻ **OBEN** Die Behausungen der Höhlenbewohner von Matmata erwiesen sich für feindliche Stämme als uneinnehmbar. **SEITEN 106–109** In diesem Wohnumfeld gibt es nur wenige Möbel – die Natur sorgt für das Nötigste. ✻ **CI-DESSUS** Les habitations troglodytes de Matmata ont toujours résisté aux tribus hostiles. **PAGES 106–109** Peu de meubles dans cet habitat – la nature pourvoit aux besoins.

Adrere Amellal

Murad Grace

Raouf Mishriki

Egypt

Dar El Baarat

Al Moudira

Zeina Aboukheir

Adrere Amellal
Siwa Oasis

Herodotus called this place the "Island of the Blessed".
Today, it's home to a hotel of Biblical purity.

It's a day's drive over tracks from Cairo to Siwa, a Berber fortress standing against the waves of sand rolling in from the Libyan Desert. The oasis clings to a white mountain, moored to the silvery bank of a broad salt lake.

It has all the beauty of the Berber village it used to be; palm fronds clothe its roofs and new *pisé* covers its walls, now that the original Berber order has returned. The owner, Mounir Neamatalla, has made his dream come true – he has created an ecological village, the first in Egypt. His hotel was built without plans but following ancestral intuition, nestling harmoniously in a hollow of the nearby palm grove. Its eight buildings contain 34 bedrooms without telephone or electricity. With its terraces, high walls, narrow alleys and vegetable garden, the site has real authenticity, not to mention organically-grown food and the option of olive oil massages and incense-scented steam baths. There is even a meditation room.

Von Kairo muss man einen ganzen Tag auf den Pisten einplanen. Dann taucht Siwa auf, eine Berberfestung vor den Sandwogen der Lybischen Wüste. Dicht an den hohen Sanddünen und am silbernen Ufer eines riesigen Salzsees gelegen, präsentiert sich die Oase in der ganzen Pracht eines alten Berberdorfes.

Bei den auf traditionelle Art gebauten Häusern bestehen die Dächer aus Palmblättern und die Mauern aus Lehm. Der Eigentümer der Anlage, Mounir Neamatalla, verwirklicht hier seinen Lebenstraum: das erste Öko-Dorf Ägyptens. Das Hotel, das nicht auf dem Reißbrett sondern nach Art der Vorfahren entworfen wurde, liegt harmonisch in einer Senke neben einem Palmenhain. 34 Zimmer ohne Telefon und Elektrizität sind auf acht Gebäude verteilt. Mit den Terrassen, den hohen Mauern, engen Gassen und dem Gemüsegarten wirkt die Anlage wie ein Dorf aus vergangenen Zeiten. Die Gäste werden mit Biokost versorgt. Im Hammam werden Massagen mit Olivenöl und Aroma-Dampfbäder angeboten. Auch ein Meditationsraum ist vorhanden, in dem man erfährt, dass bereits Alexander der Große in Siwa war. Er wollte das Orakel befragen, ob er wirklich Zeus' Sohn sei.

Du Caire, il faut emprunter les pistes pendant une journée. Alors Siwa se devine, forteresse berbère où les vagues de sable du désert libyque viennent suspendre leur course. Accrochée à la montagne blanche, amarrée au rivage argenté d'un vaste lac salé, l'oasis dévoile la beauté d'un ancien village berbère.

Dans l'ordre retrouvé des habitations traditionnelles, les palmes habillent les toits, le pisé couvre les murs. Le propriétaire des lieux, Mounir Neamatalla, réalise ici son rêve: la naissance d'un village écolo, le premier d'Égypte. L'hôtel, bâti sans plans mais avec l'intuition ancestrale, est lové harmonieusement au creux de la palmeraie voisine. Ses huit bâtiments abritent 34 chambres sans téléphone ni électricité. Avec ses terrasses, ses hauts murs, ses ruelles étroites et son potager, le site a le charme d'un village d'antan. Le voyageur n'a plus qu'à découvrir les aliments bio. Au hammam, il apprécie les massages à l'huile d'olive et les bains de vapeur à l'encens. Il ne peut manquer la salle de méditation. On y apprend qu'Alexandre le Grand s'était rendu à Siwa pour consulter l'oracle et savoir s'il était bien le fils de Zeus.

❋ **ABOVE** A natural spring, in use for thousands of years, feeds the swimming pool. Meals are taken under the palm trees, a few yards from the tank. **BELOW** In places the hotel juts directly from the belly of the white limestone mountains behind it. ❋ **OBEN** Eine natürliche Quelle, die seit über tausend Jahren angezapft wird, speist den Swimmingpool. Nur wenige Meter vom Becken entfernt liegt der Frühstücksbereich. **UNTEN** Stellenweise ist das Hotel direkt in den Berg aus weißem Kalkstein gebaut. ❋ **EN HAUT** Une source naturelle utilisée depuis des milliers d'années alimente la piscine. On déjeune sous les palmiers, à quelques mètres du bassin. **EN BAS** Par endroits, l'hôtel sort du ventre de la montagne de calcaire blanc.

✳ **ABOVE** On the flank of the white mountain (*Adrere Amellal* in the Berber language), the hotel – which is conceived as an ecological village – is in perfect osmosis with its surrounding landscape. **BELOW** From the terraces above the bedrooms, nature is visible in all her primeval grandeur. ✳ **OBEN** Das an den weißen Berg (*Adrere Amellal* in der Berbersprache) gebaute Hotel, ein »Öko-Dorf«, verschmilzt mit der Landschaft. **UNTEN** Von den Terrassen aus, die die Zimmer überschatten, kann man das Schauspiel der Natur gut beobachten.
✳ **EN BAS** À flanc de la montagne blanche (*Adrere Amellal* en langue berbère), l'hôtel, pensé comme «un village écologique», joue l'osmose avec le paysage. **EN HAUT** Des terrasses qui surplombent les chambres, on contemple à chaque instant le spectacle de la nature.

※ **ABOVE** The olive-wood furniture was made by Siwa craftsmen. The ochre stones in the walls alternate with partitions in *kershef*, a rough mixture of lake salt and clay from nearby. **FACING PAGE BELOW LEFT** Delicious bread is made in this oven, using traditional techniques. ※ **OBEN** Handwerker aus Siwa stellen diese Möbel aus Olivenholz her. Die ockergelben Mauersteine kontrastieren mit den Zwischenwänden aus *kershef*, einem Gemisch aus dem Salz des Sees und Lehm aus der Nachbarschaft. **RECHTE SEITE UNTEN LINKS** Das köstliche Brot wird nach traditionellen Rezepten gebacken. ※ **CI-DESSUS** Le mobilier en bois d'olivier est réalisé par les artisans de Siwa. Les pierres ocre des murs alternent avec des cloisons en *kershef*, un enduit rugueux, mélange de sel provenant du lac et des terres argileuses voisines. **PAGE DE DROITE EN BAS À GAUCHE** Un pain succulent est fabriqué dans le four selon les techniques traditionnelles.

✳ **ABOVE** The traditional furniture in the bedrooms was all made by the craftsmen of the oasis. The walls are made of yellow sand and clay. **FACING PAGE** At dusk, Siwa is magnified by the soothing light of paraffin lamps. ✳ **OBEN** Die althergebrachte Einrichtung der Zimmer wird ausschließlich von den Handwerkern der Oase hergestellt. Die Mauern bestehen aus hellgelbem Sand und Lehm. **RECHTE SEITE** Öllampen tauchen die Oase bei Sonnenuntergang zusätzlich in ein warmes Licht. ✳ **CI-DESSUS** Le mobilier traditionnel des chambres est entièrement conçu par les artisans de l'oasis. Les murs sont faits de sable blond et d'argile. **PAGE DE DROITE** Au crépuscule, Siwa est magnifiée par la lueur apaisante des lampes à pétrole.

Murad Grace

Gizeh

When functionalism meets the best local traditions,
the result is a shadow play of different epochs.

The acclaimed architect Hassan Fathy has been working for decades to accomplish the intellectual rehabilitation of his country's architectural traditions.

In his determination to find an oriental vocabulary for functionalism, he is convinced that his entire nation possesses a genius for architecture. The house of Murad Grace and his wife, off the Sakkarah Road at the edge of Cairo, is an example of his theory. It is sited away from the din of the city among shady palm trees, with the pyramid of Gizeh well in sight. The spaces are simple and freely articulated for maximum interplay. The house is very compact, but its studied use of vaulting makes it seem larger than it is. With a blend of lime and chalk, shallow domes and windows overlooking a kidney-shaped pool, it stands in stark contrast to the opulent houses of old Cairo. And yet when you see the old stones and beautiful objects all around you, there's no room for doubt: this house belongs here, in the Egypt of the Pharaohs.

Der mit Auszeichnungen überhäufte Architekt Hassan Fathy setzt sich seit Jahrzehnten für die intellektuelle Ehrenrettung des architektonischen Erbes seines Heimatlandes ein.

Er fördert einen orientalisch geprägten Funktionalismus, weil er davon überzeugt ist, dass sein Volk grundsätzlich über architektonisches Genie verfügt. Ein gutes Beispiel dafür ist das Haus von Murad Grace und seiner Frau an der Sakkarah Road in einem Außenbezirk von Kairo. Abseits der unruhigen Metropole liegt es im Schatten der Palmen mit direktem Blick auf die Pyramiden von Gizeh. Obwohl das Haus kompakt ist, lassen die vielen Gewölbe es größer erscheinen. Die niedrigen Kuppeln aus einer Kalk-Krei-de-Mischung, deren Fenster zum Swimmingpool (in Form einer Bohne) hinausgehen, stehen in starkem Kontrast zu den üblichen Behausungen in der Altstadt von Kairo. Doch wenn der Blick die Steine liebkost oder auf den schönen Objekten ruht, wird spürbar, wie sehr dieses in der Nähe der Pharaonen gelegene Haus in Ägypten verwurzelt ist.

Bardé de récompenses, l'architecte Hassan Fathy s'est engagé pendant des années dans la réhabilitation intellectuelle du patrimoine architectural de son pays.

Dans sa volonté de décliner un fonctionnalisme à l'orientale, il est convaincu que son peuple, tout entier, possède un génie architectural. À la périphérie du Caire, sur Sakkarah Road, la demeure de Murad Grace et sa femme a valeur d'exemple. Elle est située loin des turbulences de la ville, à l'abri des palmiers, avec les pyramides de Gizeh dans la ligne de mire. Les volumes sont simples, articulés selon des plans d'une grande liberté, qui tendent à l'interpénétration des espaces. La maison est très compacte, mais le recours aux voûtes a permis de décupler la sensation d'espace. Avec son mélange de chaux et de craie, ses dômes peu profonds et ses fenêtres donnant sur une piscine en forme de haricot, le contraste est sensible pour celui qui débarque des maisons du vieux Caire. Et pourtant, quand l'œil caresse les pierres, quand il se pose sur de beaux objets, le doute n'est plus permis la demeure est en terre d'Égypte, non loin des pharaons.

※ **ABOVE** As converts to the functionalist theories of the architect Hassan Fathy, the owners have decorated their house with ancestral objects such as these pieces of Nile pottery. **FACING PAGE** Arches and cupolas around the broad patio. ※ **OBEN** Die Besitzer ließen sich von den funktionalistischen Theorien Hassan Fathys überzeugen und statteten ihre Räume mit antiken Gegenständen aus wie diesen Tonwaren, die in der Umgebung des Nils häufig gebraucht werden. **RECHTE SEITE** Bögen und Kuppeln rund um den Patio. ※ **CI-DESSUS** Convertis aux théories fonctionnalistes de l'architecte Hassan Fathy, les propriétaires ont habillé les lieux d'objets ancestraux telles ces poteries traditionnelles du Nil. **PAGE DE DROITE** Succession de voûtes et de coupoles autour d'un grand patio.

❋ **ABOVE** The serenity of the *moucharabiehs* contrasts with the dusty street adjoining. **FACING PAGE** The walls are daubed with *helba* juice, to preserve the colour of the stone. ❋ **OBEN** Die gelassene Ausstrahlung der *moucharabiehs* steht in starkem Kontrast zur angrenzenden staubigen Straße. **RECHTE SEITE** Die Mauern wurden mit Helbasaft eingepinselt, damit die ursprüngliche Farbe der Steine erhalten bleibt. ❋ **CI-DESSUS** La sérénité des *moucharabiehs* contraste avec la poussiéreuse rue voisine. **PAGE DE DROITE** Les murs sont badigeonnés de jus d'*helba*, afin de préserver la couleur originelle de la pierre.

Raouf Mishriki

Sakkarah

The vast necropolis of Memphis has more to it than pyramids – as this house with its olive groves attests.

At the foot of the Pyramid of Djoser stands a house surrounded by 15 acres of olive groves. It's a breathtaking spot, with the olive trees, which are drenched in sunshine for 300 days a year, forming a natural barrier against the dunes of the Sahara.

Like the pharaohs who lived here before him, Raouf Mishriki venerates this delicate ecosystem. On his property, known as the Horus Estate, he built a house ten years ago whose absolute priority was harmony with its surroundings. Almost entirely composed of elements dating from the turn of the 19th century, it was modelled on a family property built a hundred years ago just north of Luxor. The finest craftsmen in the area were called in to refresh the dominant Arab and Turkish style, and in his concern for total authenticity Raouf Mishriki studiously avoided modern chrome and tiles; the pool in which he refreshes himself is a sacred one, like the ones in the old temples. Mishriki is as happy with his objects as he is with his olives, whose fruit is harvested here in just the same way as it was in antiquity. For him, the symbolic strength of a living tree is worth more than any museum piece.

Das Haus am Fuß der Djoser-Pyramide ist von einer sechs Hektar umfassenden Olivenpflanzung umgeben. Die Lage ist atemberaubend schön: Die Olivenbäume, die jährlich 300 Tage Sonne bekommen, bilden einen natürlichen Wall gegen die orangefarbenen Dünen der Sahara.

Raouf Mishriki, der hier am gleichen Ort lebt wie früher die Pharaonen, begeistert sich stets von neuem für dieses empfindliche Öko-System. Als er auf seinem nach dem Gott Horus benannten Landgut vor gut zehn Jahren ein Haus errichtete, stand die Harmonie mit der unmittelbaren Umgebung im Vordergrund seiner Überlegungen. Dabei inspirierte ihn ein Familienbesitz, der vor hundert Jahren im Norden Luxors gebaut worden war. So besteht das neue Haus fast ausschließlich aus wieder verwerteten Elementen aus dem 19. Jahrhundert. Mishriki musste sich an die besten Handwerker Ägyptens wenden, um dem dominanten arabisch-osmanischen Stil neue Impulse zu geben. Im Sinne der Authentizität verzichtete er auf Chrom und moderne Fliesen. Gebadet wird deshalb in einem heiligen Becken wie in den alten Tempeln. Der Hausherr schwärmt nicht nur von seinem Gut allgemein, sondern im Einzelnen von den Holzvertäfelungen, den Objekten und nicht zuletzt von den Olivenbäumen, deren Früchte auf althergebrachte Weise geerntet werden. In seiner symbolischen Aussagekraft ist ihm ein Baum mindestens ebenso viel wert wie ein Museumsstück.

Au pied de la pyramide de Djoser, la maison se dresse au milieu d'une oliveraie de six hectares. La beauté du site coupe le souffle. Baignés de soleil 300 jours par an, les oliviers forment un rempart naturel aux dunes orangées du Sahara.

À l'enseigne des pharaons, Raouf Mishriki vénère cette nature à l'écosystème si délicat. Sur son domaine dit d'Horus, il a édifié il y a une dizaine d'années une maison dont la priorité reste l'harmonie avec son environnement immédiat. Presque entièrement composée d'éléments de récupération datés du tournant du 19e siècle, elle s'inspire d'une propriété familiale édifiée il y a un siècle au nord de Louxor. Il a fallu recourir aux meilleurs artisans du pays pour rafraîchir le style arabo-turc dominant. Dans un souci d'authenticité, Raouf Mishriki a évité le piège des chromes et carreaux modernes. C'est donc dans un bassin sacré, à l'image de ceux des temples, que l'on se rafraîchit. Épris de son domaine, le propriétaire vénère tout autant ses boiseries et ses objets que ses oliviers dont les fruits sont récoltés comme dans l'Antiquité. Car ici, la valeur d'un arbre, dans sa force symbolique, vaut bien celle d'une pièce de musée.

Dar El Baarat
Luxor

A stone's throw from the Valley of the Queens,
this fortress hides its whimsy under vaults and domes.

In the end, the house took root on the left bank of the Nile, where the dead are – which is anything but a bad augury in Egypt since according to tradition the dead sustain the living. It was something of a feat to get it built at all.

Chronic shortage of building materials, disputes with neighbours, sandstorms – Christian Louboutin, Parisian shoemaker and darling of the jet set, has survived them all. With its corner tower, its cupolas and its *pisé* walls, the casbah (which in this case really means citadel) is situated near the ruins of a village and a Coptic monastery. A disciple of Hassan Fathy, Egypt's most eminent architect (see the previous pages on the house of Murad Grace), Olivier Sednaoui conceived it in the oldest and noblest material known to man: mother earth. Its interior breathes the fantasy which has made Louboutin so famous as a maker of beautiful shoes. As soon as the gates open, you see the whole thing around you from the courtyard and its outside fireplace. Five bedrooms and two large living rooms share a succession of raised arches and domes. The colours are simple, the furniture stately, the site matchless.

Endlich steht dieses Haus am linken Nilufer, am Ufer der Toten – kein schlechtes Omen, nicht in Ägypten, wo die Toten traditionell die Lebenden nähren. Der Stoßseufzer »endlich« bezieht sich darauf, dass der Bau dieses Hauses eine große Leistung war.

Materialmangel, Streit mit den Nachbarn, häufige Sandstürme – Widrigkeiten, mit denen Christian Louboutin, der berühmte Pariser Schuhdesigner, der die Füße des Jetset kleidet, inzwischen bestens vertraut ist. Die Kasbah (im Sinne von Zitadelle) steht mit ihrem Eckturm, den Kuppeln und Lehmmauern nahe bei den Ruinen eines alten Dorfes und eines koptischen Klosters. Olivier Sednaoui, ein Schüler Hassan Fathys, des bekanntesten Architekten Ägyptens (siehe das Anwesen von Murad Grace), plante das Haus aus dem edelsten und ältesten Material der Welt: Mutter Erde. Innen spiegelt das Haus die Fantasie, die auch die Schuhkreationen des Designers bestimmt. Kaum ist man vom Hof mit seinem Außenkamin ins Haus getreten, erfasst der Blick die gesamte Raumordnung. Eine Flucht von Kuppeln und Gewölben verteilt sich auf fünf Zimmer und zwei große Salons. Wie eine Einladung zu biblischen Ursprüngen wirken die Schlichtheit des Tons und die Noblesse der Einrichtung auf uns.

Finalement, la maison s'est enracinée sur la rive gauche du Nil, celle des morts, ce qui n'est nullement mauvais signe en Égypte, puisque, selon la tradition, les défunts nourrissent les vivants. Le «finalement» s'impose car la bâtir a relevé de l'exploit.

La pénurie de matériaux, les querelles entre voisins, les fréquentes tempêtes de sable – Christian Louboutin, célèbre chausseur parisien qui habille les pieds de la jet-set, a tout connu. Avec sa tour d'angle, ses coupoles et ses murs en pisé, la casbah (au sens premier de citadelle) se trouve proche des ruines d'un ancien village et d'un monastère copte. En disciple d'Hassan Fathy, l'architecte égyptien le plus reconnu (voir pages précédentes la demeure de Murad Grace), Olivier Sednaoui l'a conçue dans le matériau le plus noble et le plus vieux du monde: notre mère la terre. À l'intérieur souffle la fantaisie qui préside aux créations du chausseur. Sitôt les portes ouvertes, de la cour où se dresse la cheminée extérieure, l'œil embrasse l'ensemble. Cinq chambres et deux grands salons se partagent une succession de voûtes et de coupoles échafaudées. Simplicité des tons sobres, noblesse du mobilier, nous sommes conviés à un retour aux origines bibliques.

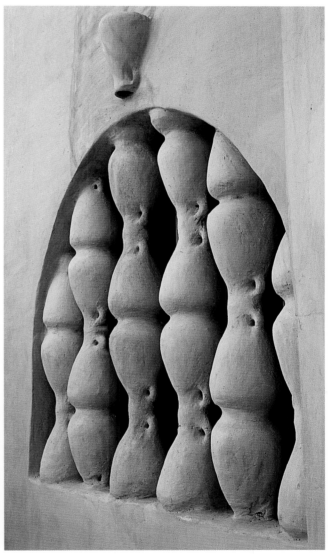

❋ **FACING PAGE** The building consists of a series of arches and domes constructed around a broad courtyard. **ABOVE** Unhappy with his *claustras*, Christian Louboutin replaced them with urns piled in front of the windows. ❋ **LINKE SEITE** Das Gebäude besteht aus einer Ansammlung von Gewölben und Kuppeln, die um den großen Hof herum gebaut wurden. **OBEN** Christian Louboutin gefielen die üblichen durchbrochenen Mauern (*claustras*) vor den Fenstern nicht, stattdessen wählte er Tonkrüge. ❋ **PAGE DE GAUCHE** L'édifice est une succession de voûtes et de coupoles échafaudées autour de la grande cour. **CI-DESSUS** Mécontent de ses claustras, Christian Louboutin les a remplacés par des jarres empilées devant les fenêtres.

❋ **ABOVE** Bead-covered Nigerian chair and Cameroon table. **FACING PAGE** Sofa, chairs, giant copper chandeliers, *moucharabiehs*, Islamic inscriptions on marble, furniture inlaid with ivory and mother of pearl: Christian Louboutin seems to have stripped the souks of Cairo bare. ❋ **OBEN** Sessel aus Nigeria und Tisch aus Kamerun, mit Perlen besetzt. **RECHTE SEITE** Christian Louboutin hat die Souks in Kairo geplündert: Sofa, Stühle, gigantische Kupferlüster, *moucharabiehs*, islamische Inschriften in Marmor, Möbel mit Elfenbein- und Perlmuttintarsien. ❋ **CI-DESSUS** Fauteuil du Nigeria et table du Cameroun ornée de perles.
PAGE DE DROITE Sofa, chaises, lustres géants en cuivre, *moucharabiehs*, inscriptions islamiques sur marbre, meubles incrustés d'ivoire et de nacre: Christian Louboutin a dévalisé les souks du Caire.

❋ **FACING PAGE** The courtyard, which is huge, has an immense open air fireplace. **ABOVE** A lantern from a Damascus mosque (early 19th century) illuminates the entrance hall. ❋ **LINKE SEITE** Der weitläufige Ehrenhof mit dem mächtigen Außenkamin. **OBEN** Die Laterne aus einer Moschee in Damaskus (Anfang 19. Jahrhundert) beleuchtet die Eingangshalle. ❋ **PAGE DE GAUCHE** La cour d'honneur, aux volumes imposants, impressionne surtout par son immense cheminée en plein air. ❋ **CI-DESSUS** La lanterne d'une mosquée de Damas (début 19ᵉ) illumine le hall d'entrée.

Zeina ABOUKHEIR LUXOR

A queen and her realm in the shadow of the Theban hills.

To lose, or to find oneself? Travel always leaves its addicts drained, at once stronger and more vulnerable, but always nearer to their own private truth.

After growing up in Lebanon and going all over the world, Zeina Aboukheir, a photographer and jewellery designer, came to rest at Luxor in a house adjoining the hotel she owns. Visiting its huge rooms is like reading Zeina's travel notebooks, and one delights in her furniture and antiques as if one were leafing through a record of her childhood. Take the salon and the dining room, where the history of the Near and Middle East is unfolded before one's eyes. Antique embroidered fabrics from Syria, of the type that were given to young married couples, cover the table and the cushions strewn on the banquettes. On a Caucasian kilim discovered in Jordan stand various items of *Retour d'Égypte* furniture dating from the 1930s. A painting from 1920 flirts with a ceiling lamp that bears the Ottoman insignia. On the walls, the frescoes by Mario Dahabi are a blend of eastern motifs and arabesques. On the floor, the cement tiles attest to the sheer willpower that went into the building of this place – for Zeina Aboukheir found some old moulds and engraved their original motifs herself. A true lover of Egypt, *la patronne* (as she is known to her workers) has set out to make the desert burst into flower. It may be that they have found a new queen in Luxor.

Die einen verlieren sich, die anderen finden sich – Reisende erleben sich stets ein wenig entrückt, mal stärker und mal schwächer, jedenfalls kommen sie ihrer eigenen Wahrheit näher.

Die Fotografin und Schmuckdesignerin Zeina Aboukheir wuchs im Libanon auf. Nachdem sie die Welt kennen gelernt hatte, blieb sie in Luxor – neben ihrem damaligen Hotel liegt heute ihr Haus. Wenn man durch die großen Räume schreitet, ist es, als lese man die Reisetagebücher der Künstlerin. Wer sich für ihre Möbel und die Antiquitäten begeistert, scheint in ihren Kindheitserinnerungen zu blättern. Nehmen wir zum Beispiel das Esszimmer: Vor unseren Augen präsentiert sich die Geschichte des Nahen und Mittleren Orients. Alte bestickte Stoffe aus Syrien, die früher jung verheirateten Paaren mitgegeben wurden, liegen auf dem Tisch und den Bankpolstern. Auf einem kaukasischen Kelim, den sie in Jordanien aufgetrieben hat, stehen Möbel im ägyptisierenden Stil der 1930er Jahre. Ein Gemälde von 1920 flirtet mit einer Deckenleuchte mit osmanischen Wappen. In den Fresken der Wände hat der Maler Mario Dahabi Wölbungen und Muster miteinander verwoben. Die Zementfliesen am Boden zeugen von der Hartnäckigkeit, die beim Bau dieses Hauses an den Tag gelegt wurde. Zeina Aboukheir besorgte sich alte Gussformen und ließ die Originalmuster eingravieren. Die »Herrin«, wie sie von den Bauarbeitern genannt wird, liebt Ägypten und würde am liebsten die Wüste begrünen. Ist sie die neue Königin?

Se perdre, ou se trouver – le voyage laisse toujours ses disciples un peu dépouillés, plus forts et plus faibles à la fois, mais toujours plus près de leur vérité.

Après avoir grandi au Liban et parcouru le monde, Zeina Aboukheir, photographe et dessinatrice de bijoux, a stoppé sa course à Luxor, dans cette maison qui jouxte son hôtel. On y découvre les vastes pièces comme on lirait ses carnets de voyage. On s'enthousiasme pour ses meubles et ses antiquités comme on feuilletterait ses souvenirs d'enfance. Prenez le salon et la salle à manger: l'histoire du Proche-Orient et du Moyen-Orient défile sous les yeux. De vieux tissus syriens brodés que l'on offrait aux jeunes mariés recouvrent la table et les coussins des banquettes. Sur un kilim caucasien découvert en Jordanie, des meubles «retour d'Égypte» des années 1930. Un tableau de 1920 flirte avec un plafonnier aux armes ottomanes. Au mur, les fresques peintent par Mario Dahabi mêlent courbes et motifs. Sur le sol, des carreaux de ciment témoignent de l'obstination déployée pour édifier les lieux. Zeina Aboukheir s'est procuré d'anciens moules et a fait graver les motifs originaux. Amoureuse de l'Égypte, «la patronne», selon les ouvriers du chantier, voulait fleurir le désert. Ont-ils trouvé une nouvelle reine?

❊ **FOLLOWING PAGES** The salon, with its 1930s *Retour d'Égypte* furniture, mocks frontiers with its wooden *sourra* (ceiling), its chandelier with Ottoman insignia, and its carpet from the Caucasus. ❊ **FOLGENDE DOPPELSEITE** Im Salon, der mit ägyptisierenden Möbeln aus den 1930er Jahren eingerichtet wurde, werden geografische Grenzen ignoriert, wie ein *sourra* (eine Deckenleuchte) aus Holz, ein Kronleuchter mit osmanischen Wappen und ein kaukasischer Kelim bezeugen. ❊ **DOUBLE PAGE SUIVANTE** Le salon, autour d'un mobilier «retour d'Égypte» des années 1930, ignore les frontières avec sa *sourra* (plafonnier) en bois, son lustre aux armes ottomanes et son kilim caucasien.

AL MOUDIRA Luxor

On the shores of eternity, an oasis of peace in the grand tradition of Arabian palaces.

Zeina Aboukheir has realised a childhood dream with her hotel, an intricate complex of domes, columns, awnings and arabesques.

It stands on the West Bank of Luxor, at Thebes, birthplace of Hercules – and it is a wondrous blend of pleasure and refinement. With the architect Olivier Sednaoui (see also the house of Christian Louboutin) Zeina Aboukheir personally directed a building site of 150 labourers and craftsmen. There are hundred-year-old wood carvings brought here from grand ruined houses, along with ceramics, wrought iron and marquetry. The walls, painted in natural pigments, cover the entire range of ochres, red and blues formerly used for Egyptian houses and temples. Fountains add their music and their touch of freshness to the shaded calm of the pavilions. A short distance from the building, an enormous swimming pool with colonnades and fountains merges with the vegetation; and all around is a 20-acre garden burgeoning with lemon trees, mandarin orange trees, mangoes and goyabas. The brick alleys running through it are edged with palms, hibiscus and eucalyptus. This, unquestionably, is the best place hereabouts from which to view the sunset.

Zeina Aboukheir hat sich durch dieses Hotel mit all seinen Kuppeln, Bögen, Säulen, Vordächern und Arabesken einen Jugendtraum erfüllt.

Am Westufer von Luxor, in Theben, wo Herkules das Licht der Welt erblickte, gehen seitdem Freude und Raffinesse eine glückliche Verbindung ein. Das war nicht immer so! Gemeinsam mit dem Architekten Olivier Sednaoui (siehe das Haus von Christian Louboutin) leitete Zeina Aboukheir drei Jahre lang eine Baustelle mit 150 Arbeitern und Handwerkern. Die allgegenwärtigen Holzschnitzereien, die aus verfallenen Villen stammen, verbinden sich mit der Keramik, dem Schmiedeeisen und den Intarsienarbeiten. Die mit natürlichen Pigmenten gefärbten Mauern präsentieren die gesamte Palette von Ocker über Rot zu Blau, die bereits die alten Ägypter für ihre Häuser und Tempel benutzten. Brunnen unterstreichen plätschernd und erfrischend die schattige Ruhe der Pavillons. Ein wenig abseits fügt sich das große Becken des Pools, umgeben von Säulen und einem Brunnen, in die prächtige Landschaft. Im Hotelgarten wachsen Zitronen- und Mandarinenbäume, Orangen-, Mango- und Guajavabäume. Dazu kommen Palmen, Hibiskus in leuchtenden Farben sowie Eukalyptus, die den Rand der Ziegelpfade zieren. Von hier aus hat man einen wunderbaren Blick auf den Sonnenuntergang.

C'est un rêve de jeunesse que réalise Zeina Aboukheir en recevant dans son hôtel, cet entrelacs de coupoles, d'arcs, de colonnes, d'auvents et d'arabesques.

Sur la rive ouest de Louxor, à Thèbes, là où Hercule vit le jour, plaisir et raffinement se conjuguent désormais. C'est nouveau. Qu'on se le dise! Avec l'architecte Olivier Sednaoui (voir également la maison de Christian Louboutin), Zeina Aboukheir a dirigé pendant trois ans un chantier de 150 artisans et ouvriers. Partout, des bois sculptés centenaires, provenant de riches demeures délabrées, jouent à cache-cache avec la céramique, le fer forgé et la marqueterie. Les murs colorés de pigments naturels conjuguent la palette d'ocres, de rouges et de bleus autrefois utilisée pour les habitations et les temples égyptiens. Des fontaines ajoutent leur musique et leur note de fraîcheur au calme ombragé des pavillons. À l'écart, le vaste bassin de la piscine, avec ses colonnades et ses fontaines, s'intègre au décor végétal. Autour, le jardin de huit hectares mélange citronniers, mandariniers, orangers, manguiers et goyaviers. Palmiers, flamboyants, hibiscus et eucalyptus bordent les allées de brique. C'est d'ici que l'on apprécie le coucher du soleil.

❋ **FACING PAGE** In the dining room, chandeliers of glass and copper, with wrought iron tables from all over Egypt. **BELOW** An immense Syrian frame, with 18th century Ottoman-Italian motifs, overlooks the bar with its sofas and Karabakh kilim. ❋ **LINKE SEITE** Im Esszimmer hängen Kristall- und Kupferlüster über schmiedeeisernen Tischen. **UNTEN** Ein riesiger syrischer Rahmen mit italo-osmanischen Mustern aus dem 18. Jahrhundert hängt über der sofabestückten Bar. Kelim aus Karabach. ❋ **PAGE DE GAUCHE** Dans la salle à manger, des lustres en verre ou cuivre, ainsi que des tables en fer forgé choisis aux quatre coins d'Égypte. **CI-DESSOUS** Un immense cadre syrien, aux motifs italo-ottomans du 18e siècle, domine le bar avec ses sofas et son kilim du Karabakh.

Sirocco House

Alan Donovan

The Giraffe Manor

Kitengela Glass

Anna Trzebinski

Dodo's Tower

Hippo Point

Armando Tanzini

Katharina Schmezer
& Hermann Stucki

Yago Casado

kenya

Anna Trzebinski
Nairobi

At the edge of a reserve, this warm interior
offers a happy blend of cosiness and wild nature.

Only 25 minutes from Nairobi, this cottage faced in pale wood is a combination of scattered influences from the African and European continents.

Yes, this is Kenya, but there is a certain English charm about this spot; Russian, too, to judge by the bare and massive tree trunks nearby, which make you think of dachas and Anna Karenina; and Indian, when you see the delicate Indian fabrics inside. Anna Trzebinski, the owner, will tell you that amid the immense freedom of the land she lives in, these odd collisions generate a sense of eternity. Her husband Tonio, born in Africa of Polish parents, spent much of his life on safari (the Swahili word means "journey") in the great plains of East Africa. The contemporary furniture, which he created for himself, was all cut straight from tree trunks to evoke the idea of nature. Mission accomplished. From the terrace overlooking the forest, giraffes can often be seen feeding on the nearby foliage. Here we are close to the bush, and the sound of rain pattering on the corrugated iron roof is balm to the soul.

Das Cottage aus hellem Holz, von Nairobi mit dem Auto in nur 25 Minuten zu erreichen, vereint Einflüsse aus Europa und Afrika. Stimmt, wir sind in Kenia. Aber ist es nicht stellenweise reizend englisch?

Und diese mächtigen Säulen aus nackten Baumstämmen, beschwören sie nicht eine Datscha, aus der jeden Moment Anna Karenina und die Ihren hervorkommen könnten? Anna Trzebinski selbst glaubt, dass die ungeheure Freiheit des Ortes, die klaren Gegensätze, ein Gefühl von Ewigkeit schüren. Ihr Mann Tonio, ein gebürtiger Afrikaner polnischer Abstammung, war schon oft auf Safari (das Kisuaheliwort bedeutet »Reise«) in den weiten Ebenen Ostafrikas. Die modernen Möbel, die er selbst entworfen hat, werden direkt aus Baumstämmen geschreinert, um so natürlich wie möglich zu wirken. Das ist ihm gelungen. Von den Terrassen, die den Blick in den Wald freigeben, kann man Giraffen beobachten, die sich von den Blättern der umstehenden Bäume ernähren. Der Busch ist nah; hier hat selbst der Regen eine angenehme Melodie. Sein Prasseln auf dem Wellblechdach beruhigt auch nervöse Gemüter.

À tout juste 25 minutes de Nairobi, le cottage paré de bois blond rassemble des influences éparses entre les continents africain et européen. Oui, nous sommes au Kenya. Mais ici et là ne flotte-il pas un charme à l'anglaise?

Et ces puissantes colonnes de troncs d'arbre nus, n'évoquent-elles pas une datcha d'où surgiraient Anna Karénine et les siens? Et que dire de ces délicates étoffes indiennes? Interrogez Anna Trzebinski, elle vous dira que l'immense liberté des lieux, cette collision limpide, génère un sentiment d'éternité. Enfant d'Afrique d'origine polonaise, son mari Tonio a passé une bonne partie de sa vie en safari (mot swahili signifiant «voyage») dans les grandes plaines de l'Afrique orientale. Les meubles contemporains qu'il a lui-même créés ont été taillés dans des troncs d'arbre afin d'évoquer la nature. Mission accomplie. Des terrasses qui surplombent la forêt, il n'est pas rare d'observer les girafes qui se nourrissent aux branches voisines. On est à proximité de la brousse. La pluie est mélodieuse. Son cliquetis sur le toit en tôle ondulée calme même les plus agités.

✳ **FACING PAGE** Built on two levels, the house has a broad ground floor living room, bedrooms on the first floor and an attic at the top. **ABOVE** The living room opens onto the terrace. The flooring is made of mahogany. ✳ **LINKE SEITE** Das zweigeschossige Haus besteht aus einem großen Wohnzimmer im Erdgeschoss, einigen Zimmern auf der ersten Etage und einem Speicher unterm Dach. **OBEN** Der Salon geht auf die Terrasse hinaus. Das Parkett ist aus Mahagoni. ✳ **PAGE DE GAUCHE** Bâtie sur deux niveaux, la maison comporte un large living au rez-de-chaussée, des chambres à l'étage et un grenier au sommet. **CI-DESSUS** Le salon s'ouvre sur la terrasse. Le parquet est en acajou.

❊ **FACING PAGE AND LEFT** The low table cut from tree trunks serves as a glass cabinet containing Trzebinski's safari souvenirs. **BELOW** On the bookshelves in the living room, a collection of local headrests – used by men and women at night so their elaborate coiffures won't be spoiled. ❊ **LINKE SEITE UND LINKS** In den niedrigen aus Baumstämmen geschnittenen Vitrinen liegen Souvenirs von verschiedenen Safaris. **UNTEN** In der Bibliothek ist eine Sammlung von Kopfstützen verschiedener Stämme ausgestellt. Darauf legen die Frauen und Männer nachts den Nacken, damit die Frisur nicht leidet. ❊ **PAGE DE GAUCHE ET À GAUCHE** Les tables basses taillées dans des troncs d'arbre sont des vitrines qui abritent des souvenirs de safari. **CI-DESSOUS** Dans la bibliothèque du salon, une collection de repose-tête régionaux, la nuit les femmes et les hommes y appuient la nuque afin de ne pas abîmer leurs coiffures.

❋ **PREVIOUS PAGES** The bed, also cut from tree trunks, is protected by a mosquito net affixed to the ceiling with a series of curtain rods. The safari trunks picked up in Nairobi give the bedroom the air of a camp in the bush. **ABOVE** An ethno-chic touch in the bathroom, with these Indian silk curtains. **FACING PAGE** The wooden kitchen building stands apart from the house. Small openings all round the roof create a pool of light below. In the midst of all the African utensils stands a wooden Indian kitchen table. ❋ **VORHERGEHENDE DOPPELSEITE** Über dem aus Baumstämmen geschreinerten Bett hängt ein an mehreren Stangen befestigtes Moskitonetz. Die in Nairobi erstandenen Safarikoffer geben dem Raum den Anstrich eines Zeltlagers. **OBEN** Die Vorhänge aus indischer Seide verleihen dem Bad einen Hauch von Ethno-Chic. **RECHTE SEITE** Die in Holz eingerichtete Küche liegt neben dem Haus. Die kleinen Oberlichter rundherum sorgen für genügend Helligkeit. In dem Sammelsurium afrikanischer Küchenutensilien steht ein indischer Holztisch. ❋ **DOUBLE PAGE PRÉCÉDENTE** Le lit taillé dans des troncs d'arbres est surmonté d'une moustiquaire fixée au plafond par une série de tringles. Les malles de safari chinées à Nairobi font de la chambre un véritable campement. **CI-DESSUS** Touche ethno-chic dans la salle de bains avec ces rideaux en soierie indienne. **PAGE DE DROITE** La cuisine en bois est indépendante de la maison. De petites ouvertures percées autour du toit créent un puits de lumière. Au milieu des ustensiles africains, une table indienne en bois.

Kitengela Glass

Nairobi

This family creates fantasies that might have been inspired by Antoni Gaudí or Niki de Saint-Phalle – out of glass, and against all expectations.

How on earth does the Kitengela factory survive, at the end of a rocky track that breaks up in the dry season and washes away in the wet? How do its glasses, vases, plates and carafes resist the onslaught of Africa's capricious outback?

Nani Croze has a ready answer: "We work among the animals, under the shade of bouganvilleas and acacias. The beauty of this place protects and inspires us." The visitor, already hypnotized by a broad palette of colours that includes cobalt blue and deep greens, discovers sculptures and wrought iron gates; even the workshops are multi-hued. In the "metal shop", Francis the blacksmith adds the final touches to a gigantic mirror destined for a Nairobi hotel. Farther on, like red mushrooms pushing out of the ground, are the bead and glass workshops, and beside these is a small shop in which the "village people" come to pick up supplies when the rhythm of their work allows. There's no shortage of work here: orders come in from all over the world. Seconded by her son Anselm and her daughter Katrineka, a specialist in jewellery made of blown glass, Nani Croze is part of a real working community. One wonders, how do the words *Sagrada Família* translate into Masai?

Warum in aller Welt liegt die Fabrik Kitengela an einer steinigen Piste, die in der Trockenzeit voller Schlaglöcher ist und in der Regenzeit im Schlamm versinkt? Wie halten die Gläser, Vasen, Teller und Karaffen diese Schocktherapie der launischen afrikanischen Natur aus?

Darauf antwortet Nani Croze: »Wir arbeiten mitten unter den Tieren, im Schatten der Bougainvillea und Akazien. Die Schönheit des Ortes schützt und inspiriert uns ganz außerordentlich.« Der Besucher ist zunächst geradezu hypnotisiert von der Farbpalette, deren Schwerpunkt auf Kobaltblau und dunklen Grüntönen liegt. Dann entdeckt er die Skulpturen, die schmiedeeisernen Portale und als I-Tüpfelchen die bunten Ateliers. Im »Metal Shop« legt Francis, der Kunstschmied, letzte Hand an einen riesigen Spiegel, ein Auftragswerk des größten Hotels in Nairobi. Etwas entfernt liegen wie sprießende rote Pilze das Atelier, in dem mit Perlen und Glas gearbeitet wird, und der kleine Laden, in dem die »Dorfbewohner« ihren Bedarf decken – je nach Geschmack und Angebot. An Arbeit mangelt es nicht, aus der ganzen Welt gehen Aufträge ein. Nani Croze arbeitet gemeinsam mit ihrem Sohn Anselm und ihrer Tochter Katrineka, die sich auf Glasbläserei-Schmuck spezialisiert hat. Also, wie übersetzt man Sagrada Família in die Sprache der Massai?

Par quel mystère la fabrique de Kitengela s'est-elle retrouvée au-delà d'une piste rocailleuse défoncée en saison sèche et submergée par les torrents en saison humide? Comment verres, vases, assiettes et carafes résistent-ils aux traitements de choc de la capricieuse nature africaine?

Réponse de Nani Croze: «Nous travaillons parmi les animaux, à l'ombre des bougainvilliers et des acacias. La beauté des lieux nous protège et nous donne une incroyable inspiration.» En visite, hypnotisé par une large palette de couleurs où dominent le bleu cobalt et les verts profonds, le voyageur découvre des sculptures, des portails en fer forgé ou, encore, des ateliers multicolores. Dans le «métal shop», Francis le ferronnier donne la dernière touche à un gigantesque miroir destiné au plus grand hôtel de Nairobi. Plus loin, tout droit sorti de terre comme les champignons rouges, l'atelier de perles et de verre, jouxte la mini-épicerie dans laquelle les «villageois» viennent s'approvisionner à leur guise, selon le rythme des créations du moment. Le labeur ne manque pas: les commandes viennent du monde entier. Secondée par son fils Anselm et par sa fille Katrineka, spécialiste des bijoux en verre soufflé, Nani Croze travaille en communauté. Au fait, comment traduit-on Sagrada Família en langue Massaï?

※ **FACING PAGE** In the shower, bottle bottoms filter the light. **ABOVE** The family architect, the youngest son Lengai, designed the house of his sister Katrineka on the basis of a hut. ※ **LINKE SEITE** In der Dusche filtert eine Ansammlung von Flaschen das Licht. **OBEN** Der jüngste Sohn Lengai ist gleichzeitig der Architekt der Familie. Er hat das Haus seiner Schwester Katrineka in Form einer Hütte gestaltet. ※ **PAGE DE GAUCHE** Dans la douche, les culs de bouteille renversés filtrent la lumière. **CI-DESSUS** L'architecte de la famille, le fils cadet Lengai, a dessiné la maison de sa sœur Katrineka sur la base d'une hutte.

❋ **ABOVE** Nani Croze, who was born into a family of artists, learned to paint and sculpt in her childhood. In its forms and materials, her house is inspired by Masai tradition. ❋ **OBEN** Aus einer Künstlerfamilie stammend beschäftigte sich Nani Croze schon als Kind mit Malerei und Bildhauerei. Ihr Umfeld orientiert sich in den Formen und Materialien an den Traditionen der Massai. ❋ **CI-DESSUS** Née dans une famille d'artistes, Nani Croze a appris la peinture et la sculpture dès l'enfance. Dans ses formes comme dans ses matériaux, l'habitat est inspiré des traditions Massaï.

❋ **FOLLOWING PAGES** The sight of mosaics, sculpture and fantastically-shaped houses comes as a shock in the middle of the bush. In the garden stands a huge mosaic dragon. ❋ **FOLGENDE DOPPEL-SEITE** Der Anblick von Mosaiken, Skulpturen und Phantasie-Häusern erstaunt in der Savanne. Im Garten steht ein Drache aus Mosaiksteinen. ❋ **DOUBLE PAGE SUIVANTE** Voir des mosaïques, des sculptures et des maisons fantaisistes surprend dans la savane. Au centre du jardin, un immense dragon en mosaïque annonce la couleur.

ALAN DONOVAN
NAIROBI

This American, who has lived in Kenya for 30 years,
is responsible for the famous African Heritage Collection.

Alan Donovan has found a mission of his own: a dedicated servant of the arts, he exports African craftwork all over the world.

In 1969, disillusioned with his US State Department job administering famine relief in the breakaway Nigerian region of Biafra, he quit government service, bought a VW bus in Paris, and went off to discover the rest of Africa. Years later he founded The African Heritage, a complex including pan-African galleries, gift shops, restaurants, craft centres and a festival which travels the world promoting African tourism and culture. The heart of Donovan's company beats in a house facing Mount Kilimanjaro. Built far out in the bush to his own design, and to plans by architect David Bristow, it responds to its owner's obsession with integrating traditional African art into a contemporary living space. Donovan's treasures, bought from a multitude of African countries, unite to form a concentrated gallery of the continent he loves; in all likelihood, he says, the house will become a museum after he is gone. May the Gods grant him many more years to show the world the wonders of Africa.

Alan Donovan hat seine Mission gefunden: Im Dienst der Künste exportiert er afrikanisches Kunsthandwerk in die ganze Welt.

Desillusioniert von seiner Arbeit, im Dienst des US-Außenministeriums Hungerhilfe für Kinder im separatistischen Biafra in Nigeria zu leisten, gab er 1969 seinen Job auf, kaufte in Paris einen VW-Bus und machte sich auf den Weg, das restliche Afrika zu entdecken. Viele Jahre später gründete er die African Heritage, ein komplexes Unternehmen aus panafrikanischen Gallerien, Geschenkboutiquen, Restaurants, Handwerksbetrieben und einem Festival zur Förderung der Kultur und des Tourismus in Afrika. Das Herz dieses Unternehmens schlägt in einem Haus in der Savanne – in Sichtweite des Kilimandscharo. Donavans Entwurf und die Pläne des Architekten David Bristow berücksichtigen die Besessenheit des Hausherrn und integrieren die traditionelle afrikanische Kunst in ein modernes Umfeld. Bunt zusammengewürfelte Schätze aus den unterschiedlichsten afrikanischen Ländern sind hier derart konzentriert versammelt, dass man das Haus mühelos in ein Museum verwandeln könnte, wenn der Besitzer einmal nicht mehr da wäre. Mögen die afrikanischen Gottheiten noch viele Jahre über Alan Donovan wachen, damit er auch weiterhin der Welt die Wunder Afrikas zeigen kann.

Alan Donovan s'est trouvé lui aussi une mission: au service des arts, il exporte dans le monde entier l'artisanat africain.

Déçu par son travail au Département d'État dans le service de l'Aide alimentaire pour les enfants du Biafra, région séparatiste du Nigeria, il démissionne en 1969, s'achète un minibus à Paris et part à la découverte de l'Afrique. Bien des années plus tard, il fonde African Heritage, une société complexe recouvrant des galeries panafricaines, des boutiques de souvenirs, des restaurants, des entreprises artisanales et un festival visant à promouvoir la culture et le tourisme africains. Le cœur de cette société bat dans une maison édifiée dans la savane, à portée de vue du Kilimandjaro. Le projet de Donavan et les plans de l'architecte David Bristow préservent l'obsession du maître des lieux: intégrer l'art traditionnel africain dans un espace contemporain. Des trésors hétéroclites glanés un peu partout évoquent un concentré d'Afrique, au point que la maison pourrait se transformer en musée à la disparition de son propriétaire. Puissent les divinités vernaculaires veiller encore longtemps sur Alan Donavan pour qu'il continue à nous montrer les merveilles de l'Afrique.

❊ **ABOVE** The house has a glorious view across the Nairobi National Park to Kilimanjaro. **FOLLOWING PAGES** The swimming pool, built of Mazeras stone from the Kenyan Coast. The pool house has a roof made of *makuti* palm leaves. ❊ **OBEN** Das Haus bietet einen großartigen Ausblick auf den Nairobi Nationalpark und den Kilimandscharo. **FOLGENDE DOPPELSEITE** Das Schwimmbad aus Mazeras-Steinen von der Küste Kenias. Das Dach des Pool House besteht aus *makuti* (Palmfasern). ❊ **CI-DESSUS** La maison dispose d'une vue superbe sur le parc national de Nairobi et le Kilimandjaro. **DOUBLE PAGE SUIVANTE** La piscine, en pierre de Mazeras de la côte du Kenya. La *pool house* est surmontée d'un toit en fibres de *makuti*.

※ **PREVIOUS PAGES** In the salon, the walls are painted with ethnic motifs and the beams encrusted with pebbles which create a mosaic effect. The floors are covered with woven palm mats.
FACING PAGE A Moon Mask from Burkina Faso. ※ **VORHERGEHENDE DOPPELSEITE** Ethnische Motive zieren die mit Pigment gestrichenen Mauern im Salon, während die Kieselintarsien auf den Balken wie Mosaike wirken. Geflochtene Palmmatten bedecken die Böden. **RECHTE SEITE** Mondmaske aus Burkina Faso. ※ **DOUBLE PAGE PRÉCÉDENTE** Dans le salon, les murs sont peints de motifs ethniques et les poutres incrustées de cailloux dessinent une mosaïque. Sols recouverts de feuilles de palmier tressées. **PAGE DE DROITE** Masque-lune du Burkina Faso.

❋ **FACING PAGE** The four-poster bed is draped with Kuba ceremonial fabrics from the Congo. **BELOW** One of the bathrooms has its own garden, while the other has a tub set into stone from Masai Mara. ❋ **LINKE SEITE** Über dem Himmelbett liegen festliche Kuba-Stoffe aus dem Kongo. **UNTEN** Eines der Bäder hat eine Tür zu einem eigenen Garten, während das andere über eine Badewanne verfügt, die etwas erhöht in Orginalsteine aus dem Massai-Mara-Nationalpark eingelassen ist. ❋ **PAGE DE GAUCHE** Le lit à baldaquin est revêtu de tissus de cérémonie Kuba provenant du Congo. **CI-DESSOUS** Une des salles de bains est agrémentée d'un jardin extérieur, tandis que l'autre bénéficie d'une baignoire encastrée dans une estrade de pierre originaire du Massaï Mara.

THE GIRAFFE MANOR
NAIROBI

An archetypal British manor house –
and a charming reminder of the colonial past.

This Elizabethan house with neo-Gothic influences is worth the journey to East Africa all on its own. Fortified by the secular canons of good taste that are the preserve of Her Majesty's subjects, its owners have carefully maintained the country house atmosphere of their residence ever since 1932.

It has geometrical pediments, regulation brick masonry, a heavy front door, and plenty of noble materials and Gothic vaulting; indeed in every way it is a hymn to Britannia, despite being 4,500 feet above sea level. The giraffes are visibly appreciative. In the park, visitors may sit on a circular platform nine feet above the ground and proffer buckets of oats to these enormous creatures. It's a unique opportunity to observe their tongues – which are 18 inches long – as well as the sunset over the Rift Valley and the perfectly aligned tea and coffee plantations. Traces of some of the earliest human ancestors were found near this spot.

Schon dieses elisabethanische Haus mit neugotischen Zügen ist eine Reise wert. Die Eigentümer, die sich jenem Ideal des guten Geschmacks verpflichtet haben, das die Untertanen Ihrer Majestät geprägt hat, bemühen sich seit 1932, die »Landhaus«-Atmosphäre ihrer Villa zu erhalten.

Die geometrischen Frontgiebel, die traditionellen Ziegel britischer Häuser, die Eingangstür aus Massivholz, die Verbindung edler Baumaterialien, gotische Kreuzrippengewölbe – da scheint in 1500 Metern Höhe »Rule Britannia« zu erklingen, so patriotisch wirkt das Gebäude. Den Giraffen gefällt es offenbar. Im Park können die Touristen den großen Tieren von einer drei Meter hohen runden Plattform aus Eimer mit Getreide anbieten. Wo kann man schon wie hier ihre 45 Zentimeter lange Zunge aus nächster Nähe bewundern? In der Abenddämmerung geht die Sonne über dem Rifttal und den sorgsam angelegten Tee- und Kaffeeplantagen unter. In dieser Gegend wurden die Spuren von einigen der ältesten menschlichen Vorfahren gefunden.

Située au cœur de l'Afrique orientale, cette maison élisabéthaine aux influences néogothiques est, à elle seule, un but de voyage. Portés par l'idéal séculaire du bon goût que l'on prête aux sujets de Sa Majesté, ses propriétaires veillent depuis 1932 à préserver l'atmosphère «maison de campagne» de leur résidence.

Frontons aux lignes géométriques, briques traditionnelles des demeures britishs, porte d'entrée en bois massif, association de matériaux nobles, ogives gothiques, c'est un chant aux accents patriotiques très «Rule, Britannia» qui s'élève à cette altitude (nous sommes à plus de 1500 mètres). Les girafes, visiblement, apprécient. Dans le parc, depuis une plateforme circulaire située à trois mètres au-dessus du sol, le visiteur peut tendre à ces géantes des seaux pleins de céréales. Une chance unique d'observer de près leur langue longue de 45 centimètres! À la nuit tombée, le soleil se couche au-dessus de la vallée du Rift et des plantations de thé et de café soigneusement alignées. On a découvert ici les traces des plus anciens ancêtres des hommes.

❋ **ABOVE** The giraffes are used to hotel guests and peer right into the living room to greet them. **FACING PAGE** The entrance leads to the largest room in the house, with high arches that allow the air to circulate. The ivory-coloured walls set off the yellow wood. In the background, a chair and a footstool on a floor of local boards. Above the chimneypiece, a portrait from the 1920s. ❋ **OBEN** Die Giraffen haben sich an die Hotelgäste gewöhnt und begrüßen sie durch Fenster und Türen. **RECHTE SEITE** Durch die Eingangstür betritt man direkt den größten Raum, unter dessen Bögen die Luft zirkulieren kann. Die elfenbeinfarbenen Wände bringen das helle Holz gut zur Geltung. Im Hintergrund steht ein Sessel mit Fußstütze auf dem Parkett aus hiesigem Holz. Über dem Kamin hängt ein Porträt aus den 1920er Jahren. ❋ **CI-DESSUS** Les girafes sont habituées aux clients de l'hôtel et viennent les saluer jusque dans le salon. **PAGE DE DROITE** L'entrée donne directement sur la pièce la plus vaste de la maison avec ses arches qui permettent à l'air de circuler. Les murs ivoire mettent en valeur le bois blond. Au fond, un fauteuil et son repose-pied sur un parquet en bois local. Au-dessus de la cheminée, un portrait des années 1920.

❋ **FACING PAGE** A colonial era telephone. **ABOVE** The classic mahogany library, in perfect harmony with the English sofa, where you can take your ease after a safari in the neighbouring game park. **BELOW** A complete Art Deco bathroom. ❋ **LINKE SEITE** Ein Telefon aus der Kolonialzeit. **OBEN** Das englische Sofa passt gut in die klassisch angelegte Bibliothek aus Mahagoni. Hier kann man sich nach einer Safari im benachbarten Nationalpark ausruhen. **UNTEN** In den Bädern dominiert der Art-déco-Stil. ❋ **PAGE DE GAUCHE** Un téléphone de l'époque coloniale. **CI-DESSUS** La bibliothèque de facture classique fabriquée en acajou, s'harmonise avec le canapé anglais où l'on peut s'étendre après un safari dans le parc voisin. **CI-DESSOUS** Dans les salles de bains règne le «total look» art-déco.

Sirocco House
Lake Naivasha

This Art Deco villa built on a lake shore beloved of hippos has a past as romantic as anything in *Out of Africa*.

Think of Mozart's music played over the harsh cries of a hippo colony. That, according to its owner, is as good a definition of Sirocco House as any.

No reference to the 1930s architecture and furnishings; no, the place itself, like an auditorium, draws its majesty from a melody that is to be found nowhere else on the planet. "When she built this property, my mother was dreaming of a space entirely dedicated to music in the middle of the bush," says Oria Douglas-Hamilton, who with her husband Ian has restored the house over a period of seven years. In the beginning there was the shared passion for Africa between an artist, Giselle Bunau-Varilla, and her Italian aviator husband Mario Rocco. The year was 1930, and the villa was built according to plans by the French modernist architect Hervé Bazin. It was a simple design: big bedrooms on the first floor surrounded by a wide veranda, a roof supported by thick octagonal cedar trunks, a living room opening on another veranda, and an estate of 3,000 hectares. The couple lived in this paradise for over 50 years. After her parents died, Oria Douglas-Hamilton picked up the gauntlet and opened her "farm" to visitors. Far from the agitation of Nairobi, life at Sirocco House still has the power to evoke the Africa of Karen Blixen.

Eine Mischung aus einer Mozartpartitur und dem Grunzen der Flusspferde – diese Beschreibung würde Sirocco House am ehesten gerecht, meint die Hausherrin selbst.

Weder die Architektur aus den 1930er Jahren noch die Einrichtung aus derselben Zeit spielen ihrer Meinung nach die Hauptrolle. Nein, der Ort leite wie ein Auditorium seine Großartigkeit von einer einzigartigen Melodie her. »Beim Bau ihres Hauses schwebte meiner Mutter ein von Musik erfüllter Ort mitten in der Savanne vor«, erklärt Oria Douglas-Hamilton, die das Gebäude gemeinsam mit ihrem Mann Ian sieben Jahre lang restauriert hat. Alles begann mit einer leidenschaftlichen Begeisterung für Afrika, die die Künstlerin Giselle Bunau-Varilla und ihren Mann, den italienischen Flieger Mario Rocco, verband. Wir schreiben das Jahr 1930, die Villa wird nach Entwürfen des französischen Architekten Hervé Bazin gebaut. Die Aufteilung ist schlicht: Eine große Veranda umgibt die geräumigen Zimmer auf der ersten Etage, dicke achteckige Zedernstämme tragen das Dach, ein Salon mit eigener Veranda – das Ganze auf einem nahezu 3000 Hektar großen Anwesen. Mehr als 50 Jahre verbringen die Eheleute in ihrem Paradies. Nach dem Tod ihrer Eltern eröffnet Oria Douglas-Hamilton eine »Farm« für Reisende, die eine gemütliche Atmosphäre schätzen. In sicherer Entfernung von der Hektik Nairobis fühlt man sich im Sirocco House in die Zeit von Karen Blixen zurückversetzt.

Une fusion entre une partition de Mozart et le chant rauque des hippopotames. Voici, selon sa propriétaire, la définition la plus juste de Sirocco House.

Aucune référence à l'architecture des années 1930 ni à l'ameublement de même époque, non, l'endroit, pareil à un auditorium, tiendrait sa majesté d'une mélodie unique au monde. «En érigeant son domaine, ma mère rêvait d'un espace dédié à la musique au milieu de la savane», confie Oria Douglas-Hamilton qui, aux côtés de son époux Ian, a restauré l'endroit pendant sept années. À l'origine, il y a la passion commune pour l'Afrique d'une artiste, Giselle Bunau-Varilla, et de son mari Mario Rocco, aviateur italien. Nous sommes en 1930, la villa est édifiée d'après les plans de l'architecte moderniste français Hervé Bazin. L'ensemble est simple: de grandes chambres à l'étage entourées d'une vaste véranda, un toit soutenu par d'épais troncs de cèdres octogonaux, un salon ouvert sur sa véranda et, surtout, un domaine de près de 3000 hectares. Le couple vit dans son paradis plus de 50 ans. Après la disparition de ses parents, Oria Douglas-Hamilton reprend le flambeau et ouvre sa «ferme» aux voyageurs épris d'intimité. Loin de l'agitation de Nairobi, vivre à Sirocco House c'est se retrouver à l'époque de Karen Blixen.

❋ **PREVIOUS PAGES** All the Art Deco furniture in the house was designed in the 1930s by Giselle Bunau-Varilla. **ABOVE** The living room still has its original Art Deco authenticity. The Afghan kilims are certified mid-19th century. ❋ **VORHERGEHENDE DOPPELSEITE** Sämtliche Art-déco-Möbel wurden in den 1930er Jahren von Giselle Bunau-Varilla entworfen. **OBEN** Der Salon im authentischen Art déco. Die afghanischen Kelims stammen verbürgtermaßen aus der Mitte des 19. Jahrhunderts. ❋ **DOUBLE PAGE PRÉCÉDENTE** Les meubles Art Déco de la maison ont tous été dessinés dans les années 1930 par Giselle Bunau-Varilla. **CI-DESSUS** Le salon garde son authenticité Art Déco. Les kilims afghans son certifiés milieu du 19ᵉ siècle.

DODO'S TOWER
Lake Naivasha

An oriental pagoda in the midst of the forest.
Or rather an inhabited tree, which is how its creator sees it.

There's a strong likelihood that tourists in the centuries to come will view this brainchild of one woman, Dodo Cunningham-Reid, with the same interest that we feel nowadays for 18th century English follies.

There's something rather breathtaking about a 100-foot tower entirely furnished with European antiques in the middle of an African forest. With its cypress-wood shingles, the house is as tall as the huge acacias that surround it. And it's only a step from the vegetable to the animal world, since giraffes, gazelles, zebras and pink flamingoes, among other things, live on the 600-acre surrounding property. An architect, George Wade, working from the drawings made by Dodo Cunningham-Reid, supervised a laborious construction project that took four years to complete (the hippos that systematically laid waste the plumbing are still a burning memory). But the form of this building is more than matched by its interior. To the inherited furniture of an old English family have been added other beautiful things made in Nairobi. As a legacy to future generations, the tower is also a delight that is shared, because it is occasionally rented to amateurs of remarkable houses. In the bedroom are bunches of roses from the garden in crystal vases, the final touch of romantic luxury.

Jede Wette, dass die Touristen in den nächsten Jahrhunderten diese Ausgeburt der weiblichen Fantasie, Dodo Cunningham-Reids Meisterwerk, mit der gleichen Begeisterung betrachten werden, die wir heute der englischen Exzentrik des 18. Jahrhunderts entgegenbringen.

Schließlich ist ein 35 Meter hoher Turm mitten im afrikanischen Busch, möbliert mit europäischen Antiquitäten, durchaus etwas Besonderes. Der mit Zypressenholz verkleidete Wohnsitz versteckt sich zwischen den riesigen Akazien seiner Umgebung. Auf dem 250 Hektar großen Anwesen leben überdies Giraffen, Gazellen, Zebras und rosa Flamingos, um nur einige der Tiere zu nennen. Anhand der Zeichnungen von Dodo Cunningham-Reid wurde der Turm unter der Leitung des Architekten George Wade innerhalb von vier mühsamen Jahren gebaut. Form und Einrichtung dieser Residenz suchen ihresgleichen. Das von einer alteingesessenen englischen Familie geerbte Mobiliar wurde durch weitere in Nairobi hergestellte Möbelstücke ergänzt. Der Turm ist nicht nur ein Vermächtnis für zukünftige Generationen, bereits heute hat er Fans unter den Liebhabern außergewöhnlicher Häuser gefunden. In den Zimmern erblühen in Kristallvasen Rosen aus dem eigenen Garten – ein Detail des romantischen Luxus. Ist dies ein neuer Turm von Babel?

Il y a fort à parier que les touristes des siècles à venir visiteront ce produit de l'imagination d'une femme, Dodo Cunningham-Reid, avec le même enthousiasme que nous éprouvons aujourd'hui devant les «folies» anglaises du 18e siècle.

Il faut dire qu'une tour de 35 mètres de hauteur, en pleine forêt africaine, meublée d'antiquités européennes, a de quoi étonner. Revêtue de bois de cyprès, l'habitation joue la complémentarité avec les immenses acacias qui l'entourent. Du végétal à l'animal il n'y a qu'un pas puisque girafes, gazelles, zèbres et flamants roses, entre autres, vivent sur les 250 hectares de la propriété. C'est l'architecte George Wade qui, suivant les dessins de Dodo Cunningham-Reid, a supervisé une laborieuse construction de quatre années (on se souvient des hippopotames qui détruisaient systématiquement la plomberie!). Mais la forme de l'habitation n'a d'égale que sa décoration. Au mobilier hérité d'une vieille famille anglaise ont été ajoutées d'autres créations fabriquées à Nairobi. Legs aux générations futures, la tour est aussi un plaisir partagé, car cette «folie» est louée aux amateurs de maisons exceptionnelles. Dans les chambres, les roses du jardin, détails d'un luxe romantique, s'épanouissent dans des vases en cristal. Une nouvelle tour de Babel?

✳ **PAGE 216** The great English tradition of the "folly," reinvented in an African forest. Every year the tower is re-varnished to preserve its honey colour. **ABOVE AND FACING PAGE** The staircase runs up the whole tower, which narrows towards the top and ends in the meditation room painted in *trompe l'œil* by David Merrian. ✳ **SEITE 216** Im Herzen des Waldes wurde die große Tradition englischer Exzentrik wiederbelebt. Der Turm wird jedes Jahr frisch lackiert. So bewahrt er seine schöne Honigfarbe. **OBEN UND RECHTE SEITE** Die Treppe zieht sich durch den gesamten Turm, der sich nach oben hin verjüngt bis zum Meditationsraum, welcher von David Merrian im Trompe-l'œil-Stil ausgemalt wurde. ✳ **PAGE 216** La grande tradition anglaise des «folies» a été réinventée au cœur de la forêt. Chaque année, la tour est revernie pour préserver sa couleur miel. **CI-DESSOUS ET PAGE DE DROITE** L'escalier grimpe le long de la tour qui se rétrécit jusqu'à la salle de méditation peinte en trompe-l'œil par David Merrian.

✳ **ABOVE** Portrait of Dodo Cunningham-Reid. **BELOW** In the dining room, mahogany panelling and cedar-wood floor. The olive-wood Biedermeier chairs are made with ebony inlays. It's hard to reconcile all this with the idea that hippos gambole by dark under the windows. ✳ **OBEN** Dodo Cunningham-Reid. **UNTEN** Mahagoni-Vertäfelung und Zedernholzboden im Esszimmer. Die Olivenholzstühle aus dem Biedermeier sind mit Ebenholzintarsien verziert. Unvorstellbar, dass sich bei Dunkelheit unter den Fenstern Flusspferde vergnügen. ✳ **CI-DESSUS** Portait de Dodo Cunningham-Reid. **CI-DESSOUS** Dans la salle à manger, boiseries en acajou et sol en cèdre. Les chaises en bois d'olivier de style Biedermeier sont incrustées d'ébène. Comment imaginer que les hippopotames gambadent sous les fenêtres à la tombée de la nuit?

✻ **BELOW** In its cocoon of panelling, a small bedroom with a 19th century bedstead. **FOLLOWING PAGES** In the master bedroom on the fourth floor, an 18th century gilt wood bed. On the embroidered linen sheets, Indian cushions. ✻ **UNTEN** Wie in einem holzvertäfelten Schmuckkästchen: ein kleines Zimmer mit einem Bett aus dem 19. Jahrhundert. **FOLGENDE DOPPELSEITE** Im Zimmer der Dame des Hauses auf der vierten Etage steht ein vergoldetes französisches Holzbett aus dem 18. Jahrhundert. Auf der Bettwäsche aus besticktem Leinen liegen indische Kissen. ✻ **CI-DESSOUS** Dans un écrin de boiseries, une petite chambre et son lit 19e. **DOUBLE PAGE SUIVANTE** Dans la chambre de maître située au quatrième étage, un lit français 18e en bois doré. Sur les draps en lin brodés, des coussins indiens.

❋ **BELOW** In this bathroom, a varnished cedar ceiling and polished mahogany panelling. On the towel rack, the linen is embroidered with the arms of the house. **FACING PAGE** A lavatory, decorated with little Chinese towers. **FOLLOWING PAGES** Breakfast, served with old crockery on a teak table. The pavilion in the trees is used as a massage room. Close to Lake Naivasha with its abundant fauna, the tower is also within reach of the Aberdare Mountains. ❋ **UNTEN** Badezimmer mit polierter Mahagonivertäfelung; die Zimmerdecke ist aus lackiertem Zedernholz. Die Bade- und Handtücher auf den Halterungen sind mit dem Wappen des Hauses bestickt. **RECHTE SEITE** Kleiner Waschraum, dekoriert mit chinesischen Türmchen. **FOLGENDE DOPPELSEITE** Großes Frühstück mit altem Geschirr auf einem Teaktisch. Der Pavillon unter den Bäumen dient als Massageraum. In der Nähe des Naivasha-Sees mit seiner großartigen Tierwelt steht der Turm in direkter Nachbarschaft zu den Bergen von Aberdare. ❋ **CI-DESSOUS** Dans cette salle de bains, cèdre verni au plafond et boiseries en acajou poli au papier de verre. Sur le porte-serviettes, le linge de maison est brodé aux armes de la maison. **PAGE DE DROITE** Cabinet de toilette décoré de petites tours chinoises. **DOUBLE PAGE SUIVANTE** Sur une table en teck, un petit-déjeuner chic dans une vaisselle ancienne. Le pavillon dans les arbres sert de salon de massage. Tout près du lac Naivasha où la faune est abondante, la tour voisine avec les montagnes de l'Aberdare.

Hippo Point
Lake Naivasha

A cottage in Kent, vintage 1930? Not a bit of it.
Those aren't sheep, they're hippos.

Hippo Point is another vestige of the colonial era, a Tudor-style house by the architect Sir Edwin Lutyens with an English lawn in front.

The garden is geometrically perfect, the grass so impeccably cut that you'd swear it had been snipped with scissors; and the house itself, built in 1933, is now an eight bedroom hotel belonging to the owner of the magnificent Dodo's Tower (see previous pages). A few years ago, the façade was still daubed in a tar-coloured rendering. This was patiently removed by Dodo Cunningham-Reid, to reveal the kind of half-timbering that was typical of 1930s England (though in this case the wood was cedar). With her romantic pink-hued 'cottage' and its carefully decorated bedrooms, Dodo has reinvented the original style of this place, in a distinctive way that oscillates between classical and modern. The dining room furniture is teak; the china is a vestige of European aristocracy, like the linen sheets, which were made in Russia and brought to England before coming to rest in Kenya. Even the wild animals all around – antelopes, gazelles and zebras – seem to have trotted out of a romantic novel. But don't go too close – they're real enough, and sometimes they forget their manners.

Hippo Point, ein Relikt aus der Kolonialzeit mit breitem englischen Rasen, trägt den Tudor-Stil des Architekten Sir Edwin Luytens stolz zur Schau.

Der Garten ist geometrisch, der Rasen makellos wie mit der Schere geschnitten. Die 1933 erbaute Anlage beherbergt inzwischen ein Hotel mit acht Zimmern, das der Eigentümerin von Dodo's Tower gehört (siehe vorhergehende Seiten). Noch vor wenigen Jahren zierte teerfarbener Rauputz die Fassade, der von Dodo Cunningham-Reid in geduldiger Kleinarbeit entfernt wurde, bis die Balken aus Zedernholz zum Vorschein kamen, die für das edwardianische England der 1930er Jahre charakteristisch sind. Die Eigentümerin verwandelte das Gebäude in ein romantisches, rosa gestrichenes Cottage mit liebevoll eingerichteten Hotelzimmern. Heutzutage würde man es als eine gelungene Mischung aus klassischem und modernem Stil bezeichnen. Die Gäste speisen in einem Teakholz-Ambiente von altem Geschirr. Die aus Russland stammende Leinenwäsche, ein Vermächtnis der europäischen Aristokratie, wurde nach England exportiert, bevor sie schließlich nach Kenia kam. Selbst die wilden Tiere, Antilopen, Gazellen und Zebras scheinen einem romantischen Märchen entsprungen zu sein. Aber Vorsicht! Sie sind echt und haben nicht immer die besten Manieren.

Vestige de l'époque coloniale, Hippo Point arbore fièrement son habitat de tradition «Tudor» édifié devant une pelouse anglaise par l'architecte Sir Edwin Luytens.

Jardin géométrique, vert impeccable d'une herbe que l'on jurerait taillée au ciseau, ce domaine, édifié en 1933, est désormais un hôtel de huit chambres appartenant à la propriétaire de la magnifique Dodo's Tower (voir pages précédentes). Il y a quelques années, la façade était encore recouverte d'un crépi couleur goudron. Dodo Cunningham-Reid l'a patiemment ôté, faisant apparaître ces poutres en bois de cèdre typiques de l'Angleterre édouardienne des années 1930. Avec son cottage romantique aux teintes roses et ses chambres décorées avec soin, elle a même réinventé la place. Aujourd'hui, sa marque distinctive oscille entre classique et moderne. On dîne sur un mobilier en teck, dans des vaisselles anciennes, ces vestiges d'une aristocratie européenne que l'on retrouve jusqu'aux draps en lin, fabriqués en Russie, importés en Angleterre, avant d'atterrir au Kenya. Même les animaux sauvages, antilopes, gazelles, et autres zèbres semblent sortir tout droit d'un conte romantique. Mais défense de s'en approcher! Eux sont bien réels, et manquent parfois de savoir-vivre.

❋ **FACING PAGE** The Tudor style, typical of England in the 1930s, is exemplified by this hotel, built to original plans by Sir Edwin Lutyens. **ABOVE** Under the watchful eye of a French chef, the food is prepared using products from the vegetable garden, or the neighbouring farms, all of which are certified organic. ❋ **LINKE SEITE** Nach Plänen von Sir Edwin Luytens wurde dieses Hotel im Tudor-Stil errichtet, der im England der 1930er Jahre vorherrschte. **OBEN** Der französische Chefkoch sorgt dafür, dass jeder Gast nach seinen Wünschen bekocht wird. Die Lebensmittel stammen sämtlich aus biologischem Anbau, entweder aus dem eigenen Garten oder von den Bauernhöfen der Umgebung. ❋ **PAGE DE GAUCHE** Style Tudor, typique de l'Angleterre des années 1930 pour cet hôtel édifié sur les plans de Sir Edwin Luytens. **CI-DESSUS** Sous la conduite du cuisinier français, les plats sont réalisés selon les goûts de chacun à partir des produits du jardin ou des fermes voisines, tous certifiés bio.

※ **PREVIOUS PAGES** The best suite at Hippo Point, with its dark wood floor and dresser. **ABOVE AND FACING PAGE** All the bathroom furniture was designed by Dodo Cunningham-Reid and made by craftsmen in Nairobi. ※ **VORHERGEHENDE DOPPELSEITE** Von der Kommode bis zum Parkett ist diese Suite in dunklem Holz ausgestattet. Sie hat die schönsten Zimmer des Hotels. **OBEN UND RECHTE SEITE** Die Einrichtung des Badezimmers wurde nach Entwürfen von Dodo Cunningham-Reid in Nairobi angefertigt. ※ **DOUBLE PAGE PRÉCÉDENTE** Avec ses bois sombres qui courent de la commode au parquet, la suite est l'endroit privilégié de Hippo Point. **CI-DESSUS ET PAGE DE DROITE** Les meubles de la salle de bains, exécutés par des artisans de Nairobi, ont tous été dessinés par Dodo Cunningham-Reid.

Armando Tanzini
Malindi Coast

This colonnaded house open to the sea-breeze is a delicious mix of the ethnic and the classical.

As so often happens, it was love at first sight between Kenya and this particular European traveller, with art as the bridge between them.

Born in Tuscany, Armando Tanzini now proclaims himself Italian-Kenyan because his work, which he defines as classical and primitive, straddles both continents. His house on the seashore at Malindi, a majestic colonnaded old building with a typical East African *makuti* roof, reflects this precisely. The floors and doors were designed by Tanzini himself; the warm shades of the wooden floorboards and ceilings blend with those of the panelling and the old Chinese, Indian and Lamu furniture. The care taken with every detail here is pure delight. Like his masters Henri Matisse, Pablo Picasso, Constantin Brancusi and Alberto Giacometti, Tanzini acknowledges the primacy of African sculpture, which he mixes with his own Florentine inheritance. Armando carries Africa in him (even his name sounds a little like Kenya's southern neighbour Tanzania) and he looks for an artistic rebirth in the original birthplace of mankind. It is no surprise that he defines his house as a temple of inspiration, and has started a foundation called "Do not forget Africa".

Im Leben passieren die erstaunlichsten Dinge, zum Beispiel dass sich ein europäischer Tourist für ein Land wie Kenia begeistert und eine künstlerische Verbindung herstellt.

Der gebürtige Toskaner Armando Tanzini weist sich selbst als Italo-Kenianer aus, weil sein Werk, das er als klassisch und zugleich primitiv bezeichnet, einen Spagat zwischen den Kontinenten darstellt. Sein Refugium an der Küste in Malindi beförderte diese Entwicklung. Das alte Gebäude mit dem *makuti* gedeckten, für Ostafrika charakteristischen Dach entfaltet mit seinen vielen Säulen eine eigenartig majestätische Wirkung. Der Hausherr selbst gestaltete die Böden und Türen. Die warmen Farben der Bodendielen und der Holzdecken passen gut zur Holzvertäfelung und den antiken Möbeln aus China, Indien und Lamu. Die Aufmerksamkeit für jedes Detail wird auch den Gästen zuteil. Wie seine Vorbilder Henri Matisse, Pablo Picasso, Constantin Brancusi und Alberto Giacometti pflegt der Künstler eine Vorliebe für afrikanische Skulpturen, die er mit seinem florentinischen Erbe kombiniert. Afrika klingt sogar in Armandos Nachnamen an (Tanzini klingt ein wenig wie Tansania, der Nachbarstaat). Er plädiert für eine Wiedergeburt der Künste, mit der die Odyssee des Homo sapiens begann. Kein Wunder, dass er diesen Ort als einen Tempel der Inspiration bezeichnet und die Stiftung »Do not forget Africa« gründete.

Comme il en existe entre les êtres, ce fut un coup de foudre entre le Kenya et un voyageur européen, avec l'art pour les réunir.

Né en Toscane, Armando Tanzini s'affiche désormais italo-kenyan puisque son œuvre, qu'il définit comme classique et primitive, fait le grand écart entre les continents. Pratiquement en bord de mer, son refuge de Malindi développe encore cette influence. La bâtisse ancienne au toit en *makuti*, typique des habitations de l'Est africain, déploie une majesté tout en colonnes. Les sols et les portes ont été dessinés par le propriétaire. Les teintes chaudes des planchers et plafonds en bois se mêlent à celles des boiseries et des meubles anciens de Chine, d'Inde ou de Lamu. Le souci apporté au moindre détail transfigure le séjour des hôtes. À l'image de ses maîtres Henri Matisse, Pablo Picasso, Constantin Brancusi ou Alberto Giacometti, l'artiste plébiscite les sculptures africaines qu'il mêle à un patrimoine florentin. Armando porte l'Afrique jusque dans son nom (Tanzini sonne un peu comme Tanzanie, le pays voisin), pour une renaissance des arts, là même où s'amorça l'odyssée des homos sapiens. Pas étonnant que l'endroit se définisse comme un temple de l'inspiration sous la forme d'une fondation baptisée «Do not forget Africa».

✳ **ABOVE AND FACING PAGE** A four-poster bed found in Kenya and veiled in immaculate silk. The armchair was bought in Lamu; the painting is by Armando Tanzini, in whose work the female form is a central element. ✳ **OBEN UND RECHTE SEITE** Tanzini entdeckte dieses mit strahlend weißer Seide verschleierte Himmelbett in Kenia, den Sessel fand er in Lamu. Frauenbildnisse sind ein zentrales Thema im Werk des Künstlers. ✳ **CI-DESSUS ET PAGE DE DROITE** Lit à baldaquin découvert au Kenya et voilé de soie immaculée. Fauteuil chiné à Lamu et représentation féminine, élément central du travail de l'artiste.

KATHARINA SCHMEZER & HERMANN STUCKI

LAMU

A riot of colours offsets the blinding white geometry of this 18th century house in the purest Swahili style.

More often than not, the purchase of a house is the result of a stroke of luck that occurs quite by chance. Towards the end of the 1970s the painter Hermann Stucki had just sold a series of drawings and collages in Nairobi.

His pockets were full of Kenyan shillings, a currency which cannot be taken out of the country. As luck would have it, he found himself in Lamu Town, a tumbledown port near the Somali border, built centuries ago in the mangrove swamp by Moorish slave traders. In the maze of streets lived a tiny cosmopolitan crowd originating from Persia, Yemen, Oman, Malaysia, India, Portugal, and the African mainland. In a quiet corner Stucki and his companion Katharina Schmezer found a house in the Arab colonial style, empty and for sale. The couple plunged into a renovation adventure that was to last for the next 15 years. In Europe, they both work, among others, for Fabric Frontline, a company specializing in finest silks, which collaborates with the most famous fashion and interior designers. Hermann designs fabric prints and Katharina represents the company in Paris. Naturally enough, the walls of their "White House" are set off by vibrant coloured fabrics, which billow in the ocean breeze. Now that their house is finished, the couple have launched themselves into the renovation of other ruins. With their excellent knowledge of the local language, they are a veritable mine of information for any newcomer who succumbs to the island's charm.

Der Kauf eines Hauses hängt oftmals mit einem unerwarteten Glückstreffer zusammen. Der Maler Hermann Stucki konnte Ende der 1970er Jahre in Nairobi unverhofft eine Reihe von Zeichnungen und Collagen verkaufen.

Als er also gerade im Besitz dieses kleinen Vermögens in kenianischen Schilling war, das er nicht ausführen durfte, entdeckte er Lamu, eine heruntergekommene Hafenstadt, die unweit der somalischen Grenze vor Jahrhunderten von Sklavenhändlern in die Mangrovensümpfe gebaut worden war. Im Labyrinth der Gassen lebte eine kleine Gemeinschaft von Kosmopoliten, die aus Persien, dem Jemen, Oman, Malaysia, Indien, Portugal und vom afrikanischen Festland stammten. An einer idyllischen Straßenecke erwartete ein Haus im arabischen Kolonialstil seine neuen Besitzer. Voller Energie stürzten sich Hermann Stucki und Katharina Schmezer in die Renovierung, ein Abenteuer, das 15 Jahre in Anspruch nehmen sollte. Das Ehepaar arbeitet unter anderem für Fabric Frontline, eine Schweizer Firma, die luxuriöse Seidenstoffe herstellt und die berühmten Modehäuser beliefert. Hermann Stucki entwirft für sie Stoffdessins, während Katharina Schmezer die Firma bei den großen Couturiers in Paris vertritt. So ist es nicht verwunderlich, dass leuchtend bunte Seidenstoffe die Wände ihres „weißen Hauses" hervorheben. Seitdem sie ihr Haus fertig gestellt haben, kümmert sich das Ehepaar um die Renovierung weiterer verfallener Häuser. Sie sprechen die Landessprache Kisuaheli und öffnen somit jedem Liebhaber der Insel Tür und Tor bei den Einheimischen.

Souvent, l'achat d'une maison procède d'un hasard heureux. Peintre, Hermann Stucki rencontre un joli succès avec une série de collages et dessins vendus à Nairobi.

À la tête d'une petite fortune en shillings kenyans, monnaie qu'il ne peut sortir du pays, il découvre, vers la fin des années 1970, Lamu Town, un port déglingué érigé il y a des siècles dans la mangrove par des négriers maures. Dans l'entrelacs de ruelles vit une petite communauté cosmopolite originaire de la Perse, du Yémen, d'Oman, de Malaisie, d'Inde, du Portugal et du continent africain. Dans un coin pittoresque, une maison de style colonial arabe attend ses nouveaux propriétaires. Hermann Stucki et Katharina Schmezer se lancent pleins d'enthousiasme dans l'aventure d'une rénovation. Une aventure qui durera 15 ans! En Europe, le couple travaille entre autres pour la maison Fabric Frontline, fabricant suisse de tissus de soie luxueux, qui collabore avec les grands couturiers et décorateurs d'intérieur. Katharina la représente sur Paris, et Hermann dessine pour ses tissus imprimés. Tout naturellement, les murs de la «maison blanche» sont relevés par les vibrantes couleurs d'étoffes gonflées par les vents marins. Leur maison achevée, le couple se lance dans l'aménagement d'autres ruines. Familiers de la langue du pays, le swahili, ils sont un sésame pour quiconque succombe aux charmes de l'île.

※ **ABOVE** The inner courtyard gives access to the main building with its three rooms in a row. The battle against humidity never ceases in Lamu; even the wall renderings have to be protected by a layer of wax. **FOLLOWING PAGES** Beside the deep well, the traditional pool, stocking water for the plants, brings a touch of modernity to the tropical garden. **PAGES 250-251** A loggia covered with plaited palm leaves filters Lamu's relentless sunshine. ※ **OBEN** Der Innenhof führt ins Hauptgebäude mit den drei hintereinander liegenden Zimmern. Der Kampf gegen die Feuchtigkeit gehört in Lamu zum Alltag, deshalb schützt eine Wachsschicht den Mauerbewurf. **FOLGENDE DOPPELSEITE** Das traditionelle Wasserbecken neben dem tiefen Ziehbrunnen dient als Reservoir zur Bewässerung und verleiht dem tropischen Garten einen modernen Akzent. **SEITEN 250-251** Eine mit Kokospalmblättern gedeckte Laube hält das mörderische Sonnenlicht ab. ※ **CI-DESSUS** Depuis la cour intérieure on accède au bâtiment principal avec ses trois pièces en alignement. Se battre contre l'humidité est une bataille sans fin à Lamu: l'enduit des murs est protégé par une couche de cire. **DOUBLE PAGE SUIVANTE** À côté du puits profond, le bassin traditionnel, qui sert de réservoir d'eau d'arrosage donne au jardin tropical une touche de modernité. **PAGES 250-251** Une tonnelle couverte de feuilles de palmes tressées filtre le soleil assassin de Lamu.

✳ **FACING PAGE AND BELOW** Hermann Stucki designed the living room furniture himself and had it made by Husseini, today the most talented carpenter in Lamu, a neighbour whom he and Katharina have known since he was a child. The beams are painted black and vermilion, native style, with white inlaid lines filled with plaster made from shell-lime. **RIGHT** The wall, pocked with 130 *zidaka* or stucco niches, is typical of feudal Swahili buildings; before the renovation work, it was covered by a thick layer of plaster. ✳
LINKE SEITE UND UNTEN Die Möbel im Salon hat Hermann Stucki entworfen und von seinem Nachbarn Husseini, heute der begabteste Schreiner in Lamu, den er und Katharina seit seiner Kindheit kennen, anfertigen lassen. Die Balken sind in der suahelischen Tradition schwarz und ochsenblutrot bemalt, versehen mit weißen vertieften Linien, die mit Muschelgips gefüllt sind. **RECHTS** Vor der Renovierung waren die *zidaka*, die für die feudalen Häuser oder kleinen Paläste der Suaheli typischen, in einer Mauer eingelassenen Stucknischen, hier 130 Stück, mit einer dicken Mörtelschicht zugekleistert. ✳
PAGE DE GAUCHE ET CI-DESSOUS Dans le salon, Hermann Stucki a lui-même dessiné des meubles fabriqués par Husseini, un voisin menuisier, aujourd'hui le plus doué à Lamu, que le couple connaît depuis son enfance. Les poutres sont peintes dans la tradition swahili en noir et vermeil, avec des sillons garnis d'un enduit blanc de poudre de coquillage. **A DROITE** Les *zidaka* sont des niches en stuc (ici au nombre de 130) creusées dans un mur des maisons féodales swahili; avant la rénovation, elles étaient recouvertes d'une épaisse couche d'enduit.

❋ **PREVIOUS PAGES** A bed of woven palm fronds. The bedcovers in the house are made of precious silks in an ethnic style, as are the curtains, hanging on 18th century wooden curtain-rails and dividing up the rooms. The floors are covered with traditional mosque-mats. **ABOVE** Shisham dresser, mirror and lamp. **FACING PAGE** This 19th century four-poster bed, found on the island, is upholstered in duchess silk, the bedcover is made from a sari. Lying by the bed is a gorgeous *mkeka*, a rare handmade Tanzanian rug made of palm fronds. ❋ **VORHER-GEHENDE DOPPELSEITE** Eine Liegestatt aus geflochtenen Palmwedeln. In diesem Haus sind die Tagesdecken und raumunterteilenden Vorhänge, die an massiven Holzstangen aus dem 18. Jahrhundert hängen, aus Seidenstoffen im Ethno-Stil gefertigt. Herkömmliche Moschee-Matten schmücken die Böden. **OBEN** Kommode, Spiegel und Lampe aus ostindischem Palisander. **RECHTE SEITE** Das Himmelbett aus dem 19. Jahrhundert stammt von der Insel selbst. Die Decke ist aus Saristoff, der Betthimmel in Duchesseseide gepatched. Unter dem Bett liegt ein wunderschöner *mkeka*, ein aus Palmwedeln handgefertigter, seltener Teppich aus Tansania. ❋ **DOUBLE PAGE PRÉCÉDENTE** Couchette en tressage de palmes séchées. Les dessus-de-lit de la maison sont réalisés dans des soieries type ethno ainsi que les rideaux, pendus sur des tringles 18ᵉ en bois massif, qui divisent les grandes pièces. Sols habillés d'une natte traditionnelle de mosquée. **CI-DESSUS** Commode, miroir et lampe en palissandre indien. **PAGE DE DROITE** Le baldaquin du lit, certifié 19ᵉ, découvert sur l'île, est habillé de soie duchesse, le couvre-lit est réalisé avec un sari. Sous le lit, un magnifique *mkeka*, tapis rare de Tanzanie tissé main à partir de feuilles de palmier.

✳ **PREVIOUS PAGES, ABOVE AND RIGHT** In the kitchen, a successful marriage between the romance of a traditional house and the contemporary character of this interior, with its cement floor. The roof is surfaced with plaited coconut palmleaves. Traditional local crockery. ✳ **VORHERGEHENDE DOPPELSEITE, OBEN UND RECHTS** Die Küche kombiniert die Romantik des alten Hauses mit hochmodernen Elementen, zum Beispiel dem Zementboden. Das Dach ist aus Kokospalmwedeln. Traditionelles Geschirr. ✳ **DOUBLE PAGE PRÉCÉDENTE, CI-DESSUS ET À DROITE** Dans la cuisine, mariage réussi entre le romantisme d'une maison traditionnelle et la puissante touche contemporaine de son espace intérieur avec son sol en ciment. Toit en feuille de cocotier tressée. Vaisselle traditionnelle.

❊ **ABOVE** There is very little water in Lamu, therefore the bathrooms, for instance, have pools, called *birika,* to store the water. To take a shower, one draws directly from the pool by using a coconut shell ladle. ❊ **OBEN** In Lamu gibt es nicht überall fließendes Wasser. Deshalb wird es, zum Beispiel für das Badezimmer, in gemauerten Becken, den *birika* gespeichert. Daraus schöpft man direkt das Duschwasser mittels einer aus Kokosschale hergestellten Kelle. ❊ **CI-DESSUS** L'eau courante n'est pas évidente à Lamu. Dans les maisons typiques elle est stockée, par exemple à la salle de bains, dans des bassins, les *birika*. Une louche fabriquée avec une noix de coco sert à se doucher, en puisant l'eau directement du bassin.

❋ **ABOVE** Small fishes are swimming in the *birika* to keep the water clean and to eliminate the mosquito-larvae. ❋ **OBEN** In der *birika* schwimmen kleine Fische, die das Wasser sauberhalten und die Mückenlarven fressen. ❋ **CI-DESSUS** Dans les *birika* des petits poissons gardent l'eau propre et éliminent les larves de moustiques.

yago casado
Lamu

This house, built in 1720 in the purest local style,
has been decorated throughout by its owner, a Spanish painter based in Milan.

Originally constructed in the 18th century, when the slave trade between Yemen and Zanzibar was at its height, this building is something of a labyrinth.

The open vestibule is a place of welcome, but also of defence. Its L-shape creates a dead end designed to resist an attack, or at least to allow a retreat back into the house. Dominated by a 100-foot tall palm tree, the latter has an interior garden, a fountain and a well of its own. This area lies to one side of a two-storey building; the ground floor area, which is characteristic of the Swahili style with its 18-foot ceiling, has beautiful columns decorated with flower motifs. There are no doors or windows; everything is wide open to the sea breeze. An outside staircase leads to the first floor; higher up, there is another large bedroom giving onto a terrace. Yago Casado says that the view across Lamu combined with the austere lines of his house have had a revelatory effect on him. "One is different in Africa. Here your identity gradually melts away and you approach a kind of spirituality. In the end, our search is not for a place to live, but a place to die." Love at first sight? Most definitely!

Das Haus wurde von einem reichen Sklavenhändler erbaut – vom Jemen bis Sansibar erreichte der Sklavenhandel seinen Höhepunkt im 18. Jahrhundert.

Das Gebäude ist außergewöhnlich verschlungen und verwinkelt. In dem offenen Vorhof fühlt sich der Besucher willkommen, gleichzeitig jedoch herausgefordert. Die L-Form führt in eine Sackgasse, die im Falle eines Angriffs die Feinde aufhalten und den Bewohnern erlauben sollte, ins Haus zu flüchten. Vor dem Gebäude steht eine 35 Meter hohe Palme und im Innenhof erblüht ein Garten mit Fontäne und eigenem Brunnen. Darüber liegt das zweistöckige Wohnhaus. Im Erdgeschoss mit seinen für den Suaheli-Stil charakteristischen, sechs Meter hohen Decken ragen stolze, mit Blumenmustern verzierte Säulen in die Höhe. Türen und Fenster gibt es nicht – der Seewind weht ungehindert durchs Haus. Eine Außentreppe führt in die erste Etage. Ein Stockwerk höher befinden sich die Terrasse und ein weiterer großer Raum. Mit Blick auf Lamu gesteht Yago Casado freimütig, dass ihm die Strenge seiner Behausung neue Sehweisen erschließt. »In Afrika wird man ein Anderer«, sagt er. »Hier löst sich die Identität langsam aber sicher auf, man nähert sich einer gewissen Spiritualität. Genau genommen sucht man nicht etwa einen Platz zum Leben, sondern einen Ort zum Sterben.« Liebe auf den ersten Blick? Das kann man wohl sagen!

Construit par un riche négrier (la traite des Noirs connut au 18e siècle son apogée entre le Yémen et Zanzibar), l'édifice impose d'emblée ses méandres.

Le vestibule ouvert accueille le visiteur, mais le défie aussi. Sa forme en L forme un cul-de-sac destiné à résister en cas d'attaque, ou tout au moins à se réfugier dans l'habitation. Dominée par un palmier de 35 mètres, celle-ci est agrémentée d'un jardin intérieur, d'une fontaine et d'un puits. Ce passage est situé à l'orée du bâtiment de deux étages. L'espace du rez-de-chaussée, caractéristique du style swahili avec ses 6 mètres sous plafond, arbore des colonnes décorées de motifs floraux. Ni portes ni fenêtres – l'ensemble est ouvert au vent marin. Un escalier extérieur grimpe au premier étage. Plus haut, la terrasse abrite encore une grande chambre. D'ici, avec vue sur Lamu, Yago Casado confie volontiers que les lignes austères de sa demeure agissent sur lui comme un révélateur. «On est différent en Afrique», dit-il. «Ici, l'identité se dissout progressivement, on se rapproche d'une certaine spiritualité. En fin de compte, on ne cherche pas un endroit pour vivre, mais un endroit pour mourir.» Un coup de foudre? C'est peut dire!

✳ **ABOVE** On the walls are paintings of Arab traders by Yago Casado. **FACING PAGE** The artist's studio. **FOLLOWING PAGES** In the chambers formerly reserved for the father and eldest son of the family, note the lovely Swahili baby cradle and the *zidaka* alcoves above the beds. On the floor, a Jambi palm mat. ✳ **OBEN** Die Bilder von Yago Casado stellen arabische Händler dar. **RECHTE SEITE** Das Atelier des Malers. **FOLGENDE DOPPELSEITE** In den Zimmern, die früher Vater und Sohn vorbehalten waren, befindet sich eine schöne suahelische Wiege. Oberhalb der Betten sind die typischen Nischen – *zidaka* genannt, auf dem Boden liegt ein Teppich aus Palmenfasern. ✳ **CI-DESSOUS** Aux murs, les tableaux signés Yago Casado représentent des marchands arabes. **PAGE DE DROITE** L'atelier du peintre. **DOUBLE PAGE SUIVANTE** Dans les chambres autrefois réservées au père et au fils de la famille, on remarque un beau berceaux swahili.

✳ **ABOVE** One of the painter's models, carefully posed in his traditional dress. **FACING PAGE** The house has three bathrooms, all restored in the style of the island. The beams in the ceiling are painted black, white and vermilion in the Swahili tradition. ✳ **OBEN** Das Modell des Malers ist nach einheimischer Art geschmückt und gekleidet. **RECHTE SEITE** Die drei Bäder des Hauses wurden im Stil der Insel restauriert. Die Deckenbalken sind in den Farben der Suaheli Schwarz, Weiß und Karminrot gestrichen. ✳ **CI-DESSOUS** Le modèle, coiffé et paré de son habit traditionnel, pose pour le peintre. **PAGE DE DROITE** La maison abrite trois salles de bains restaurées dans l'esprit de l'île. Au plafond, les poutres sont peintes dans la tradition swahilie de noir, blanc et vermeil.

Ngorongoro Crater Lodge

Mnemba Island Lodge
⊛

⊛
Emerson & Green

TANZANIA

Ngorongoro Crater Lodge

Ngorongoro Conservation Area

This extraordinary palace stands at the lip of one of the world's oldest volcanoes.

What on earth are they doing here, these minarets among the prowling carnivores? Where are we? There's nothing else anywhere near, and the Cessna has been in the air for 45 minutes since leaving the airport.

How can we explain such a folly, seen from an altitude of 8000 feet? In the beginning was the ambition of the Conservation Corporation Africa (ccafrica.com) to install itself in the continent's most magnificent places. Then there was a meeting between two men, the architect Silvio Rech and the decorator Chris Brown. It took them a year and a force of 450 Tanzanian workers and craftsmen to create this masterpiece, which is doubtless the most beautiful hotel in Africa. Amazingly, most of the Lodge, from its structural elements to the details of its interior, was made on the spot. There was a carpentry shop for the woodwork (*mnenga* walls, *mokoro* floors), a smithy for the metals, and so on – right down to details like the copper-coil chandeliers plaited by an assembly of Masai. In the evenings, the sense of mirage returns when a troop of Masai spearmen appear in their traditional dress. And in the morning thousands of flamingos take wing against the sunrise.

Ist das eine Erscheinung? Wozu dienen mitten im Busch diese seltsamen Minarette? Wo sind wir gelandet? Rundherum nichts – nach einem 45-minütigen Flug mit der Cessna von einem kleinen Flughafen aus.

Begonnen hat alles mit dem Ehrgeiz der Conservation Corporation Africa (ccafrica.com), sich an einem der schönsten Orte Afrikas niederzulassen. Dann begegneten sich zwei Männer: der Architekt Silvio Rech und der Dekorateur Chris Brown. Sie brauchten ein Jahr und 450 tansanische Arbeiter und Handwerker für die Verwirklichung dieses Meisterwerks, des wahrscheinlich schönsten Hotels in Afrika. Dabei ist die gesamte Lodge vom Aufbau bis zur kleinsten Dekoration direkt auf der Baustelle entstanden. Die Schreinerei war für die Holzvertäfelung zuständig (Wände in *mnenga*, Parkett in *mokoro*), die Kunstschmiede bis ins Detail für die Metallarbeiten, beispielsweise für die Kronleuchter aus Kupferdraht, die von einer Gruppe Massai hergestellt wurden. In der Abenddämmerung glaubt man weiter an Wunder, wenn aus dem Busch diese Krieger auftauchen – eine Lanze in der Hand, in voller Tracht – und morgens Tausende von rosa Flamingos aus dem Krater in die aufgehende Sonne fliegen.

On dirait une apparition. Mais que viennent faire ici, au voisinage des grands fauves, ces étranges minarets? Où sommes-nous? Rien alentour, le Cesna a volé 45 minutes depuis le petit aéroport.

Comment expliquer une telle folie à 2400 mètres d'altitude? À l'origine, il y a l'ambition de la Conservation Corporation Africa (ccafrica.com), décidée à s'implanter dans les plus beaux espaces d'Afrique. Et puis cette rencontre entre deux hommes, Silvio Rech, architecte, et Chris Brown, décorateur. Il leur a fallu une année et la force de travail de 450 ouvriers et artisans tanzaniens pour réaliser ce chef-d'œuvre, peut-être le plus bel hôtel d'Afrique. Étonnamment, l'ensemble du Lodge, de sa structure à la décoration intérieure, a été fabriqué sur les pentes même du chantier. L'atelier menuiserie s'est occupé des boiseries (murs en *mnenga*, parquet en *mokoro*), l'atelier ferronnerie des métaux, et ainsi de suite jusqu'aux plus infimes détails comme ces lustres en fil de cuivre tressés par une assemblée de Massaï. À la nuit tombée, la sensation de mirage se poursuit lorsque apparaissent ces guerriers de la brousse, lance à la main, en grande tenue traditionnelle. Au matin, dans le cratère, des milliers de flamants roses s'envolent dans le soleil naissant.

※ **PREVIOUS PAGES** In the dining room, the ceilings decorated with mirrors and gilded metal sunbursts were designed by the architect Silvio Rech. Under the great glass-bead chandeliers, the chairs are all upholstered with cotton damask. **ABOVE** The zinc basins have mirrors edged with gold leaf. ※ **VORHERGEHENDE DOPPELSEITE** Die Decken des Esszimmers sind mit Spiegeln und vergoldeten Metallsonnen verkleidet – eine Idee von Silvio Rech. Die Stühle unter den gläsernen Kronleuchtern wurden mit Baumwolldamast bezogen. **OBEN** Die Spiegel über den Waschbecken aus Zink sind mit Blattgold verziert. ※ **DOUBLE PAGE PRÉCÉDENTE** Dans la salle à manger, les plafonds ornés de miroirs et de soleils en métal doré ont été dessinés par l'architecte Silvio Rech. Sous les grands lustres à pampilles de verre, les chaises sont habillées de damassé de coton. **CI-DESSUS** Les lavabos en zinc sont ornés de miroirs dorés à la feuille.

❊ **ABOVE** A mirror found in a London flea market. **FACING PAGE** The bathtubs, each embellished with a piece of carved wood, are set in concrete. On the walls are wooden panels attached with big nails hammered out in the Lodge's workshop. ❊ **OBEN** Ein Spiegel vom Londoner Flohmarkt. **RECHTE SEITE** Die in einen Betonblock eingelassenen Badewannen sind mit Holz-schnitzerei verziert. Die Holzpaneele sind mit starken Nägeln (aus den Werkstätten der Lodge) an den Wänden befestigt. ❊ **CI-DESSUS** Miroir chiné aux Puces de Londres. **PAGE DE DROITE** Les baignoires ornées d'une pièce de bois ciselé sont intégrées dans un bloc de béton. Au mur, des panneaux de bois césuré sont fixés par de gros clous, martelés dans les ateliers du Lodge.

✳ **ABOVE** A bedroom with its banana leaf ceiling. The bed is very broad, inspired by the Indian and Arabian art of neighbouring Zanzibar. ✳ **OBEN** Ein Schlafzimmer unter einem Dach aus Blättern der Bananenstaude. Das große Bett kombiniert Stilelemente der indischen und arabischen Kultur der nah gelegenen Insel Sansibar. ✳ **CI-DESSUS** Une chambre blottie sous les feuilles de bananier. Un large lit inspiré des arts indien et arabe de l'île voisine de Zanzibar.

※ **FOLLOWING PAGES** A breakfast table, with chairs of brightly-coloured cotton velours. The view takes in the crater, with bush country in the foreground. ※ **FOLGENDE DOPPELSEITE** Man frühstückt mit Blick auf den Krater und den Busch. Die Stühle sind mit Baumwollsamt in leuchtenden Farben bezogen. ※ **DOUBLE PAGE SUIVANTE** Le petit-déjeuner sur des chaises habillées de velours de coton aux teintes vives est servi avec vue sur le cratère et la brousse.

Emerson & Green Zanzibar

The Sultan of Oman's palace, restored with deep respect for the blend of cultures and religions which epitomizes Zanzibar.

The past of this building is closely associated with an extravagant period of the 19th century when Zanzibar reached the height of its prosperity under the sultans.

Built around the traditional enclosed garden of a Moorish palace, it is a marriage of different styles, with lacy balconies, galleries of fretted wood, and round-topped window embrasures encrusted with coloured glass. Arthur Rimbaud, among others, was fascinated by Zanzibar, though he never came here; and the Emerson & Green house has retained much of what the great French poet dreamed of. The new owners have imported some novelties. In the bedrooms, coloured cement floors contrast with dark wooden furniture, and in the mazy passageways the walls change colour half way up, while the rounded vaulting is painted in pastel shades. The island breeze has carried the heavy scent of spices for centuries past, and it still invades the tall, square building. All around, the ruins of Stone Town are gradually coming to life and every year new arrivals come to decorate them.

Die Geschichte des Hauses ist mit der des 19. Jahrhunderts eng verknüpft, als Sansibar unter der Herrschaft des Sultans von Oman eine Epoche großen Wohlstands erlebte.

Wie bei maurischen Palästen üblich, wurde das Gebäude um den traditionellen Garten im Innenhof erbaut und verbindet die unterschiedlichsten Stilrichtungen miteinander, wie Balkone mit Holzspitzenbrüstung, Gänge mit festonierter Holzspitze und oben abgerundete, grün bemalte Fenster bezeugen. Der Zauber dieser glorreichen Vergangenheit – gern besungen von romantischen Dichtern wie Arthur Rimbaud, der, obwohl er nie in Sansibar war, dennoch ständig den Namen der Insel im Munde führte – wurde für die Gegenwart bewahrt und um moderne Impulse ergänzt. In den Zimmern kontrastieren farbige Zementböden mit dunklen Holzmöbeln. Im Labyrinth der Winkel und Ecken wechseln die Wände auf halber Höhe die Farbe, während die Rundung der Rippengewölbe in Pastellfarbe erscheint. Schwere Düfte und würzige Aromen, die seit Jahrhunderten vom Inselwind hergetragen werden, strömen in das hohe viereckige Haus. Inzwischen werden nach diesem Vorbild weitere Häuser in Stone Town wieder hergerichtet. Jährlich kommen neue Antiquitätenhändler, um sie neu zu dekorieren.

La mémoire de la maison est chevillée aux fastes du 19e siècle, époque de grande prospérité pour Zanzibar, celle du règne des sultans d'Oman.

Édifiée autour du traditionnel jardin intérieur des palais maures, elle marie de nombreux styles avec ses balcons de bois dentelés, ses galeries festonnées de dentelles de bois, et ses ouvertures arrondies incrustées de verre coloré. De ce temps révolu, chanté par les écrivains romantiques, notamment par Arthur Rimbaud, qui n'y vint jamais mais qui ne cessait de répéter le nom de Zanzibar, l'Emerson & Green a conservé les attraits. Pourtant, et c'est encore là une affaire de charme, les nouveaux propriétaires ont apporté ici et là quelques traces des temps nouveaux. Dans les chambres, les sols de ciment coloré contrastent avec les meubles en bois foncé. Dans les dédales des couloirs, les murs changent de couleur à mi-hauteur et l'arrondi des ogives est peint dans des couleurs pastel. Et puis les parfums lourds et les saveurs épicées, portés depuis des siècles par le vent de l'île, envahissent la haute maison carrée. Autour d'elle, à son image, les ruines de Stone Town se redressent. Et, chaque année, de nouveaux antiquaires viennent les décorer.

✳ **PREVIOUS PAGES** In the bedroom suite, the carved wooden furniture typical of Zanzibar, along with touches of colour from the rounded windows and stained glass. Traditional Zanzibar wooden bed, with its mattress nearly three feet from the floor. **ABOVE** The bathtub is made of coloured and polished cement. ✳ **VORHERGEHENDE DOPPELSEITE** Die Holzschnitzerei in der Suite ist charakteristisch für Sansibar. Farbkontraste mit den abgerundeten Fenstern. Zirka ein Meter hohes traditionelles Holzbett aus Sansibar. **OBEN** Die Badewanne ist aus gefärbtem und poliertem Beton. ✳ **DOUBLE PAGE PRÉCÉDENTE** Dans la suite, des meubles en bois ciselé typique de Zanzibar. Touches colorées avec des fenêtres arrondies à vitraux. Lit en bois traditionnel de Zanzibar avec son sommier perché à près d'un mètre du sol. **CI-DESSUS** La baignoire de la salle de bains est en béton teinté et poli.

MNEMBA ISLAND LODGE
near Zanzibar

On this private island, the world's most exclusive Robinson Crusoes go barefoot in the sunshine.

This is a place where you can jog along very well with just a few books, fewer clothes, and a man or woman Friday in attendance.

What you'll have as backup is the maximum luxury of this African seaside hotel. Imagine an atoll in turquoise waters protected by a barrier of coral – and ten bungalows built in the tradition of Zanzibar fishermen's huts, with decoration entirely entrusted to local artisans. The benches are made of coconut wood and hemp. The roofs and walls of the bungalows were mostly plaited on the spot. What could be more simple and luxurious? You can walk round the island in 20 minutes. There are no cars, no scorpions and no malarial mosquitoes – nothing but white sand and palm trees. Out to sea, closely ranked schools of dolphins weave their way among the multicoloured sailing dhows, playing and leaping. In the evening you lie around on white cotton poufs and talk about the exotic fishes you saw that afternoon, or – if you're lucky – the whales that throng around Mnemba in the mating season. Whales are a sign of good fortune on this African side of the Indian Ocean.

Auf Mnemba Island braucht man nur Bücher, zwei, drei Kleider und natürlich einen »Freitag« – egal welchen Geschlechts.

Das afrikanische Luxushotel liegt direkt am Strand, auf einem Atoll im türkisfarbenen Meer, geschützt von einem vorgelagerten Korallenriff. Auf der Insel stehen zehn Bungalows im Stil der Fischerhütten von Sansibar, die von den Handwerkern der Umgebung gebaut wurden. Die Liegestühle werden aus Kokosholz und Hanfseilen gefertigt. Dächer und Wände der Bungalows aus Palmenblättern werden teilweise direkt vor Ort geflochten. Kann man sich Luxus schlichter vorstellen? Die Insel ist zu Fuß in 20 Minuten umrundet, es gibt weder Autos noch Skorpione noch Malaria – nur weißen Sand und Palmen. Auf hoher See, zwischen den Daus aus Sansibar, diesen Segelbooten mit buntem Rumpf, schwimmen Delphine in dichten Schwärmen. Einer nach dem anderen springt verspielt aus dem Wasser. Abends sitzt man zusammengesunken auf einem mit weißer Baumwolle gepolsterten Hocker und erzählt von den bunten Fischen, die man am Nachmittag gesehen hat oder, wenn man richtig Glück hatte, von den Walen, die während der Paarungszeit mit Mnemba flirten. Ein gutes Omen im Indischen Ozean, der die afrikanischen Küsten umspielt.

On vit ici avec quelques livres, deux ou trois vêtements, sans oublier, à portée de main, Vendredi – homme ou femme.

Luxe maximal pour cet hôtel africain de bord de mer. Imaginez un atoll aux eaux turquoise protégées par une barrière de corail. Dix bungalows construits dans la tradition des maisons de pêcheurs de Zanzibar. Une décoration confiée aux artisans des villages voisins. Les bancs sont en bois de cocotier et en corde de chanvre. Les toits et les murs de bungalows en feuille de palme sont en partie tressés sur place. Peut-on rêver plus luxueuse simplicité? On fait le tour de l'île en 20 minutes à pied. Il n'y a ni voitures ni scorpions ni paludisme ... rien que du sable blanc et des palmiers. Au large, entre les *dhows* (boutres) de Zanzibar, ces voiliers à coques en bois multicolores, des dauphins filent en bandes serrées et sautent à la queue leu leu. Le soir, affalé sur un pouf de coton blanc, on parle des poissons multicolores observés dans l'après-midi ou – pour les plus chanceux – des baleines qui flirtent avec Mnemba pendant la saison des amours. De bon augure dans cet océan Indien qui caresse les côtes de l'Afrique.

❋ **ABOVE** A glass bead shower curtain made at Kitengela. **BELOW** *Mkadi*, a local fruit, and Kitengela carafes. **FACING PAGE** In the bedrooms, thatched roofs and coconut-wood furniture designed by the decorator Chris Brown. ❋ **OBEN** Duschvorhang aus Glasperlen, hergestellt in Kitengela. **UNTEN** Ein *mkadi*, eine Frucht, und Karaffen aus Kitengela. **RECHTE SEITE** Der Dekorateur Chris Brown richtete die Zimmer ein: Bananenblattdächer und Kokosholzmöbel. ❋ **EN HAUT** Rideau de douche en perles de verre fabriqué à Kitengela. **EN BAS** Le *mkadi*, un fruit de la région, et des carafes de Kitengela. **PAGE DE DROITE** Dans les chambres, toit en feuille de bananier et mobilier en cocotier dessiné avec simplicité par le décorateur Chris Brown.

Maison de Beau Séjour

Various Houses

SEYCHELLES, MAURITIUS

Salim Currimjee

VARIOUS HOUSES SEYCHELLES

These colonial houses are beautiful in their simplicity
and their promise of good living.

The *cases* built of wood or uncut stone in the Seychelles are the heritage of French and British colonial times.

By tradition, visitors are invited onto their broad, shady verandas to sit in a planter's chair and talk. A glance at the rattan furniture and the colonnades of tropical *sapele* wood and you immediately understand the logic that has guided the island's builders for centuries past: why, for instance, there are comparatively few closed-in spaces here, and why there are so many windows. The insides of the *cases* are as bare as possible, constantly refreshed by the sea breezes, while the heat of the sun is kept out by wooden lattice blinds. There are marble floors, straw mats and in the more primitive constructions *latanier* thatched roofs overhead. The Mahé museum, open to the public, offers the best example of a colonial building as one might have imagined it in the late 18th century. The little fishermen's houses and their small plots of garden are just as traditional; but they are scattered over the wild hills, and their horizon consists of the turquoise sea and a lavender-blue sky. They are entirely at one with the vegetation, the white sand, the coconut trees and the *takamakas* by the water.

Schon von der Veranda der Häuser aus Holz oder unbehauenem Stein werden die Spuren der französischen oder englischen Kolonisation offensichtlich.

Tradition verpflichtet, deshalb werden Besucher auf der schattigen Freitreppe in einen Sessel für Plantagenbesitzer genötigt. An den traditionellen Korbmöbeln und den Säulengängen mit Pfeilern aus *sapele*, einem Tropenholz, wird ersichtlich, nach welchen Prinzipien seit Jahrhunderten auf der Insel gebaut wird. Es gibt nur wenige geschlossene Räume, dafür überall Fensteröffnungen – die karg möblierten Innenräume lassen dem frischen Seewind genügend Spielraum. Klappläden aus Holzlatten schützen die Zimmer. Hier und da trifft man auf Marmor, Stroh und auf Latanienholzdächer, die die einfachsten Behausungen decken. Das Museum von Mahé ist ein hervorragendes Beispiel für die Kolonialbauweise im 18. Jahrhundert. Der Blick von den in den beinahe unberührten Hügeln verstreuten Häuser geht auf das türkisfarbene Meer hinaus, das sich unter einem lavendelblauen Himmel bis zum Horizont erstreckt. Die Gebäude verschmelzen mit der Landschaft, dem weißen Sand, den Kokospalmenalleen und den *takamaka*-Bäumen am Strand.

Découvertes depuis leur véranda, ces «cases» en bois ou pierre brute témoignent des années de colonisation française et britannique.

Tradition oblige, c'est sur ce large perron ombragé que le visiteur est invité à s'asseoir sur un fauteuil de planteur. Un coup d'œil aux meubles traditionnels en rotin, aux colonnades de piliers en *sapele*, un bois tropical, et instantanément apparaît la logique reprise depuis des siècles par les bâtisseurs de l'île: les espaces clos sont rares, les ouvertures sont partout privilégiées, les intérieurs s'animent dans leur nudité à la brise rafraîchissante de l'air marin. Les pièces sont protégées par des persiennes en lattes de bois. On retrouve ici et là du marbre, de la paille et, au-dessus des têtes, les toits de latanier recouvrent les demeures les plus sauvages. Le musée de Mahé, ouvert au public, offre le meilleur exemple d'une demeure coloniale telle qu'on l'imaginait à la fin du 18e siècle. Les petites maisons de bois de pêcheur avec leur humble jardin sont tout aussi traditionnelles. Disséminées sur les collines sauvages, elles ont pour horizon le turquoise de la mer et un ciel bleu lavande. Ces habitations forment un tout avec la végétation, le sable blanc, les allées de cocotiers et les *takamaka* bordant les rivages.

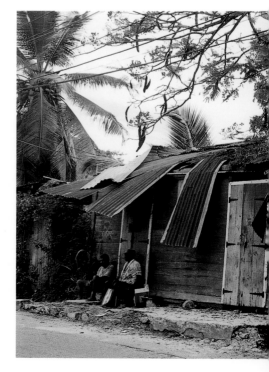

MAISON DE BEAU SÉJOUR

Mauritius

A colonial house in the north of the island has become a refined retreat that draws on several different periods.

Balanced between the ravine and the mountains, backing onto the tropical forest where ebonies and other exotic trees blend with azaleas and aromatic shrubs, Beau Séjour (as the house of the Lagesse family is called) is a testimony to the Creole life of not so long ago and the colonial epoch that reached its height in the 19th century.

Built by a Frenchman (the island had been French since the time of Louis XIV), the life of the property revolved around its immense sugar cane and banana plantations. Just as it did in Louisiana, the planter's existence so far away from the great cities of civilization led to the creation of a singular *art de vivre*. At Beau Séjour, with its traditional *varangue* (veranda) and openwork shutters to let in the cooling breezes, the façade has the look of a small palace of the kind that can still be seen from Italy to Istanbul. It is perfectly symmetrical, with carved balustrades, a comfortable *varangue* where one can sit and talk midway between house and garden, high windows, heavy shutters and light colours. The interior, recently refitted by the decorator Martine Lagesse, gives a sense of strength and finesse which is heightened by the warm, dark wood surfaces and the hunting trophies on the walls. There is a classical feel about this house which calls to mind a period engraving – or perhaps the novel *Paul et Virginie*.

Beau Séjour, so heißt das Haus der Familie Lagesse, liegt eingebettet zwischen einer kleinen Schlucht auf der einen Seite und einer Gebirgskette auf der anderen. Es schmiegt sich an einen Tropenwald, in dem zwischen Ebenholzbäumen mit Makaken darin und anderen wertvollen Hölzern Azaleensträucher und Dufthölzer stehen – ein Zeugnis der Kolonialzeit, die im 19. Jahrhundert ihren Höhepunkt erreichte.

Die von einem Franzosen gegründete Besitzung (Mauritius stand seit der Regentschaft Ludwig XIV. unter französischer Herrschaft) ist umgeben von Zuckerrohrfeldern und Bananenplantagen. Wie in Louisiana weckte die Entfernung von der modischen Welt der Städter unter den Plantagenbesitzern den Wunsch nach einem eigenen Lebensstil. Die Fassade mit der traditionell offenen Veranda und den Lamellenläden, die stets eine frische Brise durchlassen, gibt dem Haus den Anschein jener kleinen Palais, die damals von Italien bis Istanbul verbreitet waren. Eine perfekte Symmetrie der Formen, holzgeschnitzte Balustraden, eine freundliche offene Veranda, die zu Gesprächen zwischen Haus und Garten einlädt, hohe Fenster mit schweren Läden, das Ganze in hellen Farben – so vervollständigt sich das Bild. Die Dekorateurin Martine Lagesse hat die Innenräume neu gestaltet, sodass ein Eindruck von Finesse und Kraft entsteht, der die Wirkung des dunklen Holzes und der Jagdtrophäen noch hervorhebt: klassizistisch wie auf einem alten Stich. Oder aus dem Roman »Paul und Virginie«.

Entre la ravine et la chaîne de montagnes, adossée à une forêt tropicale dans laquelle les ébéniers où s'agitent des macaques et d'autres bois précieux se mêlent aux azalées et aux bois de senteur, Beau Séjour, c'est le nom de cette maison de la famille Lagesse, témoigne de la vie créole d'autrefois, cette époque coloniale qui connut son apogée au 19ᵉ siècle.

Édifié par un Français (l'île était française depuis Louis XIV), le domaine vivait tout autour de sa raison d'être: d'immenses champs de canne à sucre et plantations de bananiers. Être planteur, comme en Louisiane, éveillait chez ces sujets éloignés des modes citadines un acharnement à créer un art de vivre. Flanquée de la traditionnelle varangue et des persiennes à claire-voie qui dispensent encore une brise bienfaisante, la façade a des allures de petit palais, tels qu'on les édifiait autrefois de l'Italie à Istanbul. Symétrie parfaite des formes, balustrades ciselées, varangue confortable où l'on discute entre maison et jardin, hautes fenêtres, volets lourds, couleurs claires, voilà pour l'inspiration générale. L'intérieur, recomposé par la décoratrice Martine Lagesse, émane une impression de finesse et de force que décuplent la chaleur des bois sombres et les trophées de chasse. Un classicisme qui semble tout droit sorti d'une gravure. Ou du roman *Paul et Virginie*.

❋ **ABOVE** From the front hall, the wooden staircase and polished furniture. **FACING PAGE** Naval carpenters from France introduced the concept of the open porch to the islands of the Indian Ocean. ❋ **OBEN** Bereits im Eingangsbereich macht sich eine Vorliebe für Holz bemerkbar. Auch die Treppe und der Parkettboden betonen diesen Stil. **RECHTE SEITE** Zimmermänner von französischen Schiffen führten auf den Inseln im Indischen Ozean offene Veranden ein. ❋ **CI-DESSUS** Dès l'entrée, prédominance du bois souligné par l'escalier et le parquet. **PAGE DE DROITE** Les charpentiers marins venus de France ont introduit dans les îles de l'océan Indien les varangues, ces vérandas ouvertes.

✳ **ABOVE** The furniture shows how cosmopolitan the island became, with its armchairs and deckchairs from the Compagnie des Indes Orientales. **BELOW** The bedroom with tropical wood panels, softened by immaculately white walls. ✳ **OBEN** Die Möbel, Erinnerungsstücke der Ostindischen Kompanie, zeugen vom kosmopolitischen Geist der Inseln. **UNTEN** Das Schlafzimmer mit einer wertvollen Holzvertäfelung, die durch die strahlend weißen Wände weniger streng wirkt. ✳ **EN HAUT** Les meubles témoignent du cosmopolitisme de l'île avec ces fauteuils et méridiennes, souvenirs de la compagnie des Indes Orientales. **EN BAS** La chambre en boiserie d'essence précieuse adoucie par les murs d'un blanc immaculé.

SALIM CURRIMJEE MAURITIUS

A remarkable house built to the specifications of its architect owner, making extensive use of basic materials and plate glass windows.

Salim Currimjee's seaside holiday home is at the tranquil resort of Poste Lafayette, a place still largely undiscovered by tourists. Its owner simply calls it "the house".

This is a highly complex blend of huge glassed-in spaces with a fine atmosphere of continuity and masses of light. The fundamental, minimalist austerity of all this is a hymn to pure aesthetics and the colours of industrial raw materials. To protect the house from the boom of the sea – and thereby to preserve its intimacy – the façade runs side on to the shore. The use of white and the choice of pale stone for the floors creates a strong connection between interior and exterior, along with constantly shifting light effects in the rooms. The furniture, too, echoes this zen feeling, and the result is that Salim Currimjee's house is unique on the island, a place in which every choice of architecture and decoration has been made in function of the luxuriance of the natural environment and the glory of the view. The bedrooms, which all have terraces of their own, have a muted, turned-inward kind of light, in stark contrast to the reception areas.

Die versteckte Strandvilla liegt in dem beschaulichen Ort Poste Lafayette, der noch weitgehend von Touristen verschont geblieben ist. Der Architekt Salim Currimjee bezeichnet die Villa bescheiden als »Haus«.

Die klaren, großen Räume sind lichtdurchflutet und verstärken durch die Panoramafenster den Eindruck räumlicher Beständigkeit. Die grundsätzliche Schlichtheit, die von der minimalistischen Architektur inspiriert wird, betont die klare Ästhetik und lässt die Farben des Industriematerials hervortreten. Die parallel zum Meer ausgerichtete Fassade hält die Geräusche des Ozeans ab und schützt die Privatsphäre. Die Konzentration auf die Farbe Weiß und die Entscheidung für helle Steinböden sorgen für eine gewisse Kontinuität zwischen dem Äußeren und dem Inneren des Hauses – in den Räumen spielt der beständige Wechsel des Tageslichts eine große Rolle. Die Einrichtung richtet sich nach den Prinzipien der Zen-Philosophie. Die Villa ist auf der Insel einzigartig. Es ist ein Ort, bei dem Architektur und Inneneinrichtung von der Üppigkeit der Natur und der einzigartigen Aussicht bestimmt werden. Die jeweils mit einer Terrasse versehenen Zimmer liegen in gedämpfterem Licht als die Empfangsräume und wirken deshalb wesentlich introvertierter.

Nichée en bord de mer, cette résidence balnéaire est située à Poste Lafayette, un endroit que les touristes n'ont pas encore envahi et où l'architecte Salim Currimjee parle simplement de «maison».

Les vastes espaces dégagés et vitrés, inondés de lumière, renforcent l'impression de continuité spatiale donnée par de grandes ouvertures. La simplicité fondamentale du lieu, inspirée d'une architecture minimaliste, exalte les valeurs de l'esthétique pure et les couleurs des matériaux industriels. Pour protéger la maison de la rumeur de la mer, comme pour préserver son intimité, une façade est orientée parallèlement à l'océan. Le recours au blanc et le choix de la pierre claire des sols génèrent une impression de continuité entre l'intérieur et l'extérieur, un jeu avec des changements permanents de lumière dans les pièces. Le mobilier de celles-ci crée une référence directe à l'ambiance zen. Par son caractère unique dans l'île, cette maison à toutes les qualités d'une résidence de grand standing. C'est un décor où chaque choix a été influencé par l'exubérance de la nature et l'exigence d'une vue superbe. Pourvues de terrasses, les chambres à coucher, baignées d'une lumière plus feutrée affichent un caractère plus introverti, aux antipodes des espaces de réception.

❋ **PREVIOUS PAGES** Facing the sea, an architect's dream that is unique on the island. **ABOVE** In the living room, minimalism reigns supreme with simple sofas and a huge bookcase of pale wood. The fundamental simplicity here offsets the nearby presence of the sea. **BELOW** Plate glass windows from floor to ceiling give an effect of airy lightness and transparency. The entire house is a play of black and white. The Dalmatian, also black and white, belongs to the owner.. ❋ **VORHERGEHENDE DOPPELSEITE** Beispiellos auf der Insel: ein Architektentraum direkt am Meer. **OBEN** Sofas in strengen Formen sowie eine umfangreiche, in hellem Holz gehaltene Bibliothek bezeugen die minimalistische Haltung auch im Salon. Die natürliche Schlichtheit lässt das Meer noch präsenter erscheinen und verführt zum Träumen. **UNTEN** Die Panoramafenster reichen vom Boden bis zur Decke und verleihen dem Ambiente eine transparente Anmut. Im Inneren des Hauses herrschen die Farben Weiß, Schwarz und Grau vor – wie eine unfreiwillige Anspielung auf das Fell von Salim Currimjees Hund. ❋ **DOUBLE PAGE PRÉCÉDENTE** Face à la mer, un rêve d'architecte inédit dans l'île. **CI-DESSUS** Dans le salon, l'esprit minimaliste règne avec des canapés aux lignes sobres et une immense bibliothèque en bois clair. La simplicité fondamentale du lieu renforce la présence de la mer toute proche et incite à la rêverie. **CI-DESSOUS** Les baies vitrées qui vont du sol au plafond assurent un effet de transparence et de légèreté. Dans la maison, il y a partout un jeu de blanc, de noir et de gris, en un écho involontaire au pelage du chien de Salim Currimjee.

※ **ABOVE** The bedroom has ingenious sliding wooden shutters on its windows to protect it from the sun. **BELOW** The entrance is all cement, glass, white walls and concrete floors. The furniture is resolutely contemporary, and the huge floor-to-ceiling windows give directly on the Indian Ocean. ※ **OBEN** Ausgeklügelte hölzerne Fensterläden mit Schiebevorrichtung schützen das Schlafzimmer vor der Sonne. **UNTEN** Zement und Glas sind die bevorzugten Baumaterialien im Eingangsbereich. Ergänzt durch weiße Wände und Betonböden entstand ein lichtdurchfluteter, modern möblierter Raum. Die deckenhohen Fenster gehen auf den Indischen Ozean hinaus. ※ **CI-DESSOUS** D'astucieux volets de bois coulissants protègent la chambre du soleil. **CI-DESSOUS** Édifié avec un recours généreux au ciment et au verre, paré de murs blancs, de sols en béton, l'entrée est un espace lumineux aménagé de meubles modernes. Du sol au plafond, les grandes ouvertures donnent sur l'océan Indien.

Mombo Camp

Jao Camp

BOTSWANA

MOMBO CAMP
OKAVANGO DELTA

This camp of huts and walkways built on stilts extends across two kilometres of the African plain.

Living rooms, dining rooms and library form the epicentre of this project by Silvio Rech and Lesley Carstens, in which wood and thatch have been used as basic materials throughout – though none of the trees on the spot were cut down, for obvious reasons.

The rosewood floors are built around the acacias, ebony trees and tall palms which are home to colonies of tiny velvet monkeys. The suites, scattered through the groves of old trees, are lined with khaki canvas stretched between tall wooden pilings pointed skywards. Each tent is divided into two parts; in each one a huge brown and cream-coloured bedroom, with a desk of reddish wood, goes with its own salon area, where there's a broad sofa upholstered in white cotton. In the bathroom, the wood is pale, the light warm and the atmosphere gentle – a real place of relaxation, with tall mirrors, big basins of brown earthenware and a shower right in the middle. Outside, suspended between two palm trees, is another shower directly confronting the savannah. In the distance, vast flocks of birds wheel away into the orange evening sky. The languid outlines of a pride of lions move across the near horizon – another moment of magic in this unspoiled, faraway paradise.

Die Salons, die Speisesäle und die Bibliothek bilden den Mittelpunkt des von Silvio Rech und Lesley Carstens erbauten Gebäudes. Als Baumaterial wurden vor allem Holz und Stroh verwendet – allerdings wurden auf dem Anwesen keine Bäume gefällt, da die Natur als Teil der Einrichtung angesehen wird.

Das Parkett aus Rosenholz windet sich um die Akazien, Ebenholzbäume und hoch gewachsene Palmen, in denen kleine Affen herumturnen. Die um die hundertjährigen Bäume verstreuten Suiten sind mit Khakistoff ausgekleidet, der zwischen hoch ragende Holzpfeiler gespannt ist. Jedes dieser Zelte ist zweigeteilt: Von dem großen Zimmer in Braun- und Cremetönen ist ein kleiner Salon abgeteilt, in dem ein langes, mit weißer Baumwolle bezogenes Sofa steht. Das Badezimmer ist mit hellem Holz ausgestattet und das warme Licht lädt geradezu dazu ein, sich der Faulheit hinzugeben: Hohe Spiegel, weit geschwungene Waschbecken aus braunem Emaille und eine Dusche mitten im Raum schaffen einen Ruheraum par excellence. Eine weitere Dusche hängt zwischen zwei Palmen draußen in der Savanne. In der Ferne schwingen sich Myriaden von Vögeln in den orangefarbenen Himmel. Am Horizont zeichnen sich die Silhouetten friedlicher Löwen ab – so wirkt der Zauber des Augenblicks in diesem vor Menschen geschützten Winkel der Welt.

Les salons, salles à manger et la bibliothèque forment l'épicentre de cet édifice, réalisé par Silvio Rech et Lesley Carstens, où bois et chaume ont été utilisés comme matières premières. Ici, les arbres n'ont pas été abattus, la nature fait partie du décor.

Les parquets de bois de rose tournent autour des acacias, des ébéniers ou des hauts palmiers qu'habitent des familles de petits singes vervets. Les suites, dispersées au milieu des arbres centenaires, sont habillées de toile kaki tendue entre de hauts piliers de bois pointant vers le ciel. Chaque tente est divisée en deux parties. Une immense chambre aux tonalités de brun et de crème, avec bureau en bois cérusé, répond à un coin salon agrémenté d'un large canapé recouvert de coton blanc. Dans la salle de bains, le bois est blond, la lumière chaude, et la paresse douce: une véritable salle de repos avec ses hauts miroirs, ses grandes vasques en faïence brune et sa douche installée au beau milieu de la pièce. À l'extérieur, suspendue entre deux palmiers, on trouve encore une douche face à la savane. Au loin, une myriade d'oiseaux s'envolent dans le ciel orange. Les silhouettes de quelques lions paisibles se dessinent à l'horizon. Magie de l'instant dans ce bout du monde préservé des hommes.

※ **PREVIOUS PAGE** On the central terrace, the deck chairs offer a stunning vantage point. **FACING PAGE** On the terrace of the "Honeymoon" suite, the *sala*, made up of a daybed in the shade of the palm thatch. Here you can read a book while the big cats snooze nearby. ※ **VORHERGEHENDE DOPPELSEITE** Von den Korbsofas auf der mittleren Terrasse genießt man den freien Blick auf die Savanne. **RECHTE SEITE** Ein *sala*, ein Ruhebett im Schatten des Palmenblattdaches, auf der Terrasse der »Honeymoon-Suite«. Hier kann man vor einer Kulisse von Großwild lesen.
※ **DOUBLE PAGE PRÉCÉDENTE** Sur la terrasse centrale, des méridiennes en rotin offrent une vue imprenable sur la savane. **PAGE DE DROITE** Sur la terrasse de la suite «Honey Moon», le *sala*, formé d'un lit de repos à l'ombre d'un toit de feuilles de palme. On lit face aux grands fauves.

※ **FACING PAGE** Each bedroom has its own outside shower under the trees, as an extension of a big bathroom. **BELOW** In the bedrooms, the contemporary furniture designed by Silvio Rech is matched with objects picked up in markets all over Africa. ※ **LINKE SEITE** Als Verlängerung des großzügigen Badezimmers verfügt jedes Zimmer über eine Freiluftdusche unter den Bäumen. **UNTEN** Die moderne Einrichtung unter Federführung von Silvio Rech wird durch Objekte vom afrikanischen Kontinent aufgelockert. ※ **PAGE DE GAUCHE** Chaque chambre dispose d'une douche extérieure placée sous les arbres en prolongement de la vaste salle de bains. **CI-DESSOUS** Dans les chambres, le mobilier aux lignes contemporaines dessiné par Silvio Rech se marie aux objets chinés sur tout le continent africain.

JAO CAMP
OKAVANGO DELTA

Guests at this idyllic bush camp come to experience nature at her unspoiled best –
in conditions of high luxury.

It all started with two stubborn people, David and Cathy, authentic pioneers from Maun, the capital of the delta.

Beginning in 1938, David's grandparents too many of Europe's crowned heads on safari, and he himself is a former white hunter. Less is known of Cathy, except that she was always a keen reader of interior decoration magazines. Destiny intervened when, on the off-chance, they entered a competition organized by the government of Botswana. The challenge was to submit ideas for developing a concession in the middle of the delta – and the couple's plan came out top, out of a field of 130. David dreamed of Africa, Cathy of Bali. The South African architects Silvio Rech and Lesley Carstens undertook to bring these two worlds together in terms of architecture and décor, and the result is Jao Camp. Every bedroom opens on a broad terrace with a view of the flaming sunset. Rosewood floors and furniture, muslin mosquito nets, brown earthenware basins were all designed by Silvio Rech and made on the spot by local craftsmen. The huge open salon overlooks the river with its thousands of waterlilies, while among the Zimbabwean jars, *mokuba* cushions and Masai spears, benches and wardrobes imported from Indonesia add a touch of Asia to the décor.

Mit einer gewissen Besessenheit von David und Cathy fing alles an. Die beiden Pioniere stammen aus Maun, der Hauptstadt des Deltas.

Davids Großeltern begleiteten seit 1938 Mitglieder der königlichen Familien Europas auf Safari und er selbst war früher Jäger. Über Cathy ist nicht viel bekannt, außer dass sie aus lauter Langeweile Zeitschriften zum Thema Wohnen und Einrichten verschlang. Ihr Leben veränderte sich schlagartig, nachdem sie sich bei der Regierung von Botswana um eine Konzession mitten im Delta bewarben und unter 130 Bewerbern auserwählt wurden. David hatte nur Afrika im Sinn, sie dagegen Bali. Die südafrikanischen Architekten Silvio Rech und Lesley Carstens konnten dem Paar helfen, diese beiden Welten fruchtbar zu verbinden. Alle Zimmer verfügen über eine große Terrasse mit atemberaubender Aussicht. Nach Entwürfen von Silvio Rech wurde die Einrichtung vom Parkett über die Rosenholzmöbel und Moskitonetze aus Leinenstores bis zu den Waschbecken aus Sandstein an Ort und Stelle von ansässigen Handwerkern hergestellt. Von einem weiträumigen Salon blickt man über den Fluss mit Tausenden von Seerosen. Inmitten der Tonkrüge aus Simbabwe finden sich Kissen aus *mokuba* und Massai-Lanzen. Bänke und Schränke wurden hingegen aus Indonesien importiert, um der Einrichtung ein asiatisches Flair zu verleihen.

À l'origine, il y a l'obstination de David et Cathy, un couple d'authentiques pionniers natifs de Maun, la capitale du delta.

Ses grands-parents à lui, dès 1938, guidaient en safari les familles royales européennes. Il était autrefois chasseur. D'elle, on ne sait pas grand-chose, sinon que pour tromper l'ennui elle dévorait les magazines de décoration. Un coup du sort comme il ne s'en produit qu'un dans une vie a tout fait basculer. Par hasard, juste pour voir, David et Cathy ont proposé au gouvernement du Botswana un dossier d'aménagement d'une concession au cœur du delta. Ils ont été lauréats parmi 130 candidats! Il rêve toujours d'Afrique, elle rêve de Bali. Les architectes sud-africains Silvio Rech et Lesley Carstens ont relevé le défi de réunir les deux mondes. Chaque chambre s'ouvre sur une large terrasse qui offre, le soir, un panorama sur l'horizon flamboyant. Parquet et mobilier en bois de rose, moustiquaire en voile de lin, lavabos en grès aux teintes brunes, l'ensemble, signé Silvio Rech, a été fabriqué sur place par des artisans locaux. Un immense salon ouvert surplombe la rivière et ses milliers de nénuphars. Au milieu des jarres du Zimbabwe, des coussins en *mokuba* et des lances Massaï, les banquettes et les armoires importées d'Indonésie apportent une touche asiatique au décor.

❋ **PREVIOUS PAGES** At the entrance to the camp, which is entirely constructed on tree trunks, is a shop selling African objects. **BELOW** A teak-encircled swimming pool in its own island of greenery near the river, where the hippos sport. **FACING PAGE** When you come in from safari, it's time for a drink by the fire, in the company of an array of percussion instruments (foreground). ❋ **VORHERGEHENDE DOPPELSEITE** Am Eingang des Pfahlbaucamps, im Wirrwarr von Baumstämmen wird in einem Laden afrikanisches Kunsthandwerk verkauft. **UNTEN** Der mit Teakholz eingefasste Swimmingpool liegt im Grünen in der Nähe des Flusses, in dem die Flusspferde schwimmen. **RECHTE SEITE** Wenn man von der Safari zurückkommt, lauscht man bei einem Glas Wein am Feuer den Trommlern (im Vordergrund). ❋ **DOUBLE PAGE PRÉCÉDENTE** L'entrée du camp sur pilotis, avec son capharnaüm de troncs d'arbres, abrite une boutique d'objets africains. **CI-DESSOUS** La piscine cerclée de teck s'inscrit au milieu d'un îlot de verdure à quelques mètres de la rivière où nagent les hippopotames. **PAGE DE DROITE** Au retour du safari, on boit un verre au coin du feu au son d'instruments à percussion (au premier plan).

✳ **BELOW** In the brown salon, the atmosphere is nicely balanced between Asia and Africa. Ghanaian stools and headrests from Zimbabwe stand side by side with graceful Balinese benches and their *kuba* cushions (made of raffia with geometric motifs). **FACING PAGE** Built on stilts for security, the lodge is made up of eight suites distributed among the shady palm trees, each with a glorious view of the river. ✳ **OBEN** Der Salon ist in Brauntönen gehalten, die Atmosphäre hält die Balance zwischen Afrika und Asien. Hölzerne Hocker aus Ghana und Kopfstützen aus Simbabwe harmonieren mit anmutigen balinesischen Sitzbänken und den dazugehörigen Kissen aus *kuba* (geometrisch gemustertem Bast). **RECHTE SEITE** Die aus Sicherheitsgründen als Pfahlbau errichtete Lodge hat acht Suiten, die im Schatten der Palmen verstreut liegen, alle mit unbegrenztem Flussblick. ✳ **CI-DESSOUS** Dans le salon aux tons bruns, l'atmosphère balance entre l'Asie et l'Afrique. Des tabourets du Ghana et repose-tête en bois du Zimbabwe côtoient de gracieux bancs balinais et leurs coussins en *kuba* (raphia aux motifs géométriques). **PAGE DE DROITE** Construit sur pilotis par mesure de sécurité, le lodge est composé de huit suites dispersées à l'ombre des palmiers, avec une vue imprenable sur la rivière.

FACING PAGE An outside shower. BELOW A fine brown earthenware basin designed by Silvio Rech; note the antique bathtub, polished floor and wooden daybed in this bathroom – which is in a corner of the bedroom, there being no partitions. ✳ INKE SEITE Die Freiluftdusche. UNTEN Waschbecken aus Sandstein in angenehmem Braunton nach einem Entwurf von Silvio Rech; antike Badewanne, gewachstes Parkett und Ruhebett aus Holz im Badezimmer, das ohne Trennwand in das eigentliche Zimmer übergeht. ✳ PAGE DE GAUCHE Douche extérieure. CI-DESSOUS Lavabo en grès aux belles teintes brunes dessiné par Silvio Rech; baignoire ancienne, parquet ciré et lit de repos en bois pour cette salle de bains qui ne forme qu'une pièce avec la chambre.

Camp 5

Singita Boulders Lodge

Casa Rech

Shahn & Alice Rowe

Willie Bester

Townships

Pierre Lombart

Ndebele

Bathafarh Farm

De Oude Schuur

Gapad Cottage

Jean-Marc Lederman

Malcolm Kluk

Meerlust

Tracy Rushmere & Peter Maltbie

Jonathan Green & Marina Pretorius

SOUTH AFRICA

Camp 5
MAKALALI

From a couple of hundred yards away,
you'd never guess that these brown anthills conceal a comfortable safari lodge.

Impeccable in his bush jacket, the guide awaits you at the door of the little plane which left Johannesburg, with you aboard, about an hour earlier. In the Land Rover, there's a sign just above the game rifle on the dashboard, which reads "Makalali".

That's the name of this private 75,000-acre reserve with its four separate safari camps, as well as this erstwhile private camp, each of which has six rooms. Makalali isn't some kind of African Disneyland, but a natural reserve with facilities that take those who go there to the very source of Africa's wildlife. And even that doesn't quite do it justice; much of the originality of the place rests on the work of the architect Silvio Rech, who set out to put together something "thoroughly sensual". He has succeeded. The fabrics, the cushions, the rattan chairs and the mattresses on the floor are an enticement to relax. By night, the soft lights, the candles and the oil lamps tinge everything a rich gold. Exhausted by a full day in the bush, you find yourself falling asleep on the spot, oblivious to the savannah and its perils. The whole thing seems to be lifted straight from *Out of Africa* – only here Meryl Streep isn't at the beck and call of a film director, she's right here with you. She's spent the day at Makalali observing animals as they move about according to the direction of the wind or the ambient scent of water. And here she is, like you, back again at nightfall.

Der Führer in tadellos sitzender Buschkleidung erwartet den Reisenden vor dem kleinen Flugzeug, das eine Stunde zuvor von Johannesburg abgeflogen war. An dem Landrover weist ein Schild direkt über dem schweren Gewehr am Armaturenbrett auf »Makalali« hin.

So heißt das private Naturschutzgebiet, das auf 30000 Hektar vier separate Camps, sowie dieses ehemals private Camp 5, mit je sechs Zimmern beherbergt. Makalali ist kein afrikanisches Disneyland sondern ein Naturschutzgebiet, wo Touristen den Ursprung allen Lebens in der Wildnis erleben können. Dabei verdankt sich die Originalität der Anlage einzig und allein dem Architekten Silvio Rech. Der Künstler wollte einen sinnlichen Ort schaffen und das ist ihm gelungen. Stoffe, Kissen, Korbsessel und Matratzen direkt auf dem Boden laden zur Entspannung ein. Nachts verleiht das gedämpfte Licht der Kerzen und Öllampen dem Camp einen goldenen Schimmer. Erschöpft von einem Tag auf Safari schläft man auf der Stelle ein, ohne sich weiter um die Gefahren der Savanne zu sorgen. Man wähnt sich in der Kulisse des Films *Jenseits von Afrika*, aber Meryl Streep gehorcht der Inspiration keines Autors oder Regisseurs. Sie ist hier. In Makalali hat sie den Tag damit verbracht, zu beobachten, wie sich die Tiere am Wind oder dem Geruch der Wasserlöcher orientieren. Und nun steht sie da in der Abenddämmerung. Es sei denn …

Impeccable dans sa tenue de brousse, le guide attend le voyageur au pied du petit avion qui a quitté Johannesburg une heure auparavant. Dans la Land-Rover, juste au-dessus d'un gros fusil fixé sur le tableau de bord, une pancarte indique «Makalali».

C'est le nom de cette réserve privée de 30000 hectares formée de quatre camps bien distincts et de cet ancien camp privé, abritant chacun six habitations. Le Makalali n'est pas un Disneyland africain mais une réserve naturelle dont les racines plongent le voyageur au plus profond de la vie sauvage. L'adjectif est d'ailleurs bien faible, car l'originalité des lieux repose entièrement sur le travail de l'architecte Silvio Rech. L'artiste voulait composer un lieu sensuel, et l'entreprise est réussie! Tissus, coussins, fauteuils en rotin et matelas posés sur le sol invitent à la détente. De nuit, la lumière tamisée, les bougies et les lampes à pétrole donnent à l'ensemble une teinte dorée. Épuisé par une journée de safari, on s'endort sur-le-champ, ignorant la savane et ses périls … On jurerait le décor tiré de *Out of Africa*. Mais Meryl Streep n'obéit pas à l'inspiration d'un auteur ou d'un metteur en scène. Elle est à vos côtés. Au Makalali, elle a passé le jour à observer les animaux poussés par le vent ou l'odeur des points d'eau. Et puis, la voici à la nuit tombée. À moins que …

✳ **PREVIOUS PAGES AND FACING PAGE** The camp's miniature swimming pool. With its mosaics and domes, Makalali is a cross between something created by Antoni Gaudí, and mythical Darkest Africa. **ABOVE** The terraces in the tops of the jackalberry trees are ideal for relaxing and watching the animals come down to drink in the river. ✳ **VORHERGEHENDE DOPPELSEITE UND LINKE SEITE** Im Camp gibt es einen kleinen Swimmingpool. Makalali ist ein eigenes Universum, irgendwo zwischen Antoni Gaudí und Afrika. **OBEN** Auf den in den Jackalberry-Bäumen versteckten Terrassen kann man sich entspannen und zuschauen, wie die Tiere am Fluss trinken. ✳ **DOUBLE PAGE PRÉCÉDENTE ET PAGE DE GAUCHE** Ce camp dispose d'une piscine miniature. Avec ses mosaïques et ses dômes, le Makalali a su inventer un univers à mi-chemin entre Antoni Gaudí et l'Afrique. **CI-DESSUS** Les terrasses nichées au creux des arbres de Jackalberry sont idéales pour se détendre et observer les animaux qui s'abreuvent à la rivière.

❋ **PREVIOUS PAGES** More adventurous guests can spend the night under the stars, by the light of spirit lamps, with lions in the darkness nearby. **FACING PAGE** Framing the mosaic tub, the trees also support the roof. **ABOVE** A bedroom, with the traditional cotton mosquito net and raffia cushions. On the teak floor, a sisal mat. ❋ **VORHERGEHENDE DOPPELSEITE** Besonders Mutige können die Nacht auch ganz in der Nähe der wilden Tiere im Freien verbringen, im Licht der Öllampen. **LINKE SEITE** Die Bäume, die das Dach stützen, umringen die Mosaik-Badewanne. **OBEN** Ein Zimmer mit dem üblichen Moskitonetz aus Baumwolle sowie Bastkissen. Auf dem Teakholzboden liegt ein Sisalteppich. ❋ **DOUBLE PAGE PRÉCÉDENTE** Les plus courageux peuvent passer une nuit à la belle étoile, sous la lumière des lampes à pétrole et à proximité des grands fauves. **PAGE DE GAUCHE** Encadrant la baignoire en mosaïque, des arbres supportent le toit. **CI-DESSUS** Une chambre avec la traditionnelle moustiquaire en coton et des coussins en raphia. Sur le sol en teck, un tapis de sisal.

Singita BOULDErs LODge

SaBi SanD

A room with a view:
a camp that has been immaculately integrated into the surrounding landscape.

Before it was turned into a lodge, Singita was a private house, and it is perhaps in the one or two objects and books remaining from earlier times that the enduring charm of the place resides.

Singita, which means "miracle", overlooks a 40,000 acre reserve. Its architect, Bruce Stafford, set out to achieve a view of the plain and its fauna from a point of vantage similar to a box at the opera, from the front and from the side. He designed the buildings overlooking the site accordingly, in the conviction that man's presence should have the minimum effect on the environment. From these vantage points the illusion is perfect: the undisturbed existence of the wild, and the sophistication of mankind, create a mysterious harmony. At the heart of this Eden is a main living room that once constituted the entire original residence here and served Stafford as the blueprint for the rest of the project. Guests eat among the trees, or beside the big fireplace. There are eight thatched chalets artfully sited in the vegetation around the main house. Materials, colours, furniture and bedrooms are all handled in an elegant, ethnic style, while statuettes, glass, masks, earthenware, polished stone and fabrics play their traditional role. For the safaris, there is a choice of "targets" – the big five of African fauna are all plentiful in the reserve.

Bevor es in eine Lodge verwandelt wurde, diente Singita als Privatwohnsitz. Es mag an den Hinterlassenschaften der ehemaligen Besitzer oder auch an der Hand voll Bücher liegen, die wie ein Gebetbuch weitergegeben werden – jedenfalls ist Singita eine Lodge voller Zauber und Charme.

Singita, übersetzt ein »Wunder«, geht auf einen 15000 Hektar großen Park hinaus. Das Konzept des Architekten Bruce Stafford besteht darin, seine Gäste in einer Art Opernloge zu platzieren, mit Blick auf die Savanne und ihre Tiere. Stafford legte Wert darauf, den Eingriff des Menschen in die Natur so gering wie möglich zu halten und entwarf Gebäude, von denen man die Landschaft überblicken kann. Die wilde Welt der Tiere und die Eleganz des menschlichen Daseins verbinden sich auf geheimnisvolle Weise. Der Salon im Zentrum dieses Paradieses, der eigentlich aus der alten ansehnlichen Residenz entstand, hat Modellcharakter. Hier speist man unter Bäumen oder an dem mächtigen Kamin. Acht strohgedeckte Chalets verteilen sich auf die Landschaft. In Bezug auf das Baumaterial, die Farben und Möbel sind alle Zimmer im ethnisch-eleganten Stil eingerichtet. Kleine Statuen, Glaswaren, Masken, Keramik, polierte Steine sowie Stoffe dienen der üblichen Dekoration. Auf Safari kann man zwischen verschiedenen Schießscheiben wählen. Die berühmten »Big Five«, Büffel, Elefant, Leopard, Löwe und Nashorn leben im Reservat.

Avant d'être transformée en lodge, Singita était une résidence privée, et c'est peut-être dans les quelques objets et la poignée de livres transmis comme un bréviaire, que réside ce supplément d'âme qui fait le vrai charme.

Singita, traduisez «le miracle», s'ouvre sur un parc de 15000 hectares. Voir la savane et sa faune, comme au balcon d'un opéra, de face, de profil: tel est le concept défendu par l'architecte Bruce Stafford. Tenant d'un impact minimal de l'homme sur son environnement, il a conçu des bâtiments qui surplombent le site. De ces promontoires, l'illusion est parfaite. Le monde brut de la faune et les sophistications du genre humain se marient mystérieusement. Au cœur de cet éden, un grand salon qui n'était autre, précisément, que l'ancienne résidence cossue, fait figure de modèle. On y mange entre les arbres ou au coin de l'immense cheminée. De part en part, huit chalets au toit de chaume sont dispersés dans la végétation. Matériaux, couleurs, mobilier, les chambres ont toutes été décorées dans un esprit ethnique et élégant. Statuettes, verreries, masques, céramiques, pierre polie et tissus jouent leur rôle traditionnel. Pour les safaris, on a le choix des «cibles». Les fameux «Big five» des amateurs gambadent dans la réserve.

❋ **PREVIOUS PAGES, LEFT AND BELOW** Stone walls and wicker furniture of combined English and African styles. The space marries futurist shapes and traditional concepts, with raffia skirts from Mali used to make the cushions. **FACING PAGE** This dinner service is decorated with traditional motifs from the province of Mpumalanga. ❋ **VORHERGEHENDE DOPPELSEITE, LINKS UND UNTEN** Geschichtete Steinmauern, die wie irische Schornsteine anmuten, Korbmöbel, die stilistisch England mit Afrika verbinden – die Anlage kombiniert futuristische Formen mit traditionellen Elementen wie den mit Raffiabast aus Mali bezogenen Polstern. **RECHTE SEITE** Das Service im Ethno-Chic spielt mit Mustern aus der Provinz Mpumalanga. ❋ **DOUBLE PAGE PRÉCÉDENTE, À GAUCHE ET CI-DESSOUS** Murs en pierres superposées qui évoquent les chemins d'Irlande, meubles en osier combinant les styles africain et anglais, l'espace marie les formes futuristes et les concepts traditionnels avec ses anciens pagnes du Mali en raphia qui habillent les coussins. **PAGE DE DROITE** Le service ethno-chic reprend les motifs de la province du Mpumalanga.

❋ **PREVIOUS PAGES** The plate glass window of a suite looking across a private pool. **LEFT** Off the reception area, a stone-walled cloakroom, with an antelope horn handle on the door. **FACING PAGE** Each bedroom has its own solid jacaranda wood bed. The sisal on the floor and the green English bedcover bring a touch of strength and rigour to the romantically-draped mosquito net and the ceiling fan. In the background, the bathroom and its outside shower. ❋ **VORHERGEHENDE DOPPELSEITE** Die Suite verfügt über ein Panoramafenster und einen Privatpool. **LINKS** Ein kleiner gemauerter Waschraum an der Rezeption – der Griff an der Tür ist aus Antilopenhorn. **RECHTE SEITE** Die großen Betten in den Zimmern sind aus Palisanderholz. Der Sisalteppich und die grüne englische Tagesdecke mildern in ihrer Strenge den eher romantischen Eindruck, den das Moskitonetz und der Ventilator vermitteln. Im Hintergrund liegen das Badezimmer und die Freiluftdusche. ❋ **DOUBLE PAGE PRECEDENTE** Dotée d'une baie vitrée, cette suite donne sur une piscine privée. **A GAUCHE** À la réception, un cabinet de toilette en pierre et sa poignée en corne d'antilope. **PAGE DE DROITE** Les chambres disposent d'un lit massif en bois de jacaranda. Le sisal sur le sol et la couverture verte anglaise apportent une touche de force et de rigueur au romantisme déjà vu de la moustiquaire et du ventilateur. Au fond, la salle de bains et sa douche extérieure.

CASA RECH

JOHANNESBURG

Opting for a novel kind of ecological art de vivre, the celebrated architect Silvio Rech and his wife Lesley Carstens have built themselves a house of earth, stone and thatch.

Silvio Rech's house is a surprising thing to come across in a major South African city. In this fashionable quarter, the orderly American-style lines of villas seem to have turned away from indigenous Africa.

Silvio Rech has taken a totally different road. His entrance is hidden by a thick screen of vegetation; and when you enter his house you are literally stunned. Rech is a daring artist who has already built a raft of follies. His own home is a scale model, if you like, of many of the other things he has built and decorated. There are walls of brown earth supporting a thatched roof and floors of stained and varnished concrete; in short, Rech has built himself an authentic African dwelling equipped with every modern convenience. It has a wooden deck all round it, giving access to every room. By way of one of the glass doors framed by hand-carved wooden jambs, you can go into the bedroom with its bunk beds (little Gio and his sister Luna sleep below under a goatskin and their parents above). In the same way you can wander into the dining room, the kitchen, the hanging closet or the bathroom. The spaces all communicate with each other, and everywhere there are benches moulded from earth and simple cushions to lie on. This is a totally imaginary idea of Africa, say Rech's detractors. Not so – it's a transposition, or at the very least, a version of "reality corrected by style", in the words of Albert Camus .

Spaziergängern in der großen afrikanischen Stadt bietet sich ein erstaunlicher Anblick, denn die Villen in diesem Nobelviertel sind dermaßen amerikanisiert, dass man vergessen könnte, in Afrika zu sein.

Silvio Rech entschied sich für das genaue Gegenteil. Der Wohnsitz des interessanten Künstlers, unter dessen Federführung bereits viele andere »Verrücktheiten« entstanden, ist fulminant in seiner Andersartigkeit. Als wäre es ein Modell, erkennt man hier in allem und jedem die Inspiration des Chefs. Die Wände aus brauner Erde tragen ein Strohdach, der Boden besteht aus Zement, der mit Pigmenten und Lack marmoriert wurde – eine echte Hütte mit allem erdenklichen modernen Komfort. Ein Holzdeck verläuft einmal um das gesamte Haus, das man durch eine Glastür mit handgeschnitztem Rahmen betritt. Im Schlafzimmer stehen die Betten übereinander – oben schlafen die Eltern, unten der kleine Gio und seine Schwester Luna, unter einer Ziegenfelldecke. Weiter geht's ins Esszimmer, in die Küche, den eingebauten Kleiderschrank und das Badezimmer. Die Räume kommunizieren miteinander und überall laden die im Boden verankerten Bänke und schlichten Kissen zur Meditation ein. Kritiker sehen in dieser Architektur ein Bild von Afrika, das mit der Realität angeblich nichts zu tun hat. Dabei handelt es sich um eine Transposition oder zumindest um eine »durch Stil verbesserte Wirklichkeit«, wie sie schon von Albert Camus beschrieben wurde.

C'est une découverte inattendue pour qui se balade dans la grande ville sud-africaine. Dans ce quartier chic, les villas ordonnées à l'américaine semblent oublier la terre d'Afrique.

Silvio Rech a pris le chemin résolument inverse. Ici, une végétation épaisse dissimule l'entrée. On reste stupéfait devant la demeure de l'artiste un peu allumé et déjà coupable de multiples folies. En modèle réduit, toute l'inspiration du chef est là. Soutenue par des murs en terre brune, protégée par un toit de chaume, posée sur un sol en ciment marbré de pigments et de vernis, l'habitation est une véritable hutte équipée du confort moderne. Sa galerie de circulation en bois, le deck, tourne autour de chaque pièce. Par une porte vitrée encadrée de bois sculptés à la main, on entre, au choix, dans la chambre avec ses lits superposés (les parents en hauteur, le petit Gio et sa sœur Luna, en bas, sous une peau de chèvre), dans la salle à manger, la cuisine, la penderie ou la salle de bains. Les espaces communiquent entre eux et partout des bancs moulés dans la terre ou de simples coussins invitent à la méditation. Voilà une Afrique imaginaire diront les détracteurs. On leur répliquera qu'il s'agit là d'une transposition ou, tout au moins, du «réel corrigé par le style» dont parlait l'écrivain Albert Camus.

✳ **FACING PAGE** This room with its two traditional bells is positioned between the bedroom and the bathroom. It serves as both antechamber and living room. **ABOVE** In the bedroom, the circular bench moulded out of clay is surmounted by a shelf. African masks and Asante-style stools provide basic furniture.
✳ **LINKE SEITE** Dieser Ruheraum zwischen Schlafzimmer und Bad, der gleichzeitig als Vorzimmer und Salon dient, steht ganz im Zeichen der beiden großen Glocken. **OBEN** Über der runden in die Erde eingelassenen Bank hängt ein Regal. Afrikanische Masken und Hocker nach Aschanti-Art – das ist auch schon die gesamte Einrichtung. ✳ **PAGE DE GAUCHE** À la fois antichambre et salon, cette pièce de repos que dominent deux cloches traditionnelles est située entre la chambre et la salle de bains. **CI-DESSUS** Dans la chambre, la banquette circulaire moulée dans la terre est surmontée d'une étagère. Masques africains et tabourets d'inspiration Ashanti meublent sommairement l'espace.

※ **ABOVE, RIGHT, AND FACING PAGE** In the dining room, the wooden dishes are placed on a *kuba* raffia piece. The chandelier by Silvio Rech is inspired by the shape of an elephant's tusk and woven from brass wire. The furniture and the stone fireplace cohabit with contemporary lamps. ※ **OBEN, RECHTS UND RECHTE SEITE** Das Geschirr im Esszimmer steht auf *kuba*-Bast. Elefantenstoßzähne inspirierten Silvio Rech zu dem Kronleuchter aus geflochtenem Messingdraht. Die Möbel und der gemauerte Kamin passen gut zu den Lampen, die dem Raum einen moderneren Anstrich geben. ※ **CI-DESSUS, À DROITE ET PAGE DE DROITE** Dans la salle à manger, la vaisselle en bois est posée sur un raphia *kuba*. Le lustre réalisé par Silvio Rech est inspiré d'une défense d'éléphant et tressé en fil de laiton. Meubles et cheminée en pierre cohabitent avec des luminaires qui affirment un accent plus contemporain.

✳ **FACING PAGE AND BELOW** Thatch, wicker and brick give a gentle ambiance to the kitchen, along with metal utensils and a Philippe Starck lemon squeezer. In the background, a zinc basin. **RIGHT** Like a column, a living tree grows straight from the marbled cement floor. ✳ **LINKE SEITE UND UNTEN** Ziegelwände und geflochtene Körbe sorgen für eine warme Atmosphäre in der Küche. Neben Küchengerätschaften aus Metall steht die Zitronenpresse von Philippe Starck. Im Hintergrund das Spülbecken aus Zink. **RECHTS** Wie eine Säule ragt der Baum aus dem Zementboden mit dem marmorierten Finish. ✳ **PAGE DE GAUCHE ET EN BAS** Le chaume et l'osier mêlés à la brique assurent une douce ambiance dans la cuisine dont les ustensiles en métal côtoient le presse-citron de Philippe Starck. Au fond, lavabo en zinc. **A DROITE** Tel une colonne, l'arbre vivant surgit du sol en ciment au fini marbré.

❋ **ABOVE** The lavatory beside the bathroom is topped by a metal plaque and a conical ceiling with corbelled brickwork. **RIGHT** A basin designed by Silvio Rech. **FACING PAGE** The massive bathtub is on a level with the surroundings outside. The French windows give on to the circular deck. ❋ **OBEN** Hinter der Toilette, die neben dem Badezimmer liegt, hängt eine Metallplatte, über der sich die kegelförmige Decke wölbt. **RECHTS** Das Waschbecken hat Silvio Rech entworfen. **RECHTE SEITE** Die riesige Badewanne wurde ebenerdig eingelassen. Die Fenstertüren führen auf die Terrasse. ❋ **CI-DESSUS** Le cabinet de toilette qui jouxte la salle de bains est surmonté d'une plaque de métal et d'un plafond conique strié de briques en encorbellement. **A DROITE** Une vasque dessinée par Silvio Rech. **PAGE DE DROITE** L'immense baignoire encastrée est à hauteur du paysage. Les portes-fenêtres donnent sur le deck circulaire.

SHAHN & ALICE ROWE

JOHANNESBURG

This house incorporates some of the most beautiful features of the African village –
no easy task in a residential district of Johannesburg

With its brown earth walls and surrounding exotic vegetation, the building so strongly resembles a mud dwelling that the neighbours call it "Rowes' Village".

To create it, Shahn and Alice Rowe worked as a team with the architect Kate Otten, whose master is the great Egyptian architect Hassan Fathy. All his life, Fathy proclaimed his goal of rehabilitating African functionalism by bringing back earth as a primary material. African-style, the Rowes' house was born of several different recyclings. The doors and windows come from a now-vanished house that once belonged to Shahn's parents. The massive front door is made from elements picked up at railway yards. Obsessed by the idea of adapting to Africa, and above all rejecting the dominant Californian-villa style of their district, the trio used kiaat wood, Oregon pine and Zimbabwean teak. Every object has been selected for its originality. The carpets echo the mosaics and the red floor tiles. Sun-mirrors and wrought iron lamps brighten the warm rooms, and the combination of all these things is wonderfully harmonious. In the morning, the garden is laden with the scent of flowers. Who would imagine that the big city is only a few yards away?

Die von Mauern aus brauner Erde gestützte Behausung in einer exotischen Pflanzenwelt ähnelt so sehr einer Lehmhütte, dass die Nachbarn sie schon in »Rowe-Dorf« umbenannt haben.

Beim Bau des Hauses hat das Ehepaar Rowe eng mit der Architektin Kate Otten zusammengearbeitet, die sich zur Schule Hassan Fathys zählt. Fathy hat sich als Architekt ein Leben lang dafür eingesetzt, eine Art afrikanischen Funktionalismus zu begründen, indem er die Erde als Baumaterial rehabilitierte. Auf afrikanische Art und Weise bedeutet in diesem Zusammenhang, dass das Bauwerk aus einer Menge von wieder verwertbaren Materialien besteht. Die Fenster und die Türen stammen aus Shahns inzwischen abgerissenem Elternhaus. In der mächtigen Eingangstür wurde Material verwertet, das auf Eisenbahnbaustellen gesammelt wurde. Das Trio, das sich mit dem Haus an die afrikanische Umgebung anpassen und keinesfalls den Stil kalifornischer Villen nachahmen wollte, entschied sich für Kiaatholz, Oregon-Kiefer und Teakholz aus Simbabwe. Jeder Gegenstand wurde einzeln ausgesucht. Die Teppichmuster beziehen sich auf die Mosaike und Terrakottafliesen. Spiegel in Form der Sonne und schmiedeeiserne Lampen beleuchten die in warmen Tönen gehaltenen Räume. Alles strahlt Harmonie aus. Morgens verströmt der Garten seinen betörenden Duft. Kaum vorstellbar, dass die Großstadt ganz in der Nähe liegt …

Soutenue par des murs en terre brune, protégée par une végétation exotique, l'habitation ressemble à une hutte en terre au point que le voisinage la nomme le «village des Rowe».

Pour édifier son «village», donc, le couple a véritablement travaillé en équipe avec l'architecte, Kate Otten. Celle-ci revendique comme influence principale le maître égyptien Hassan Fathy. Sa vie durant, cet homme a affiché sa volonté de décliner un fonctionnalisme à l'africaine, c'est-à-dire en réhabilitant la terre. À l'africaine, cette construction est né de nombreux recyclages. Portes et fenêtres proviennent de la maison, disparue aujourd'hui, des parents de Shahn. La porte d'entrée, monumentale, mêle des éléments glanés sur les chantiers ferroviaires. Obnubilé par l'idée de s'adapter à l'Afrique, de ne surtout pas singer les villas californiennes, le trio a utilisé les bois de kiaat, le pin d'Oregon, un teck du Zimbabwe. Chaque objet a été choisi pour son originalité. Des tapis répondent aux mosaïques et aux tomettes. Des miroirs en soleil, des lampes en fer forgé illuminent les pièces chaudes. L'ensemble est très harmonieux. Au matin, le jardin embaume. Comment imaginer que la grande ville n'est qu'à quelques minutes?

✳ **ABOVE** Made up of a photographer's studio and a living space, the Rowes' property is a homage to Africa. **FACING PAGE** The studio entrance gives on to a make-up room. ✳ **OBEN** Das Haus der Rowes – ein Teil wird als Fotostudio, der andere zum Wohnen genutzt – ist eine Hommage an Afrika. **RECHTE SEITE** Der Eingang des Studios führt zu einem Schminkzimmer. ✳ **CI-DESSUS** Formée d'un studio de photographe et d'une habitation, la propriété du couple Rowe est un hommage aux concessions d'Afrique. **PAGE DE DROITE** L'entrée du studio donne sur une salle de maquillage.

❋ **ABOVE** With its cement floor marbled with tiles, the bathroom is full of warm colours created by Alice Rowe. "We have a good spiritual environment here," they both say. **FACING PAGE** The wrought iron and wood bed is ethnically inspired. ❋ **OBEN** Das Badezimmer ist mit marmoriertem Zementboden ausgelegt; die warmen Farben hat Alice Rowe ausgewählt. »Wir leben hier in einer besonders spirituellen Umgebung«, betonen die beiden Besitzer unisono. **RECHTE SEITE** Das fein gearbeitete Bett aus Holz und Schmiedeeisen passt gut zum ethnischen Stil des Hauses. ❋ **CI-DESSOUS** Posée sur un sol en ciment marbré de carreaux, la salle de bains déploie ses couleurs chaudes créées par Alice Rowe. «Nous vivons ici dans un environnement spirituel exceptionnel», répètent en chœur les propriétaires. **PAGE DE DROITE** Le lit ouvragé marie bois et fer forgé dans un concept ethnique.

* **LEFT** A warm and intimate water closet, unconcerned with modern comforts. **BELOW AND FACING PAGE** A pool of light around the cement bathtub. Using traditional techniques, the Rowes and their architect Kate Otten have gleefully upset all the canons of their white residential area. * **LINKS** Die kleine Toilette betont mit den warmen Farben den Charakter eines stillen Örtchens. **UNTEN UND RECHTS** Ein Lichtschacht beleuchtet die Beton-badewanne. Gelassen stellen die Rowes und ihre Architektin Kate Otten den Stilkanon der weißen Viertel Johannesburgs auf den Kopf, indem sie sich von althergebrachten Techniken inspirieren lassen. * **A GAUCHE** Renforcée de teintes chaudes, le coin toilette joue la carte de l'intime en s'affranchissant du confort moderne. **CI-DESSOUS ET PAGE DE DROITE** Un puits de lumière illumine la baignoire en béton. En s'inspirant des techniques tradi-tionnelles, le couple Rowe et son architecte Kate Otten bousculent sans états d'âme les canons en vigueur dans les quartiers blancs de Johannesburg.

Pierre Lombart

Johannesburg

Secure in its treetop solitude,
this house of platforms and split-levels surveys a broad vista of sky.

This is an architect's island, shot through with light and open to all manner of inspiration. It's no mean accomplishment to dominate vast spaces such as these. You can arrive, observe, sift, appropriate what you need from this place, and come away with your life permanently enriched. "We exist in forgetfulness of all our metamorphoses," says a French poet.

Pierre Lombart, himself a Belgian architect who has lived in South Africa for fifteen years, feels that it's important to keep his memories intact. How can one not be clear and straightforward, living in a house so airy and light, with architecture so easily comprehensible? The absolute requirement here was truthfulness, confronting things full on, whereas down below in the other villas the doors and shutters are all bolted for mortal fear of a country that is going through a period of profound change. The simplicity of Lombart's materials reaffirms his need to be part of his environment. He has gone back to the basics of his craft. As a sculptor of space, he sets out to celebrate every moment of daylight. His collection of contemporary art, begun fifteen years ago, includes paintings by Patrick Mautloa, Willem Boshoff and Jane Alexander – another proof, if it were needed, of Lombard's veneration for pure creativity. And everything else is confirmed by some lines by Gérard de Nerval he keeps framed in the bedroom: "May each soul go where its fancy leads it, and shut the door behind."

Auf der kleinen lichtdurchfluteten Insel des Architekten sind Inspirationen aller Art willkommen. Der Umgang mit großen Räumen ist alles andere als einfach. Man beobachtet, sondiert und nimmt mit, was das Leben bereichert. »Wir leben im Vergessen unserer Verwandlungen«, erklärte ein französischer Dichter.

Pierre Lombart, der belgische Architekt, der bereits seit 15 Jahren in Südafrika lebt, scheint dagegen ein gutes Gedächtnis zu haben. Wie sollte man in so einer luftigen Behausung nicht auf Transparenz setzen, auf eine allgemein verständliche Lesbarkeit der Architektur? Hier gibt es eine Fülle von Wahrheiten, eine Art und Weise, den Dingen ins Auge zu sehen, anders als in den Villen weiter unten, deren Türen und Fensterläden geschlossen bleiben, nicht zuletzt aufgrund der Angst in einem Land, das genau das gerade erlebt: seine Verwandlung. Die Auswahl einfacher Baumaterialien betont ebenfalls die Tendenz mit der Umgebung zu verschmelzen. Pierre Lombart hat sich auf die Grundsätze seines Berufes besonnen. Als »Bildhauer des Raums« möchte er jeden Augenblick genießen. In der Welt der Kunst kennt er sich aus: Seine vor 15 Jahren begonnene Sammlung zeitgenössischer Kunst umfasst Werke von Patrick Mautloa, Willem Boshoff und Jane Alexander. Im Schlafzimmer hängt ein Gedicht von Gérard de Nerval: »Jede Seele soll allein nach Lust und Laune leben, und bei geschloss'ner Tür nach Erfüllung streben.«

Transpercé de lumière, l'îlot de l'architecte est ouvert aux inspirations en tout genre. Ce n'est pas rien de dominer les grands espaces. On observe, et puis on peut trier, mine de rien, faire ses provisions, avant de poursuivre son chemin dans la vie. «Nous vivons dans l'oubli de nos métamorphoses», scandait un poète Français.

Pierre Lombart, architecte Belge installé en Afrique du Sud depuis 15 ans, tient à garder bonne mémoire. Comment ne pas faire vœu de transparence dans cette habitation si aérienne, à l'architecture d'une parfaite lisibilité? Il y a ici une exigence de vérité, une manière de voir les choses en face, alors qu'en bas, dans les autres villas, les portes et les volets sont clos, dans la crainte d'un pays qui, précisément, vit sa métamorphose. La simplicité des matériaux utilisés affirme encore la double volonté de se fondre dans l'environnement. Pierre Lombart s'en est remis aux fondamentaux de son métier. «Sculpteur d'espace», il a voulu célébrer chaque instant de la journée. Sa collection d'art contemporain commencée il y a 15 ans (on retrouve Patrick Mautloa, Willem Boshoff et Jane Alexander) hisse encore le drapeau de la création. Dans la chambre, c'est un poème de Gérard de Nerval qui intime: «Allez, que le caprice emporte / Chaque âme selon son désir / Et que close après vous la porte.»

✳ **PAGE 396** An eagle's nest indeed – Overlooking a thousand square metres of garden, the house consists of three platform levels, each flooded with light. **PREVIOUS PAGE** The salon leading through to the kitchen dining room, with "Barcelona" armchairs by Ludwig Mies van der Rohe and a coffee table designed 25 years ago by the South African Willem Boshoff. **ABOVE** Brick floors and chairs around the table, designed by Pierre Lombart. **BELOW RIGHT** The staircase leading to the bedroom was made by Guy du Toit and David Rousseau out of an aeroplane wing and sundry recycled ingredients, to celebrate earth, air, fire, and water. **FACING PAGE** The footbridge leading to the study echoes the platform leading up from the roadway. Everything here is a viaduct through a world that knows no limitations. ✳ **SEITE 396** Ein Adlernest? Könnte man meinen. Oberhalb des 1000 Quadratmeter großen Gartens wird das Haus auf drei Plattformetagen von Licht durchflutet. **VORHERGEHENDE SEITE** Im Salon stehen ein »Barcelona«-Sessel von Ludwig Mies van der Rohe und der dazugehörige niedrige Tisch, den Willem Boshoff vor 25 Jahren gebaut hat. Der Raum geht in die Küche über, die gleichzeitig als Esszimmer dient. **OBEN** Die von Pierre Lombart entworfenen Stühle rollen über den Ziegelboden. **UNTEN RECHTS** Guy de Toit und David Rousseau bauten die Treppe zum Schlafzimmer aus dem Tragflügel eines Flugzeugs und anderen recycelten Dingen. Das Kunstwerk feiert die vier Elemente Feuer, Erde, Luft und Wasser. **RECHTE SEITE** Der luftige Steg führt genau bis zum Schreibtisch und betont die Idee der Plattform. Hier ist alles Viadukt, eine Welt ohne Grenzen. ✳ **PAGE 396** Nid d'aigle? Il y a de ça. Au-dessus de mille mètres carrés de jardin, la maison vit sur des plates-formes de trois étages baignées de lumière. **PAGE PRECEDENTE** Le salon avec son fauteuil «Barcelona» de Ludwig Mies van der Rohe et sa table basse créé il y a 25 ans par le Sud-Africain Willem Boshoff communique avec la cuisine-salle à manger. **CI-DESSUS** Autour de la table, les chaises créées par Pierre Lombart roulent sur les sols en brique. **CI-DESSOUS A DROITE** L'escalier qui mène à la chambre a été créé par Guy de Toit et David Rousseau à partir d'une aile d'avion et d'autres pièces recyclées, pour célébrer le feu, l'air, la terre et l'eau. **PAGE DE DROITE** La passerelle aérienne qui court jusqu'au bureau évoque la plate-forme qui grimpe depuis la route. Tout ici est viaduc, monde sans frontières.

Bathafarh Farm
near Johannesburg

Disneyland horror or folly with a touch of genius?
Opinions are divided on this "home sweet home" with ghostly overtones.

The house has the quality of a mirage – as if the size, site and architecture of Joseph Kerham's castle didn't already make it unique in South Africa.

Overlooking a residential suburb, it's the kind of high walled citadel you'd expect to see in a fairy-tale picture book. With its formal French garden and its colonnaded Trianon pool, Castle Bathafarh represents another time, one that it exists to protect from the alien rhythms of modern life. What does its tower conceal? Whatever the reason, Joseph Kerham, its provincial builder, made a decision to bring the charm of the good old days right into the city. All that was needed was a little silence, masses of old doors, windows, wardrobes, old church pews and burnt terracotta tiles to reconstitute the era of the *ancien régime*. Kerham winds up his venerable grandfather clock beneath the incredulous gaze of a row of ancestors in gilt frames. The figurative scenes in the main drawing room evoke an old house somewhere in Europe. In the master bedroom there's a profusely-draped bed with columns at each corner and a luxurious counterpane. Here's living proof that the term *ancien régime* no longer defines an epoch, but a ready-made ambiance.

Ein Wunder? Von der schieren Größe, der Lage und erst recht der Architektur her sucht das Schloss von Joseph Kerham in Südafrika seinesgleichen.

Die Zitadelle mit den hohen abweisenden Mauern thront über einem Wohnviertel – eine Atmosphäre wie in *Dornröschen*. Der Garten im französischen Stil, das Wasserbecken mit den »Trianon«-Säulen à la Versailles, alles hier brüstet sich mit einem vergangenen Lebensstil, der sich mit Händen und Füßen gegen die Moderne wehrt. Was verbirgt sich wohl hinter dem Bergfried? Joseph Kerham rechnet in typischer Provinzlermanier die Nachteile der Großstadt gegen den Zauber der »guten alten Zeiten« auf. Um das »Ancien Régime« wiederzubeleben, bedurfte es vieler Türen, ein wenig Stille, dazu kamen Fenster, antike Schränke, alte Kirchenbänke und Terrakottafliesen. Unter den ungläubigen Blicken seiner Ahnen in den goldenen Bilderrahmen zieht der Hausherr die alte Uhr auf. Selbst die gegenständliche Malerei im großen Salon zeigt eine Besitzung im alten Europa. Das von hohen Säulen umgebene Bett im Schlafzimmer des Schlossbesitzers strahlt mit den Kissen und der verführerisch weichen Tagesdecke eine zeitlose Wehmut aus. Dabei bezeichnet der Begriff »Ancien Régime« schon lange weniger eine bestimmte Epoche, als vielmehr eine häusliche Atmosphäre.

Un mirage? De par sa taille, son emplacement et son architecture, le château de Joseph Kerham est unique en Afrique du Sud.

Surplombant une banlieue résidentielle, la citadelle, avec ses hauts murs de soutènement, génère une vision fantastique digne de la *Belle au Bois dormant*. Avec son jardin à la française, son bassin à colonnes «Trianon», elle vante un art de vivre révolu tout en se protégeant du rythme de la vie moderne. Alors, que dissimule le donjon? De manière provinciale, Joseph Kerham a choisi de conjuguer les inconvénients de la grande ville et les charmes du «bon vieux temps». Il a suffi d'un peu de silence, de lots de portes, de fenêtres, d'antiques armoires, de vieux bancs d'église et de carreaux de terre cuite brûlée pour reconstituer l'époque de l'Ancien Régime. Monsieur remonte la vieille horloge sous le regard incrédule des ancêtres dans leurs cadres dorés. Même les scènes figuratives du grand salon évoquent une demeure de la vieille Europe. Dans la chambre du maître de maison, un lit bordé de larges colonnes, agrémenté d'étoffes et d'un langoureux dessus-de-lit, parle encore une langueur hors du temps. Mais il y a belle lurette que le terme d'Ancien Régime désigne davantage une ambiance qu'une époque.

※ **FACING PAGE AND ABOVE** Joseph Kerham's Trianon-style park. **FOLLOWING PAGES** An effervescence of styles in the living room – copies of 18th century chairs and an antique kilim. ※ **LINKE SEITE UND OBEN** Joseph Kerhams Park im Anklang an das »Petit Trianon« in Versailles. **FOLGENDE DOPPELSEITE** Eine Fülle verschiedener Stile wird im Salon kombiniert. Die Stühle auf dem alten Kelim imitieren den Stil des 18. Jahrhunderts. ※ **PAGE DE GAUCHE ET CI-DESSUS** Joseph Kerham a aménagé un parc aux accents «petit Trianon». **DOUBLE PAGE SUIVANTE** Foisonnement de styles dans ce salon; les chaises imitent le 18e siècle sur un kilim ancien.

NDEBELE
MPUMALANGA PROVINCE

The renowned Ndebele wall frescoes reflect the evolution of the world.

In the mid-19th century, when the Ndebele people of South Africa forsook their straw huts for houses made of earth, they discovered not only a new form of architecture but also a finger-painting technique handed down by their Sotho neighbours.

As time went by, their iconography grew richer and when in 1923 a white farmer had the bright idea of asking his agricultural workers to paint his house in bright colours against a white background, the result was a revelation. Colour replaced the patterns painted with mud and natural oxides. Later, the original geometrical shapes were influenced by the urban experiences of Ndebele artists working in industry. Today, Esther Mahlangu has become a virtuoso in the art of bridging the gulf between tradition and the new motifs linked to latter day urban development. Her frescoes show not only the beaded skirts worn by young brides, but also such ordinary modern things as sloping roofs, ladders, windows, and double-edged razor blades. She paints with feather brushes and uses traditional calabashes instead of pots for her colours. Although these paintings have no magic powers according to the Ndebele, they are nevertheless thought to protect houses against the evil eye – a belief that is widespread in Africa.

Als die Ndebele in Südafrika Mitte des 19. Jahrhunderts aus ihren Strohhütten in Häuser aus Lehm zogen, entdeckten sie gleichzeitig mit dieser neuen Architekturform die Technik der Fingermalerei bei ihren Nachbarn, den Sotho.

Im Laufe der Zeit entwickelten die Ndebele diese Technik immer weiter und als 1923 ein weißer Farmer eine seiner Landarbeiterinnen bat, die weißen Wände seines Hauses in bunten Farben zu bemalen, war die Sensation perfekt. Die früher mit Erdfarben und natürlichen Oxiden gemalten Muster waren farblich eher gedämpft. Wieder einige Zeit später veränderten sich die geometrischen Muster durch die Erfahrungen, die Ndebele-Künstlerinnen in der Stadt und bei der Arbeit in der Industrie machten. Esther Mahlangu verbindet virtuos die althergebrachte Kunst mit neuen Motiven, die mit der Verstädterung zusammenhängen. Die Wandmalerei zeigt so unterschiedliche Motive wie die mit Perlen bestickten Schürzen verheirateter Frauen, geneigte Dächer, Leitern, Fenster oder zweischneidige Rasierklingen. Zum Malen benutzt die Künstlerin Federpinsel, als Farbtopf traditionelle Kalebassen. Wenngleich diese Bilder den Ndebele zufolge keinerlei Zauberkraft haben, sollen sie doch wie in vielen afrikanischen Ländern die Häuser vor Unglück schützen.

Au milieu du 19ᵉ siècle, quand le peuple Ndebele d'Afrique du Sud abandonne ses huttes en paille pour des habitations en terre, il découvre en même temps qu'une nouvelle forme d'architecture une technique de peinture au doigt léguée par ses voisins, les Sothos.

Au fil du temps, l'iconographie gagne en richesse et, en 1923, quand un fermier blanc demande à une de ses ouvrières agricoles de peindre sa maison de couleurs vives sur fond blanc, c'est une révélation. La couleur remplace les motifs peints à la boue avec des oxydes naturels. Plus tard encore, les formes géométriques sont influencées par l'expérience urbaine de nombreux artistes Ndebele qui travaillent dans l'industrie. Aujourd'hui Esther Mahlangu est virtuose dans l'art de jeter un pont entre la tradition et les nouveaux motifs liés à l'urbanisation. Ces fresques représentent aussi bien les motifs des pagnes de perle que portent les jeunes femmes mariées que des toits en pente, des échelles, des fenêtres, ou encore des lames de rasoir à double tranchant. Pour peindre, elle utilise des pinceaux en plume et, en guise de pots, des calebasses traditionnelles. Si ces peintures n'ont aucun pouvoir magique selon les Ndebele, elles contribuent néanmoins, comme dans de nombreux pays d'Afrique, à protéger les maisons du mauvais sort.

※ **PAGE 410** Esther Mahlangu is the most famous living Ndebele artist. Her geometrical drawings are known all over the world. **ABOVE** Her house is a blend of brightly coloured symmetrical motifs and modern equipment. ※ **SEITE 410** Esther Mahlangu ist die berühmteste Malerin der Ndebele. Ihre symmetrischen Zeichnungen gehen um die Welt. **OBEN** In ihrem Haus verbindet sie geometrische Muster mit lebhaften Farben und einer modernen Einrichtung. ※ **PAGE 410** Esther Mahlangu est l'artiste Ndebele la plus célèbre. Réalisés dans la symétrie, ses dessins ont fait le tour du monde. **CI-DESSUS** Sa maison mêle les motifs géométriques de couleurs vives et l'équipement moderne.

TOWNSHIPS
Cape Town

The slum dwellers around the airport struggle perpetually against the encroaching sand – and do what they can to make their homes attractive.

Black or white – before Nelson Mandela and freedom, the simplistic horror of South Africa applied to everything from skin colour to the walls of houses.

White villas against bright African façades, as in the Malay quarter which still exists today; for years the mad theorists of apartheid imposed the difference, forcing people who didn't meet their racial criteria to move out of the central part of the Cape area. This brought about the creation of the townships. According to the prevailing wisdom, these districts were expected to separate the races, while supplying visual proof in downtown Cape Town that the myth of white South Africa was really true. The "Cape Flats" (so called to distinguish them from the residential quarters on the slopes of Table Mountain) today have a population of nearly two million, hovering just outside the city. What could be more natural today than the celebration of colour, in honour of a country that calls itself the Rainbow Nation? More often than not, the walls inside the houses are covered with advertisements for consumer products, which serve as wallpaper of a kind. Food cartons and cans are recycled, too. In summer, the tin shacks are furnace-hot, and in the winter they're so cold that entire families go to bed at six, as soon as they get home from school or work. So a touch of colour on the walls is more than welcome.

Schwarz oder Weiß – bis zu Nelson Mandelas Befreiung lief es in Südafrika schrecklicherweise stets auf die Frage nach der Hautfarbe hinaus. Für Häuser galt das Gleiche.

Weiße Villen gegen die bunten Fassaden in afrikanischem Patchwork wie in dem noch immer existierenden Viertel Malay. Über lange Zeit siedelten die fanatischen Vertreter einer Menschen verachtenden Apartheidpolitik unerwünschte Bürger nach rassischen Kriterien aus den Stadtzentren um. So entstanden die Elendsviertel am Stadtrand. Die Stadtteile sollten nach Rassen getrennt werden, auch um in der Innenstadt die Illusion eines weißen Südafrika aufrecht erhalten zu können. Die »Cape Flats« (Bezeichnung, um sie von den Wohnvierteln am Hang des Tafelbergs zu unterscheiden) am Stadtrand beherbergen heutzutage fast zwei Millionen Einwohner. Hier steht die Farbe im Mittelpunkt, wie ein Echo darauf, dass sich das südafrikanische Volk den Beinamen »Regenbogen-Nation« gegeben hat. An den Wänden hängen statt Tapeten bunte Papierrollen mit Anzeigen, die für Güter des täglichen Bedarfs werben. Dosen aller Art werden ebenfalls wieder verwertet. Im Sommer ist eine Wellblechhütte der reinste Backofen, im Winter dagegen ein Kühlschrank. Zu dieser Jahreszeit gehen manche Familien schon um sechs Uhr abends schlafen, sobald sie von der Arbeit oder von der Schule nach Hause kommen. So gestalten sie wenigstens ihre Wände ein wenig fröhlicher …

Noir ou blanc – avant la libération de Nelson Mandela, l'effroyable simplisme de l'Afrique du Sud se déclinait du pigment des peaux aux murs des maisons.

Villas blanches contre façades bariolées de patchworks africains, à l'exemple du quartier Malay qui existe encore; longtemps, les savants fous de l'apartheid ont accompli leur sale besogne, déplaçant du centre de Cape Town les populations rejetées par les critères raciaux. Ainsi sont nés les bidonvilles. Dans la mythologie d'alors, ces quartiers avaient pour vocation de séparer les races, mais aussi d'entretenir visuellement, là-bas en ville, le mythe d'une Afrique du Sud blanche. Les «Cape Flats» (ainsi désignés en opposition aux quartiers résidentiels à flanc de la Montagne de la Table) abritent aujourd'hui près de deux millions d'habitants en périphérie de la ville. Quoi de plus naturel que d'y célébrer aujourd'hui les couleurs, en écho à cette nation autoproclamée «Arc en ciel»? Les murs sont le plus souvent bariolés de rouleaux de papier à la gloire de produits de consommation courante tenant lieu de papier peint. On recycle également toutes sortes de boîtes de conserve. L'été, la cabane en tôle est une fournaise. L'hiver, c'est un frigo au point que, sitôt revenues du travail et de l'école, les familles se couchent dès six heures. Alors, un peu de gaieté aux murs…

❋ **ABOVE** The corrugated iron shacks are built on a dusty, windswept plain. Amid this scene of dire poverty, people signify their sense of belonging with brightly decorated walls. In winter, the houses are heated with paraffin, at the mortal risk of starting a general conflagration. ❋ **OBEN** Die Wellblechhütten stehen im sandigen, windigen Flachland. In diesem extremen Elend gestaltet man seine Wände höchstens mit bunten Werbeplakaten. Im Winter wird mit Paraffin geheizt – nicht selten kommt es zu verheerenden Bränden.
❋ **CI-DESSUS** Les cabanes en tôle ondulée sont édifiées sur une plaine sablonneuse battue par les vents. Dans cette misère extrême, on marque l'appartenance par des murs bariolés. L'hiver, on se chauffe à la paraffine au risque de terribles incendies.

❋ **ABOVE** Every year, the rural exodus brings hundreds of thousands more people to the capital of Cape Province. Huge construction programmes are under way to replace shanties without water or electricity. ❋ **OBEN** Jährlich führt die Landflucht dazu, dass Hunderttausende von Neuankömmlingen in die Hauptstadt am Kap strömen. Umfassende Bauvorhaben sollen dafür sorgen, dass die Menschen nicht länger in Baracken ohne Wasser und Strom hausen müssen. ❋ **CI-DESSUS** Chaque année, l'exode rural provoque l'arrivée de centaines de milliers de nouveaux habitants dans la ville du Cap. D'immenses programmes de construction visent à remplacer ces baraques sans eau ni électricité par des maisons en dur.

※ **ABOVE** Township-style, the partitions are covered with wrapping paper advertising soap, chocolate, wine; there are also recycled cigarette cartons and small match-boxes adorned with lions' heads. ※ **OBEN** Die Trennwände sind wie in den Townships üblich mit Werbung oder Verpackungen von Seife, Schokolade oder Wein beklebt. Ein Löwenkopf schmückt Zigarettenstangen und Streichholzpackungen. ※ **CI-DESSUS** À la mode des bidonvilles, les cloisons des pièces sont recouvertes de papier d'emballage récupéré à la gloire de savons, de marques de chocolat, de vin, de cartouches de cigarettes ou encore de petites boîtes d'allumettes arborant la tête d'un lion.

✳ **ABOVE** The art of survival in the townships – floors are covered with pieces of carpet and linoleum picked up in the residential areas. Things abandoned by other people are brought back into use, and religious belief is very strong. ✳ **OBEN** Überlebenskunst in den Townships: Auf den Böden liegen Teppich- oder Linoleumreste, die die Bewohner in den vornehmen Wohnvierteln aufgetrieben haben. Man richtet sich mit weggeworfenen Dingen ein. Dabei sind die Bewohner der Elendsviertel sehr gläubig. ✳ **CI-DESSUS** L'art de (sur)vivre des habitants des townships: on couvre les sols de bouts de moquette ou de lino, récupérés dans les quartiers résidentiels; on s'équipe d'objets abandonnés. Et on est très croyant.

WiLLiE BesTer

cape Town

This artist has invited the industrial world to his house –
and the result is a miniature Beaubourg on the southern tip of Africa.

It used to be a "Whites Only" suburb – a sinister label if ever there was one. The anathema applied not only to its inhabitants but also to their homes, which were all drearily alike. When the mixed-race artist Willie Bester arrived, colour arrived in his slipstream.

His house is a promising blue on the outside. Around it, a décor typical of a Karoo desert farm (the Karoo is close by) flirts with mosaics and objects salvaged and reinvented in new roles. Willie Bester himself drew up the plans for his circular house, with no corner crannies where bad thoughts could lurk. The first thing you see inside it is a steel structure strongly resembling a hot water boiler, and setting the tone for the whole house. Actually it's a column, supporting the staircase. A giant portrait of Nelson Mandela, with his eyes turned to heaven, overlooks the living room. Loftwise, the kitchen and dining room are one; the bedrooms are on the first floor, with a wing for the three children; and the studio is adjacent. Willie Bester's work has won considerable recognition in Europe, and he is now embarked on a series of new experiments. As the months go by, his 'industrial park' steadily fills with fresh creations. Viewed as life sources, his factory pipes and tubes are like so many arteries attached to an imaginary pumping heart. The organism is alive. It quivers with inspiration. One day it's a house; the next, it's a museum.

Es war einmal ein »Whites-only«-Vorort – was für eine finstere Bezeichnung. Der Bann bezog sich auf die Menschen, aber auch auf die Häuser mit ihren fahlen Fassaden. Als sich der Künstler Willie Bester hier einkaufte, brachte er die Farbe gleich mit.

Schon die bläuliche Fassade ist ein gutes Zeichen. Das Dekor wie von einer Farm in der nahe gelegenen Wüste Karoo harmoniert mit Mosaiken und neu zusammengesetzten Objekten vom Trödel. Willie Bester selbst zeichnete die Pläne für das runde Haus, wo sich böse Gedanken gar nicht erst einnisten können. Zunächst stolpert man über eine Stahlkonstruktion, die auf den ersten Blick einem Heizkessel ähnelt. Tatsächlich dient sie als Stützpfeiler für die Treppe. Im Salon hängt als Ausdruck der Verehrung ein Porträt Nelson Mandelas (mit Blick zum Himmel). Wie in einem Loft gehen Küche und Esszimmer ineinander über. Die Zimmer liegen im ersten Stock, ein separater Flügel ist den Kindern vorbehalten. Im Atelier nebenan widmet sich Willie Bester, der inzwischen auch in Europa bekannt wurde, neuen Experimenten. Nach und nach füllt sich sein »Industriepark« mit neuen Kreationen. Als eine Quelle des Lebens führen die Fabrikrohre wie Arterien zu einem imaginären Herzen – ein lebendiger Organismus im Einklang mit der Inspiration. Heute ist dies ein Haus, morgen vielleicht schon ein Museum.

C'était une banlieue «Whites only» – sinistre appellation s'il en est. L'anathème s'appliquait aux habitants mais aussi aux demeures, toutes semblables avec leur façade blafarde. Quand l'artiste métis Willie Bester a investi les lieux, la couleur se devait d'être au rendez-vous.

C'est un extérieur bleuté de bon augure qui accueille le visiteur. Autour, un décor de ferme du Karoo (le désert voisin) flirte avec les mosaïques et des objets de récupération réinventés. Willie Bester a lui-même dessiné les plans d'une maison circulaire, sans recoins pour les mauvaises pensées. On tombe alors sur une structure en acier semblable à une chaudière. Le ton est donné. C'est en vérité un pilier qui soutient l'escalier. Révérence oblige, un grand portrait de Nelson Mandela, yeux au ciel, fait face au salon. À la manière d'un loft, cuisine et salle à manger se relayent; les chambres sont à l'étage, avec une aile pour les trois enfants; l'atelier est contigu. Reconnu désormais en Europe, Willie Bester s'y livre à de nouvelles expérimentations. Mois après mois, ce «parc industriel» s'enrichit de nouvelles créations. Source de vie, les tuyaux d'usine sont des artères reliées à un cœur imaginaire. L'organisme est vivant. Il bat au gré des inspirations. Un jour, c'est une maison, un autre c'est un musée.

✳ **ABOVE** Willie Bester, 47, grew up with the prohibition against Blacks taking any part in the creative arts. He has represented his country in many foreign exhibitions. In homage to the great man, a portrait of Nelson Mandela dominates his "industrial park". ✳ **OBEN** Der 47-jährige Willie Bester erlebte noch mit, dass Schwarze vom Kunstbetrieb ausgeschlossen waren. Heute vertritt er sein Land auf zahlreichen Ausstellungen. Als Hommage hängt ein Porträt Nelson Mandelas in seinem »Industriepark«. ✳ **CI-DESSUS** Willie Bester, 47 ans, a grandi avec l'interdiction faite aux Noirs de toucher aux arts. Il a représenté son pays dans de nombreuses expositions. En hommage, un portrait de Nelson Mandela domine son «parc industriel».

✻ **FACING PAGE** The boiler recycled as a column for the staircase is emblematic of the work of this artist, who places industrial society at the centre of his creative work. **ABOVE** The chairs at his bar are recycled drains; in general, his raw materials are pieces of wood, tin cans, squashed paint tubes and other objects picked up on the streets of the townships. ✻ **LINKE SEITE** Ein als Treppenpfeiler zweckentfremdeter recycelter Heizkessel ist sinnbildlich für die Arbeiten des Künstlers, der die Industrie in den Mittelpunkt seines Schaffens stellt. **OBEN** Ausrangierte Wasserrohre bilden die Füße der Barhocker. Ausgangsmaterial für Besters Kunstwerke sind oft Holzstücke, Konservendosen, ausgedrückte Farbtuben und verschiedene andere Dinge, die er auf den Straßen der Elendsviertel sammelt. ✻ **PAGE DE GAUCHE** La chaudière recyclée en pilier pour l'escalier est emblématique du travail de l'artiste qui place la société industrielle au centre de sa création. **CI-DESSUS** Les fauteuils de son bar sont des conduites d'eau revisitées; de manière générale, ses matières premières sont des bouts de bois, des conserves, des tubes de peinture écrasés et divers objets ramassés dans les rues des bidonvilles.

MALCOLM KLUK
Cape Town

This navy-blue house in the trendy Greenpoint district
is a reflection of sky and glittering sea.

The sun beats down and the wind blows. The Cape climate is pure and violent. In imitation of the open sea, the designer Malcolm Kluk has clothed his house in blue.

Outside, it hangs over the ocean; inside it's as if one were under the surface. "My guests find this very intimate and soothing," he says. "Not surprisingly, in aurasoma therapy dark blue represents the third eye of protection and providence." The house is also a physical expression of its owner's moods. Words have been scrawled on the walls – Hope, Dreams, Desire – to form a triptych, a kind of reassuring background murmur. A line by Dylan Thomas encapsulates the attitude of Malcolm Kluk: "Rage, rage against the dying of the light." Dreams are there to come true for us, if we can only do our best. The designer draws inspiration for his art from the place in which he lives. His secret, he says, is that he "… just brings everything together; the assembled effect becomes right, because I make no effort to superimpose some kind of preordained look." Malcolm Kluk was born in Durban and knows England well, having lived there for eight years. He carries within himself a mix of influences which he seeks to express in his interior. In the future other desires will come, along with other passions, fires and colours.

Kapstadt funkelt in einem Klima, das, mit viel Wind und Sonne gesegnet, klar und brutal zugleich ist. Der Designer Malcolm Kluk hat sein Haus ganz in Blau eingerichtet, als wollte er auf die hohe See hinaus.

Das Haus selbst ragt über dem Meer empor, innen hat man dagegen eher das Gefühl, unter Wasser zu leben. »Meinen Gästen gefällt die neue Gemütlichkeit des Navy Blue. In der Aura-Soma-Therapie steht diese Farbnuance für das Dritte Auge, das für Schutz und Vorsehung zuständig ist«, erklärt der Hausherr lächelnd. Das unter solchem Schutz stehende Haus spiegelt die Stimmungen seines Bewohners wider. Wie Hinweise stehen hingekritzelt Wörter an den Wänden. »Hoffnung«, »Träume« und »Lust« bilden ein Triptychon, das die Menschen glücklich machen soll. Ein Gedicht von Dylan Thomas veranschaulicht ebenfalls Malcolm Kluks Philosophie: »Wüte, wüte gegen das Sterben des Lichts«. Es fordert dazu auf, den Träumen nachzuspüren und sie zu verwirklichen. Hirngespinste? Keineswegs. Der Designer zieht die schöpferische Kraft für seine Arbeit aus diesem Haus. Verrät er sein Geheimnis? »Ich bringe alles zusammen, so entsteht genau die richtige Wirkung, weil eben kein gewollter ›Look‹ aufgesetzt wird.« Malcolm Kluk, der in Durban geboren wurde und acht Jahre in England gelebt hat, schöpft aus den Erfahrungen mit verschiedenen Stilrichtungen, die er in seinem Haus zum Ausdruck bringen will. Später werden dann andere Wünsche, Fieberträume, Verbrennungen und andere Farben hinzukommen.

Vent et soleil intenses, Cape Town étincelle sous un climat pur et violent à la fois. Comme pour prendre le large, le styliste Malcolm Kluk a habillé sa maison de bleu.

À l'extérieur, on est suspendu au-dessus de la mer; à l'intérieur, c'est au contraire comme si on vivait sous la mer. «Mes invités se réjouissent d'une intimité retrouvée grâce au Navy blue. Dans la thérapie aurasoma, cette nuance représente le troisième œil, celui de la protection et de la providence», sourit-il. Placé sous un tel patronage, l'habitat est une représentation des humeurs de son propriétaire. Aux murs, sous forme d'avertissements, des mots ont été griffonnés. Espoir, Rêves et Désir forment un triptyque, un «mur-murs» pour rendre les gens heureux. Un poème de Dylan Thomas illustre encore la philosophie de Malcolm Kluk: «Rage, rage contre la lumière mourante», invite à poursuivre la quête des rêves et de leur accomplissement. Chimères? Pas le moins du monde. Le styliste puise l'inspiration de son art dans sa maison. Son secret? «Je pose tout ensemble et l'effet d'assemblement est juste, car il n'y a pas d'effort pour imposer un look.» Originaire de Durban, familier de l'Angleterre où il a passé huit années, Malcolm Kluk porte en lui un mélange d'influences qu'il veut reproduire dans son intérieur. Plus tard, viendront d'autres désirs, d'autres fièvres, d'autres brûlures, d'autres couleurs.

* **ABOVE** Corrugated iron roof, party walls, terrace on the street, balcony and small yard: the house is typical of this formerly working class Cape area, now fashionable. *
OBEN Wellblechdach, Brandwände, eine Terrasse zur Straße, ein Balkon und ein kleiner Hof – ein völlig normales Haus in dem früheren Arbeiterviertel, wo sich jetzt die Schickimicki-Szene von Kapstadt einnistet. * **CI-DESSUS** Toit en tôle ondulée, murs mitoyens, terrasse sur la rue, balcon et petite cour, la maison est typique de cet habitat autrefois populaire, aujourd'hui investi par les bobos de Cape Town.

❋ **ABOVE** The houses of the Cape all have a small yard contiguous to the living room, which is sheltered from the wind and used for open air dining. **FOLLOWING PAGES** The long table comes from a garage, where it was used as a work bench. Malcolm Kluk came across it when he was buying his car. ❋ **OBEN** Die meisten Häuser in Kapstadt haben als Verlänge-rung des Salons einen kleinen windgeschützten Hof, in dem man unter freiem Himmel essen kann. Als Sitzgelegenheiten dienen Malcolm Kluk weiß lackierte hohe Holzzylinder. **FOLGENDE DOPPELSEITE** Der lange Tisch stammt aus einer Garage, wo er als Werkbank benutzt wurde. Malcolm Kluk entdeckte ihn, als er sein Auto kaufte. ❋ **CI-DESSUS** Les maisons de Cape Town mettent toutes en valeur la petite cour à l'abri du vent qui prolonge le salon et sert de salle à manger à ciel ouvert. En guise de sièges, Malcolm Kluk a redécouvert ces plots de bois peints en blanc. **DOUBLE PAGE SUIVANTE** La longue table provient d'un garage où elle servait d'établi. Malcom Kluk l'a découverte en achetant sa voiture.

✳ **ABOVE** In the bedroom, the piled books have a living curve, lengthened or shortened as Kluk's reading progresses. **FACING PAGE** Keywords of good conduct on the blue-painted walls. ✳ **OBEN** Die Bücherstapel im Schlafzimmer weisen darauf hin, dass die Bibliothek stets mit Neuzugängen versorgt wird. **RECHTE SEITE** Die Worte an den blau getünchten Wänden fordern uns auf, das Richtige zu tun. ✳ **CI-DESSUS** Dans la chambre à coucher, l'empilement de livres assure à la bibliothèque une courbe vivante, rétrécie ou allongée au fil des lectures. **PAGE DE DROITE** Aux murs badigeonnés de bleus des mots soufflent un code de bonne conduite.

✳ **ABOVE AND FACING PAGE** A Victorian sofa for three and an ordinary table. A metal chandelier, of the kind that are made in the streets round the Cape, hangs from the ceiling. The furniture was patiently assembled from antique shops, markets and friends' houses. ✳ **OBEN UND RECHTE SEITE** Ein dreisitziges viktorianisches Sofa lädt dazu ein, sich an diesem klassischen Tisch niederzulassen. Von der Decke hängt einer der Metalllüster, wie sie auf den Straßen von Kapstadt hergestellt werden. Geduldig hat der Hausherr die Möbel in Antikläden, auf dem Flohmarkt oder bei Freunden gesammelt. ✳ **CI-DESSUS ET PAGE DE DROITE** Un sofa trois places victorien sert d'assise à une table des plus classique. Au plafond, un lustre en métal comme on en fabrique dans les rues de Cape Town. Le mobilier a été patiemment rassemblé auprès d'antiquaires, dans des foires ou chez des amis.

* **LEFT** The bedroom is a mix of styles, with books and personal objects. The owner views his furniture as so many photographs that precisely evoke moments in time, or people. Dream or reality? * **LINKS** Im Schlafzimmer gehen die verschiedenen Stilrichtungen eine harmonische Verbindung mit den Büchern und anderen persönlichen Dingen ein. Der Hausherr betrachtet seine Möbel wie Fotografien, die punktgenau Momente und Personen heraufbeschwören können. Traum oder Wirklichkeit? * **A GAUCHE** La chambre marie les styles avec des livres et des objets personnels. Le propriétaire considère ses meubles comme des photographies qui évoquent avec précision des moments ou des personnes. Rêve ou réalité?

Tracy Rushmere & Peter Maltbie
Cape Town

Here the influences of many continents co-exist, though Africa predominates.

An Indian spear on one side of the bed, African statues on the other – such is the norm for the owners of this house in the centre of the Cape.

The need to combine various genres is a natural one in an interior developed by Tracy Rushmere, who runs a well-known shop in town called African Image, and Peter Maltbie, a photographer of Amerindian origin. All roads intersect here, with a kilim from Turkey on the pale wood floor, a robe from the Nigerian Hausa tribe on the wall, a Ghanaian bedcover on the bed, and an ivory lion from Mozambique. While there's African art everywhere – even the sound system is kept in a Zulu meat cabinet – there are touches of the Orient and South America to complete the picture, with Indian tables, decorative stones from the Far East, and above the bed a traditional Indian shield with medicinal virtues made by Peter Maltbie. Being open to the world means not being blind to one's surroundings, and Tracy Rushmere, a South African, hasn't neglected antiques made by the Boer settlers who reached the Cape three centuries ago. An example is her 19th century wooden chair, known locally as a *boerstoel*. The space is regularly enriched with finds like this.

Auf der einen Seite des Kopfendes eine indische Lanze, auf der anderen afrikanische Statuen – deutlicher kann man den Geschmack des Hausbesitzerpaares mitten in Kapstadt nicht auf den Punkt bringen.

Beide haben das Bedürfnis, Genregrenzen zu überwinden – Tracy Rushmere, berühmt für ihr Geschäft African Image und Peter Maltbie, Fotograf indianischer Abstammung. Von Norden nach Süden kreuzen sich die Stile, wie bei dem türkischen Kelim auf hellem Holzboden oder der Robe vom Stamm der Hausa aus Nigeria an der Wand, der Tagesdecke aus Ghana oder auch den elfenbeinernen Löwen aus Mosambik. Die allgegenwärtige afrikanische Kunst (sogar die Musikanlage steckt in einem Vorratsschrank der Zulu) wird ergänzt durch östliche oder südamerikanische Einrichtungsgegenstände, durch indische Tische, Schmucksteine aus Fernost oder den über dem Bett angebrachten indianisch anmutenden Schild, der Heilkräfte besitzen soll – selbst gemacht von Peter Maltbie. Wer weltoffen ist, richtet seinen scharfen Blick auch auf die eigene Umgebung. Die Südafrikanerin Tracy Rushmere interessiert sich jedenfalls für die Antiquitäten der Buren (jener holländischstämmigen Bevölkerung, die seit über 300 Jahren am Kap siedelt), beispielsweise für diesen *boerstoel*, einen Holzstuhl aus dem 19. Jahrhundert. Nach und nach tragen die beiden Hausbesitzer immer neue Funde zusammen.

Une lance indienne d'un côté de la tête de lit, des statues africaines de l'autre, comment mieux résumer le parti pris des propriétaires de cette maison située au centre de Cape Town?

Ce besoin de marier les genres s'exprime naturellement dans l'intérieur de Tracy Rushmere, célèbre en ville pour sa boutique African Image, et de Peter Maltbie, photographe aux origines amérindiennes. Du Nord au Sud, les routes se croisent avec ce kilim de Turquie sur le sol en bois blond, cette robe de la tribu Hausa du Nigeria sur un mur, ce dessus-de-lit du Ghana, ou encore ce lion en ivoire mozambicain. Si l'art africain est partout (même la chaîne hi-fi est placée dans un garde-manger zoulou), des touches orientalistes ou sud-américaines complètent le tableau, avec les tables indiennes, les pierres décoratives d'Extrême-Orient, et toujours au-dessus du lit, ce bouclier aux vertus médicinales dans la tradition indienne fabriqué par Peter Maltbie. Être ouvert au monde ne signifie pas pour autant être aveugle à ce qui les entoure, et Tracy Rushmere, Sud-Africaine, ne néglige pas les antiquités des Boers (Hollandais ayant débarqué il y a trois siècles), avec, notamment, cette chaise en bois du 19e siècle appelée *boerstoel*. L'espace s'enrichit régulièrement de trouvailles à l'occasion d'une nouvelle pêche aux trésors.

※ **FACING PAGE AND ABOVE** The living room, like the rest of the house, is a fine mix of African artifacts (statues and stools) and Art Deco furniture, always reference for Tracy Rushmere.
BELOW The bedroom symbolizes the double culture of the owners, with its African influences (note the Ghanaian bedcover) and American Indian religious objects. ※ **LINKE SEITE UND OBEN**
Wie das Haus insgesamt bildet auch der Salon eine geschmackvolle Mischung aus afrikanischen Raritäten (Statuen und Schemel) und Art-déco-Möbeln, Tracy Rushmeres Spezialität.
UNTEN Das Schlafzimmer spiegelt die beiden kulturellen Welten der Hausbesitzer wider – die Tagesdecke kommt aus Ghana, die Kultgegenstände stammen von amerikanischen Indianern. ※ **PAGE DE GAUCHE ET CI-DESSUS** Le salon, à l'image de la maison, est un savoureux mélange de curiosités africaines (statues et tabourets) et de meubles Art Déco, période de référence pour Tracy Rushmere. **CI-DESSOUS** La chambre à coucher symbolise la double culture des propriétaires avec ses influences africaines (dessus-de-lit du Ghana) et ces objets cultuels des Indiens d'Amérique.

DE OUDE SCHUUR
CAPE TOWN

A city centre loft,
high above the celebrated Malay quarter.

When apartheid was still functioning in South Africa, the heart of Cape Town was pretty much out of bounds. Today all that's changed. The area around Long Street, Bree Street and up to Kloof Street is full of people, galleries and crowded bars. Craig Port's loft is in the middle of all this.

Like its forerunners in New York, London and Paris, the space preserves its original shape as a warehouse, though the ambience is softened by subtle decoration. At all times of day, sunshine floods across the pale wood floors. Light is the cardinal element: there are windows everywhere, looking out towards Table Mountain and the town. The walls are of brick, covered in white: they exemplify the approach of Craig Port, which has been to preserve the authenticity of the place and only to give it the thinnest veneer of covering. There's no veranda, no walkway and no unnecessary effects: this is relentless industrial chic, completely austere. All the purchases for the loft were made in Long Street, at auctions or in Cape Town second hand shops. There's nothing ostentatious, only the occasional small luxury, such as the Art Deco table picked up at Groot Schuur Hospital, the HQ of the celebrated Dr. Christian Barnard.

Zu Zeiten der Apartheid wollte niemand so recht in die Innenstadt – das ist heute anders. In der Umgebung der Long Street, der Bree Street und weiter oben zur Kloof Street hin sind Galerien und Bars stets gut besucht. Das Loft liegt mittendrin.

Wie in New York, London oder Paris wahrt es seine Lageratmosphäre, die jedoch mit Hilfe einer wohl überlegten Dekoration wohnlich gestaltet wurde. Den ganzen Tag lang wirft die Sonne ein Streifenmuster auf das helle Parkett. Helligkeit wird hier insgesamt groß geschrieben: Es gibt überall Fenster zum Tafelberg oder zum Stadtzentrum. Die weiß getünchten Ziegelwände verraten viel über Craig Ports Methode, die Ursprünglichkeit des Ortes zu wahren, indem er seine eigenen Vorstellungen kaum wahrnehmbar einbringt. Veranden, komfortable Übergänge, platzraubende Kunstsammlungen oder überflüssige Effekte sucht man hier vergebens. Der Hausherr setzt auf Industrie-Chic, auf karge, eher nüchterne Akzente. Die Einrichtung stammt aus der Umgebung der Long Street, von Auktionen, Versteigerungen oder aus vereinzelten Trödelläden. Angeben ist verpönt, aber ein wenig Luxus darf sein, wie dieser Art-déco-Tisch, den Craig Port in der Groot-Schuur-Klinik aufgetrieben hat, wo der berühmte Professor Christian Barnard einst operierte. Eine gute Wahl. Wer schlicht und einfach lebt, muss keine Herzkrankheiten fürchten …

Au temps de l'apartheid, le cœur de la cité était un lieu infréquentable. Aujourd'hui, tout a changé. C'est autour de Long Street, Bree Street et en remontant sur Kloof Street, que la ville étale sa liberté avec ses galeries et ses bars. Ce loft est au milieu de la centrifugeuse.

Comme ses modèles de New York, Londres ou de Paris, il préserve sa forme d'entrepôt et adoucit l'ambiance à l'aide d'une décoration pointue. À tout instant de la journée, les rayons du soleil strient le parquet en bois clair. La luminosité est d'ailleurs un élément essentiel: partout des fenêtres sont percées en direction de la Montagne de la Table ou du centreville. Les murs de briques recouverts de blanc témoignent de la démarche de Craig Port: préserver l'authenticité du lieu, ne revêtir l'ensemble que d'une fine pellicule. Point de véranda, de passerelles, d'encombrantes collections ou d'effets superfétatoires: on la joue industriel chic, dans la sobriété assumée. Le shopping a été réalisé autour de Long Street, aux enchères ou chez les quelques brocanteurs de la ville. Rien d'ostentatoire, juste de petits luxes, comme cette table Art Déco chinée au Groot Schuur Hospital où officiait le célèbre professeur Christian Barnard. Un bon choix. À vivre ainsi dans la simplicité, on limite les risques cardiaques…

✳ **ABOVE** The square living room with its re-upholstered sofas and club chairs purchased in the city. The sculptures on the walls are by Brett Murray, an artist from the Cape. **BELOW** The thoroughly functional kitchen has a three-door refrigerator and metal everywhere. The 1950s stools came from a Cape milk bar. ✳ **OBEN** Der viereckige Salon mit neu bezogenen Kanapees und Klubsesseln, die Craig Port in der Stadt entdeckt hat. An den Wänden Skulpturen von Brett Murray, einer Künst-lerin aus Kapstadt. **UNTEN** Die Küche ist vorwiegend funktionell eingerichtet, hier dominiert Metall. Nicht zu übersehen ist der dreitürige Kühlschrank. Die Barhocker aus den 1950er Jahren stammen aus einer Milchbar in Kapstadt. ✳ **CI-DESSUS** Le salon carré avec ses canapés rehoussés et ses clubs chinés en ville. Aux murs, les sculptures sont de Brett Murray, un artiste de Cape Town. **CI-DESSOUS** Fonctionnelle avant tout, la cuisine où domine le métal est équipée d'un réfrigérateur «Déli» à trois portes. Les tabourets des années 1950 proviennent d'un milk-bar de Cape Town.

❊ **ABOVE** Under a collection of mirrors, the owner's study – with an Art Deco table from Groot Schuur Hospital and an ostrich egg lamp designed by Trevor Dykman. **FOLLOWING PAGES** A bed found at a sale in Groote Schuur Hospital. The hanging frame was once a cake trolley. ❊ **OBEN** Viele Spiegel zieren das Büro des Hausherrn. Der Art-déco-Tisch stammt aus der Groot-Schuur-Klinik, während die medusenhäuptige Straußeneier-Lampe von Trevor Dykman entworfen wurde. **FOLGENDE DOPPELSEITE** Auch das Bett stammt aus den Beständen der Groot-Schuur-Klinik. Als Kleiderschrank dient ein ehemals für den Transport von Backwaren benutztes fahrbares Regal. ❊ **EN HAUT** Sous une collection de miroirs, le bureau du propriétaire, avec sa table Art Déco chinée au Groot Schuur Hospital, et sa lampe méduse en œufs d'autruche signée Trevor Dykman. **DOUBLE PAGE SUIVANTE** Un lit trouvé dans une vente du Groot Shuur Hospital. En guise de penderie, un trolley utilisé autrefois pour les pâtisseries.

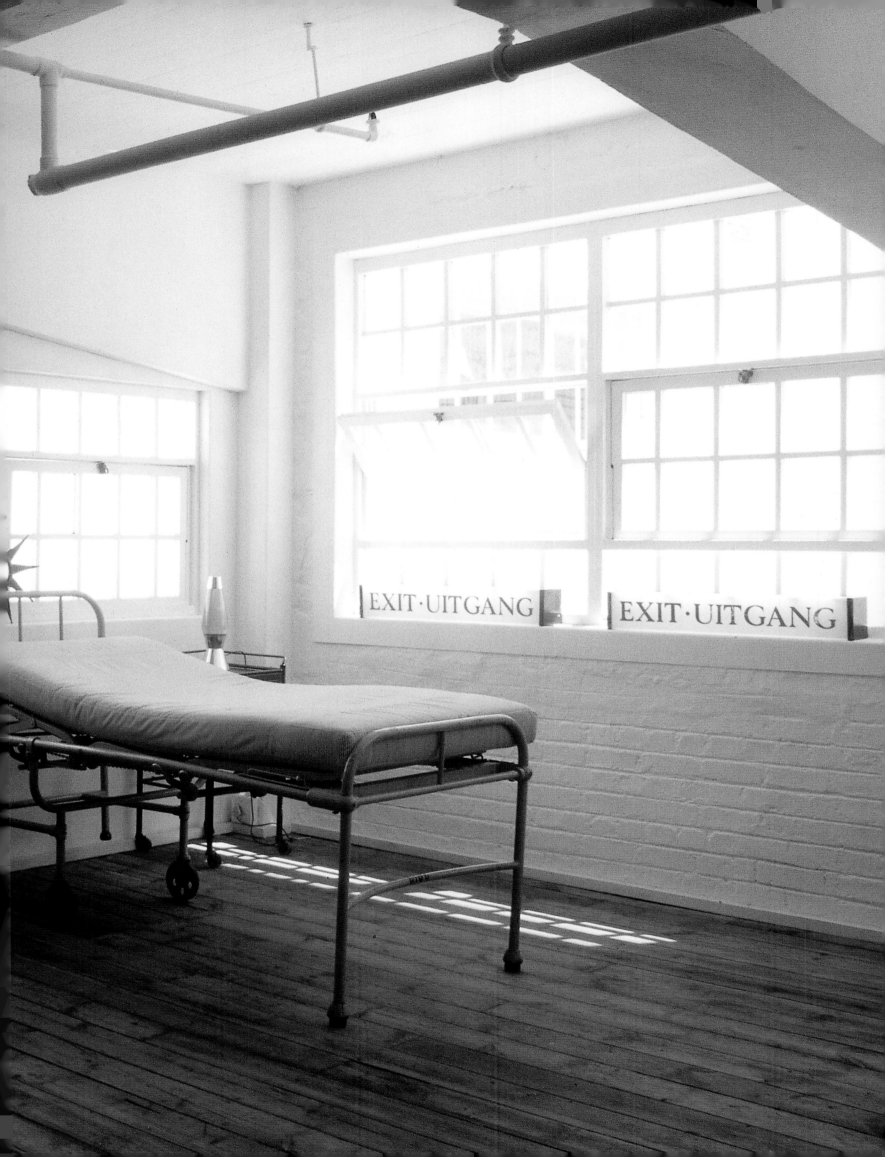

Jean-Marc Lederman

LLANDUDNO

Near the Cape,
a house of glass and concrete high above the Atlantic.

Beneath a sky of pigeon's egg blue, the outline of Jean-Marc Lederman's house stands above its protected site, one of South Africa's most famous swimming places. The sea is icy cold here, but its emerald hues and the white sandy beach that rims it attract the happy few from every corner of the globe.

Building sites are rare in the vicinity and it was only the combination of obstinacy and good luck that enabled Jean-Marc Lederman to buy one. A Frenchman who has lived at the Cape since 1994, his idea was to duplicate the simplicity and sense of space perfected by the architect Frank Lloyd Wright. After two years of work, the result is a piece of architecture remarkable for its purity, its clean lines and its open aspect, designed for living between the sky and the ocean. The walls are rough-surfaced and high metal guardrails stand between the main living room and the rest of the house. Otherwise the space is virtually unadorned, with nothing but the occasional touch of bright colour to enliven it. There are Moroccan poufs, rugs and carpets, harmonizing perfectly with pieces of furniture imported from Bali and their more modern counterparts from Paris and New York. And of course the view is breathtaking. There's nothing missing from this natural décor, so reminiscent of the Côte d'Azur in the time of Claude Monet and Paul Cézanne. But that headland a few miles to the south is the Cape of Good Hope, no less.

Die Silhouette des Hauses zeichnet sich scharf vor dem meerblauen Himmel über dem geschützten südafrikanischen Badeort ab. Das Wasser ist eiskalt, aber die Happy Few der großen weiten Welt wissen die smaragdgrünen Wellen und den weißen Sandstrand zu schätzen.

Es mangelt an bebaubaren Grundstücken und nur Glück und eine gewisse Sturheit konnten Jean-Marc Lederman dazu verhelfen. Der Franzose, der seit 1994 in Kapstadt lebt, hatte es sich in den Kopf gesetzt, ein großes und dennoch schlichtes Haus im Sinne des Architekten Frank Lloyd Wright zu bauen. Nach zwei Jahren Bauzeit konnte sich das Ergebnis sehen lassen: eine glasklare Architektur mit geraden Linien und vielen Fenstern, wie geschaffen für ein Leben zwischen Himmel und Ozean. Keine Tapeten an den Wänden; eine hohe Reling aus Metall trennt den großen Salon von den anderen Räumen. Er wirkt beinahe jungfräulich, nur hier und da leuchten sparsam eingesetzt lebhafte Farben auf. Marokkanische Teppiche, Kissen und gepolsterte Hocker harmonieren mit den aus Bali importierten Möbeln sowie moderneren Stücken aus Paris oder New York. Die Aussicht auf das Meer durch die Panoramafenster ist atemberaubend. Der Natur mangelt es an nichts, hier denkt man unwillkürlich an die Côte d'Azur zu Zeiten Claude Monets oder Paul Cézannes. Dabei ragt nur wenige Kilometer südlich das Kap der Guten Hoffnung aus den eisigen Fluten.

Sous un ciel bleu marine, la silhouette se détache sur un site protégé, haut lieu balnéaire sud-africain. L'eau est glaciale, mais ses reflets émeraude et la plage de sable blanc attirent les happy few du monde entier.

Les terrains à bâtir sont rares et ce sont les effets conjugués de la chance et de l'obstination qui ont permis à Jean-Marc Lederman d'en dénicher un. Ce Français établi à Cape Town depuis 1994 avait une idée en tête: copier les volumes et la simplicité des œuvres de l'architecte Frank Lloyd Wright. Après deux années de travaux, le résultat s'impose: une architecture très pure en lignes droites avec des ouvertures partout, pour vivre entre le ciel et l'océan. Les murs sont à l'état brut et de hautes rambardes métalliques séparent le grand salon du reste de la maison. L'espace est resté pratiquement vierge avec, ici et là, des touches de couleurs vives pour rehausser l'ensemble. Poufs, tapis et coussins marocains s'harmonisent parfaitement aux meubles importés de Bali et à ceux, plus modernes, achetés à Paris ou New York. Depuis les baies vitrées qui font face à la mer, le panorama est à couper le souffle. Rien ne manque à ce décor naturel évoquant si souvent la Côte d'Azur au temps de Claude Monet et Paul Cézanne. Et pourtant, à quelques kilomètres au Sud, c'est bien le Cap de Bonne-Espérance qui pointe son museau.

* **ABOVE** The gardens and terraces add a touch of green to the play of sunshine, blue sky and sea. **BELOW** The plate glass windows, as here in the bathroom, are an invitation to contemplate the view – the owner's favourite pastime, as it happens. * **FACING PAGE AND FOLLOWING PAGES** Overlooking the icy sea-water is a swimming pool, suspended between ocean and sky. **PAGE 468** Here the philosophy is entirely minimalist, dominated by grey and white. The whole house is decorated with sculptures and paintings by South African artists discovered by Jean-Marc Lederman in the JOAO gallery in Cape Town. * **OBEN** Die terrassenförmig angelegten Gärten legen einen Hauch von Grün über die blau getönten Licht- und Schattenspiele. **UNTEN** Wie hier im Badezimmer laden die Panoramafenster dazu ein, die Landschaft zu betrachten, eine der Lieblingsbeschäftigungen des Hausherrn. **RECHTE SEITE UND FOLGENDE DOPPELSEITE** Das lang gestreckte Schwimmbad mit Blick auf das eiskalte Meer scheint zwischen Himmel und Erde zu schweben. **SEITE 468** Minimalismus als Philosophie – Weiß und Grau dominieren. Skulpturen und Gemälde südafrikanischer Künstler, die Jean-Marc Lederman in der Galerie JOAO im Zentrum von Kapstadt entdeckt hat, vervollständigen das Bild. * **CI-DESSUS** Les jardins en terrasses ajoutent une touche verte à ces jeux d'ombre et de lumière où domine le bleu. **CI-DESSOUS** Les baies vitrées, comme ici dans la salle de bains, invitent à contempler le paysage, l'exercice favori du propriétaire. **PAGE DE DROITE ET DOUBLE PAGE SUIVANTE** Face à l'eau glacée, une piscine tout en longueur joue la suspension entre le ciel et la terre. **PAGE 468** Philosophie minimaliste où dominent le gris et blanc. L'ensemble est décoré de sculptures et de peintures d'artistes sud-africains que Jean-Marc Lederman a découvert dans la galerie d'art JOAO située au cœur de Cape Town.

JONATHAN GREEN & MARINA PRETORIUS
Greyton

Two architects worked together to renovate this simple, restful house.

Far from the vineyards and the tourist circuits is Greyton, a small village well known to the intellectuals and artists of South Africa. It's a bit like a town in France's Lubéron, suddenly transported to an area only two hours from Cape Town.

There's no sea – that would be overdoing it – only the countryside and a network of rivulets. Nothing's really changed here for about 120 years: "Greyton was a poor village which eked out a hard living selling vegetables to the missionary settlements nearby," explain Jonathan Green and Marina Pretorius. "The cottages were pretty humble ones and wherever possible we did our best to preserve the historic aspect of the place." Like the efficient architects they are, they restored their house in five months. From the "happy door" of the veranda – the chosen domain of Edgar, an Irish terrier, and Emma, a Schnauzer – there's a view of the dining and living rooms inside, then of the kitchen with its pergola off to the side. The loftiness of the ceiling, which extends right to the corrugated iron roof, is a surprise. The walls are painted a rich butter yellow whose warmth is reinforced by unpretentious wooden furniture, with only a few fittings in wrought iron to add a touch of black. The owners, who like things minimalist, seem to fear nothing but garishness and slavery to fashion.

Abseits der Weinberge und Touristenpfade, aber nur zwei Autostunden von Kapstadt entfernt, liegt das kleine Dorf Greyton, das unter südafrikanischen Intellektuellen und Künstlern sehr beliebt ist.

Kein Meer – viel zu vulgär – stattdessen ist man auf dem Land, wo viele kleine Bäche den Städter erfreuen. In den letzten 120 Jahren hat sich hier nur wenig verändert. »Greyton war ein armes Dorf, in dem sich die Menschen mühsam durch den Verkauf von Gemüse an die benachbarten Missionare über Wasser hielten«, erzählen Jonathan Green und Marina Pretorius. »Die Bauweise der Cottages war bescheiden. Wir haben uns dafür entschieden, den historischen Charakter beizubehalten.« Innerhalb von fünf Monaten restaurierte das Architektenpaar respektvoll das Haus. Durch die Verandatür, wo uns Edgar, der Irische Terrier, und Emma, die Schnauzerhündin, fröhlich kläffend begrüßen, gelangt man ins Esszimmer und in den Salon, an den sich die Küche und eine Pergola anschließen. Die beeindruckend hohen Decken reichen bis zum Wellblechdach. Die buttergelb getünchten Wände strahlen Ruhe und Gelassenheit aus, ein Eindruck, der durch die Holzmöbel noch unterstrichen wird. Nur die schmiedeeisernen Elemente tragen einen Hauch von Schwarz bei. Als leidenschaftliche Minimalisten lehnen die Hausbesitzer alles Vulgäre oder krampfhaft Moderne ab.

Bien loin des vignobles et des circuits touristiques, il y a Greyton, petit village très réputé chez les intellectuels et artistes sud-africains, quelque chose comme le Lubéron français transposé à deux heures de Cape Town.

Pas de mer – trop vulgaire – mais la campagne et ses petits ruisseaux si prompts à détendre le citadin. Ici, rien, ou presque, n'a changé en 120 ans. «Greyton était un village pauvre qui ne vivait que des légumes vendus à des missionnaires voisins», expliquent en cœur Jonathan Green et Marina Pretorius. «Les cottages étaient modestes dans leur fabrication; nous avons voulu préserver le caractère historique des lieux.» En architectes respectueux, le couple a restauré la maison en cinq mois. De «la porte heureuse» de la véranda où glapissent joyeusement Edgar, le terrier irlandais, et Emma, le schnauzer, on aperçoit la salle à manger et le salon, puis la cuisine et sa pergola dans l'alignement. La hauteur du plafond, élevé jusqu'au toit en tôle ondulée, est impressionnante. Dictés par l'envie de calme et de tranquillité, les murs affichent une belle couleur beurre frais dont la chaleur est renforcée par des meubles en bois. Seules les installations en fer forgé apportent une touche noire. Les propriétaires férus de minimalisme ne craignent que le vulgaire ou le branché.

❋ **FACING PAGE AND ABOVE** The wrought iron bed in the summer bedroom was discovered by Marina Pretorius's father during the 1970s, at Prince Albert in the Karoo Desert. The couple have decorated the house throughout with objects accumulated since their student days. ❋ **LINKE SEITE UND OBEN** Marina Pretorius' Vater entdeckte das schmiedeeiserne Bett im Sommerzimmer in den 1970er Jahren in Prince Albert, einem Ort in der Wüste Karoo. Die überwiegend schlichten Einrichtungsgegenstände haben die beiden Architekten seit ihrer Studentenzeit nach und nach zusammengetragen. ❋ **PAGE DE GAUCHE ET CI-DESSUS** Le lit en fer forgé de la chambre d'été a été découvert à Prince Albert (désert du Karoo), dans les années 1970 par le père de Marina Pretorius. Le couple a sobrement décoré la maison avec les objets accumulés depuis le temps où ils étaient étudiants.

Meerlust
Stellenbosch

Meerlust is the most famous vineyard in South Africa,
and the Cape Dutch architecture of its historic main house is nothing short of a reference.

Seven generations of the Myburgh family have lived and died under this venerable thatched roof and the present owner, Hannes Myburgh, likes to relate how each one has left its mark ever since the first pioneers arrived in the Cape region in 1669.

Meerlust was settled and founded in 1756, and ever since then the place has gradually accumulated furniture and paintings. The house now consists of some 30 rooms, distributed over two stories. In the 1970s, before becoming a winegrower, Hannes Myburgh travelled widely in Europe. When he came home he lived in the former slave quarters adjoining the main building, before inheriting the property in 1988 and endowing the house with his own contribution of African and European furniture and objects. His first decision was to make the kitchen a more convivial area. Today this is where everyone at Meerlust gathers for meals, around a big square maple wood table with a dozen leather-upholstered chairs bought at an auction years ago. There are club armchairs or a delicately faded chintz sofa, should you be feeling too enfeebled to endure a candlelit dinner. The dogs wander about unconcerned by the family ghosts, while life in the old house moves leisurely onward.

Ein Strohdach krönt die Besitzung, auf der sieben Generationen Myburghs ihre Spuren hinterlassen haben. 1669 ging der Pionier der Familie bei Kapstadt an Land; bereits 1756 wurde Meerlust erbaut.

Doch lassen wir die Vergangenheit ruhen und öffnen die Tür zur Gegenwart. Schon im Vorraum werden Möbel und Bilder aus verschiedenen Epochen kombiniert. 30 Räume verteilen sich auf zwei Etagen. Hannes Myburgh, der heutige Besitzer, ist weit gereist und lebte Ende der 1970er Jahre in Europa, bevor er Winzer wurde. Nach seiner Rückkehr wohnte er in einem Nebengebäude, in dem früher die Sklaven untergebracht waren. Als er 1988 sein Erbe antrat, richtete er sich neu ein und arrangierte ein Miteinander von europäischen und afrikanischen Möbelstücken und Objekten. Als Erstes erklärte er die Küche zu einem Ort des Zusammenlebens. Inzwischen trifft man sich auf Meerlust hier zum Abendessen, an einem großen rechteckigen Tisch aus Ahornholz mit einem Dutzend Lederstühlen, die Myburgh auf einer Auktion erstanden hat. Wer zu erschöpft ist, lässt sich auf dem Chintzsofa mit dem ausgeblichenen Blümchenmuster oder in einem der Clubsessel nieder. Das Festmahl wird bei Kerzenlicht serviert. Hunde tollen herum – die Schatten der Vergangenheit ruhen.

Depuis l'habitation coiffée d'un toit de chaume, sept générations de Myburgh vous contemplent. L'actuel propriétaire affirme volontiers que chacune d'elle y a laissé son empreinte.

Le pionnier de la famille a débarqué dans la région du Cap en 1669; Meerlust a vu le jour en 1756. Mais chassons les spectres et poussons la porte. Dès le vestibule, les époques se confondent en meubles et tableaux. Les 30 pièces se déploient sur deux étages. Avant de devenir vigneron, Hannes Myburgh a beaucoup voyagé et vécu en Europe à la fin des années 1970. À son retour, il a habité dans la partie attenante, autrefois réservée aux esclaves. Quand l'héritage a été prononcé, en 1988, il a investi les lieux en mêlant meubles et objets africains et européens. Sa première décision fut de faire de la cuisine un lieu convivial. À Meerlust, aujourd'hui, c'est là, autour d'une grande table carrée en érable, que l'on se retrouve pour dîner, assis sur une douzaine de chaises en cuir achetées aux enchères. Les plus alanguis prennent place sur un canapé en chintz fleuri, délicatement fané, ou un fauteuil club. Le festin est servi aux chandelles. Les chiens gambadent. Sans importuner les fantômes de la famille.

✳ **PREVIOUS PAGES** Meerlust is the perfect illustration of the Cape Dutch style, with its thatched roofs and columns. **ABOVE AND FACING PAGE** The traditional Dutch gables serve in Africa as simple decorative elements celebrating life on the farm. The walls are of brick, with a thick skin of lime wash. ✳ **VORHERGEHENDE DOPPELSEITE** Meerlust ist ein perfektes Beispiel für den Cape-Dutch-Stil: Die Strohdächer der Häuser ruhen auf Säulen. **OBEN UND RECHTE SEITE** Diese Giebelvoluten, die in der holländischen Architektur ihren festen Platz haben, dienen in Afrika nur der Zierde – die Darstellungen feiern die Arbeit in der Landwirtschaft. Die Ziegelwände sind mit einer dicken Kalkschicht rau verputzt. ✳ **DOUBLE PAGE PRECEDENTE** Meerlust est le témoignage parfait du style Cape Dutch avec ses habitations à toit de chaume, soutenues par des colonnes. **CI-DESSUS ET PAGE DE DROITE** Les pignons aux volutes traditionnelles dans l'architecture hollandaise sont en Afrique de simples éléments décoratifs célébrant les travaux de la ferme. Murs en briques, crépis d'une épaisse couche de chaux.

✳ **ABOVE** Austrian plaster heads dating from before the war. **FACING PAGE** The kitchen is the heart of the house, with its big maple wood table and its buffet filled with dishes, vases and farm produce put up in jars. ✳ **OBEN** Gipsköpfe aus dem Vorkriegsösterreich. **RECHTE SEITE** Die Küche ist der Mittelpunkt des Hauses – ein großer Tisch aus Ahornholz, ein Küchenschrank mit Geschirr, Vasen und Konserven aus der eigenen Produktion. ✳ **CI-DESSUS** Têtes en plâtre fabriquées avant-guerre en Autriche. **PAGE DE DROITE** La cuisine est le cœur de la maison avec sa grande table en érable et son buffet d'épicier rempli de vaisselle, de vases et de produits de la ferme en bocaux.

CAPAD Cottage
Greyton

A cottage – and a warm fireside for the cold South African winters.

Turn on your time machine, close your eyes and enter the enchanted world of Beatrix Potter's Peter Rabbit and Pigling Bland, where all the geese are distinguished-looking and pigs are clean as whistles.

There's something of this idyll in Mike Donkin's lovely cottage at Greyton. To the pure lines of the surrounding meadows and hills, he has added an interior décor that is the antithesis of his house in town. Donkin is a stout supporter of country style; his cottage has beams galore, a massive ladder leading up to the attic, old-fashioned kitchen appliances, and bare floors. Yet there's not a shred of pretension here – one of the pictures on the wall may have cost him only 25 rand (about two pounds sterling) at a local auction, but that doesn't make him any less proud of it. Similarly, elements of a watering system twine around the flamboyant candleholder on the veranda, which is dressed up with cheap glass. Old armchairs and worn cushions are always good enough for Donkin; yet if you look more closely there's a subdued theme running through the house. In every room there's some kind of reference to the sea, whether it be a candlestick with a seashell base, or a collection of model boats, or a miniature lighthouse. Maybe he misses the ocean, even though water abounds on his property, with springs, a dam and a pool. Beatrix Potter would thoroughly approve.

Ab in die Zeitmaschine, Augen schließen und schon fühlt man sich in die Zauberwelt von Beatrix Potter zurückversetzt. Wer erinnert sich nicht an Peter Hase, die Flopsi-Häschen und die bukolische Idylle mit vornehmen Gänsen und porentief sauberen Schweinen?

Mike Donkins hübsches Cottage in Greyton würde gut in diese Welt passen. Das Interieur, das in scharfem Kontrast zu Donkins ansonsten städtischem Umfeld steht, ist als Ergänzung der klaren Linien der Wiesen rundum und des sanften Schwungs der Hügel zu verstehen. Mit Snobismus hält sich Mike Donkin nicht auf, er pflegt im Gegenteil einen betont rustikalen Stil: Stolz präsentierte Holzbalkendecken, eine wuchtige Speichertreppe, veraltete Elektrogeräte im Haushalt und unbehandelte Fußböden. An der Wand hängt ein Bild, das er für 25 Rand (rund drei Euro) auf dem hiesigen Trödel gekauft hat. Der flackernde Kerzenleuchter auf der Veranda ist umgeben von Gartenschläuchen und billigen Gläsern. Alte Sessel und Kissen erfüllen ihren Zweck. In jedem Zimmer wird man auf die eine oder andere Art ans Meer erinnert, sei es durch einen Kerzenleuchter mit einem Fuß aus Muschelschalen oder eine Sammlung von Modellbooten oder einen Miniatur-Leuchtturm. Vielleicht weil der Ozean so weit entfernt ist? Das reichlich vorhandene Süßwasser lässt ihn rasch in Vergessenheit geraten, ob beim Anblick der Springbrunnen und des Stauwehrs oder im Swimmingpool. Beatrix Potter hätte es hier jedenfalls gefallen.

Mettez en route la machine à remonter le temps, fermez les yeux et retrouvez le monde enchanté de Beatrix Potter. Souvenez-vous l'histoire de Pierre Lapin, l'idylle pastorale avec ses oies distinguées et ses cochons tout propres. Vous ne voyez vraiment pas?

Alors filez à Greyton et observez le beau cottage de Mike Donkin. Aux lignes pures des prairies alentour, aux courbes douces des collines avoisinantes, il a joint une décoration intérieure aux antipodes de son habitat de la ville. Résolument attaché au style rustique avec ses poutres fièrement affichées, son échelle massive pour le grenier, ses appareils électroménagers d'un autre âge, ses sols nus, Mike Donkin ne s'encombre pas de snobisme. Telle peinture au mur a été achetée 25 rands aux enchères locales (moins de trois euros). Dans la véranda, le flamboyant chandelier est cerclé de tuyaux d'arrosage et fagoté de verreries bon marché. De vieux fauteuils et coussins usés font l'affaire. Étrangement, sous la forme d'un chandelier au pied en coquillage, d'une collection de bateaux ou d'un phare la mer est présente dans chaque pièce. Regretterait-on l'absente? L'eau douce se chargera de la faire oublier. Sur la propriété, elle abonde dans les fontaines, un barrage, et une piscine. Beatrix Potter apprécierait.

✽ **PRECEDING DOUBLE PAGE** A simple rush thatch covers the informal living room with its gay colours. The furniture, sofas and armchairs were picked up at antique shops and at auction at Sotheby's in Cape Town. **FOLLOWING PAGES** The kitchen with is massive table. Viewed as the heart of the house, it is furnished with old but indomitable electrical fittings. ✽ **VORHERGEHENDE DOPPELSEITE** Ein einfaches Rieddach deckt den formlosen, in leuchtenden Farben gestrichenen Salon. Die Möbel, Sofas und Sessel stammen aus Antiquitätenläden, vorwiegend aber von Auktionen bei Sotheby's in Kapstadt. **FOLGENDE SEITEN** Die Küche mit dem riesigen Tisch bildet den Mittelpunkt des Hauses; die Elektrogeräte sind alt aber unverwüstlich. ✽ **DOUBLE PAGE PRECEDENTE** Un simple toit de roseaux recouvre l'informel salon aux couleurs éclatantes. Les meubles, sofas et fauteuils ont été chinés chez les antiquaires et surtout achetés aux enchères de la Sotheby's à Cape Town. **DOUBLE PAGE SUIVANTE** La cuisine avec sa table monumentale est le cœur de la maison, elle se contente d'un électroménager hors d'âge mais increvable.

Obus & Various Dwellings

Chefferie Bandjoun

Emir's Palace

Susanne Wenger

CAMEROON, NIGERIA

CHEFFERIE BANDJOUN Cameroon

The Bandjoun compound is a sacred place,
a metaphor for the celestial powers.

In the Bamiléké region in western Cameroon, the people take their traditions very seriously. No power, be it colonial or central, has ever quite succeeded in dominating this remote rural area.

In the middle of it, at the end of a winding road through thick banana groves, stands a remarkable chief's compound, or *chefferie,* founded in the second half of the 17th century. Since that time, the chief in these parts has inherited all his ancestors' goods, including women and children – hence the constant necessity to find more space. The palace, decorated with sculptures, is surrounded by bamboos lashed together with raffia cord. The ceiling is held up by pillars decorated with representations of ancestors and the creation of the universe – cosmogonic art, in the scholarly definition. On either side of a central avenue, or "axis of life", are the lodgings reserved for the wives of the present chief, Joseph Ngnie Kamga, who dispenses justice from the steps of his palace. His throne stands on the lion skin which symbolizes his power. The royal chairs are adorned with cowrie shells, beads, and supporting figures in the form of leopards.

Im Gebiet der Bamiléké im Westen Kameruns wird die Tradition ernst genommen. Bereits in der Kolonialzeit ist es den Machthabern nie wirklich gelungen, diese ländliche Gegend zu unterwerfen.

Nach einer Fahrt über gewundene Straßen durch Bananenplantagen steht man erstaunt vor der Chefferie aus der zweiten Hälfte des 17. Jahrhunderts. Seitdem erbt der Häuptling alles Hab und Gut von seinem Vorfahren – inklusive Frauen und Kinder. Die Unterbringung so vieler Menschen erfordert viel Platz. Die Fassade des skulpturengeschmückten Palastes besteht aus mit Bast umwickelten Bambusstäben. Diese Pfeiler, die auch das Dach stützen, sind mit Schnitzereien verziert, die von den Ahnen und der Entstehung der Welt erzählen – so genannte kosmogonische Kunst. Auf beiden Seiten der zentralen Allee, der »Lebensachse«, stehen die Häuser der Frauen des derzeitigen Häuptlings Joseph Ngnie Kamga. Auf den Stufen seines Palastes hält er mit Hilfe eines Beraterstabes Gericht. Sein Thron steht auf einer Löwenhaut, die seine Machtfülle symbolisiert. Die königlichen Sitze sind mit Kaurimuscheln, Perlen und Stützfiguren in Form von Leoparden geschmückt.

En pays Bamiléké, à l'ouest du Cameroun, on ne plaisante pas avec les traditions. Les pouvoirs, qu'ils soient coloniaux ou centraux, n'ont jamais réellement soumis cette région rurale.

Au terme d'une route sinueuse qui progresse à travers les bananiers, on s'émerveille devant cette chefferie fondée durant la seconde moitié du 17e siècle. Depuis cette époque, le chef hérite de tous les biens de son ancêtre, femmes et enfants compris. D'où la nécessité d'étendre l'espace pour loger son monde. Le palais, décoré de sculptures, est ceint de bambous liés par des cordons de raphia. Le plafond est maintenu par des piliers décorés de représentations qui symbolisent les ancêtres et la création de l'univers, ce qu'on nomme l'art cosmogonique. De chaque côté de l'allée centrale, «l'axe de la vie», se trouve le quartier réservé aux femmes du chef actuel, Joseph Ngnie Kamga. Aux marches du «palais», tous les quatre jours, celui-ci rend la justice lors d'un conseil. Son trône est déposé sur une peau de lion symbolique de sa puissance. Les sièges royaux sont en cauris et perles avec des colonnettes de soutien en forme de panthères.

❋ **ABOVE** The building has a conical thatched roof over a loft, which formerly came in very useful. The doors are framed with carved panels. ❋ **OBEN** Über dem Palast wölbt sich ein konisches grasgedecktes Dach. Darunter liegt der Speicher, der früher eine große Rolle spielte. Die Türen sind mit skulptierten Paneelen eingefasst. ❋ **CI-DESSUS** Le bâtiment est surmonté d'un toit conique en chaume qui abrite le grenier, espace autrefois important. Les portes sont encadrées de panneaux sculptés.

❋ **ABOVE** The bamboo façades, patiently woven together with raffia, are decorated with human forms. **BELOW** The entrance to the ceremonial house, with its geometrical patterns painted on the bamboo walls. ❋ **OBEN** Plastische Figuren zieren die Bambuspfeiler, die untereinander sorgfältig mit Bast verbunden wurden. **UNTEN** Die Eingangstür zum Haupthaus, dessen Bambuswände mit grafischen Mustern bemalt sind. ❋ **CI-DESSUS** Les façades en bambou patiemment attaché avec du raphia, sont ornées de représentations humaines. **CI-DESSOUS** À l'entrée de la maison cérémoniale ornée de dessins géométriques peints sur les murs en bambou.

❊ **ABOVE** In the course of everyday life, a magical relationship is established between men and animals – hence what happens to one can happen to the other. In totem form, the animal serves as an alter ego used by ritual healers to drive out evil. ❊ **OBEN** Im Alltag besteht eine Verbindung zwischen Mensch und Tier. Was dem einen zustößt, kann auch dem anderen widerfahren. In Form eines Totems dient das Tier als wahres Alter Ego den Heilern bei den rituellen Austreibungen des Bösen. ❊ **CI-DESSUS** Dans la vie courante, une relation magique est établie entre les hommes et les animaux, et ce qui arrive à l'un peut arriver à l'autre. Représenté sous la forme d'un totem, l'animal, véritable alter ego, sert au guérisseur dans les rites d'expulsion du mal.

✻ **ABOVE** In the west of Cameroon, the number of conical roofs in a chief's compound attest to his power: some of them are veritable royal households. ✻ **OBEN** Im westlichen Teil Kameruns glitzern die Metalldächer weiterer Chefferien in der Landschaft. Je höher die Anzahl der Spitzdächer, desto bedeutender ist die Chefferie – einige haben sich zu wahren Königshöfen entwickelt. ✻ **CI-DESSUS** Dans l'ouest du Cameroun, d'autres chefferies font briller leurs demeures métalliques dans le paysage. Le nombre des toits coniques témoigne de l'autorité de la chefferie; certaines sont de véritables cours royales.

※ **ABOVE** The chief's compound has not been spared the inroads of the modern world. The outsides of the houses are changing more and more with the advent of magnificent corrugated iron roofs overhanging their bamboo facades. ※ **OBEN** Auch eine Chefferie bleibt von modernen Einflüssen nicht verschont. Das Äußere der Häuser ist Wandlungen unterworfen wie der Einführung von Wellblechdächern, die als neue Wahrzeichen der Macht über der Bambusfassade aufragen. ※ **CI-DESSUS** La chefferie n'est pas épargnée par le monde moderne. L'extérieur des cases se modifie de plus en plus avec l'apparition de toits en tôle ondulée magnifiques surmontant le rideau en bambou des façades, nouvelles formes de pouvoir.

OBUS
& various dwellings
Northern Cameroon

In this arid landscape,
people survive in the earth houses with pointed tops.

The tall *obu* dwellings, with their carefully worked, ribbed façades, are unique and famous in northern Cameroon. Elsewhere in the country, the *saré* houses, as they are called locally, are like small compounds.

The area is part of the Sahel, where the *harmattan* wind burns the landscape and dries everything to a crisp, from the scrub-covered pastureland to the village wells. Stone walls here are held together with clay. The vaulting is assembled from clay bricks, and the roof is tressed millet straw bound with raffia. There are no openings apart from a tiny door, because the main purpose here is always and forever to keep out the murderous heat. Under the thatch, there's a small grain store for the reserves of millet and ground nuts which make up the staple diet here. There's no ladder up to it, you have to pull yourself up by your arms. From a distance, the villages blend into the vegetation – the savannah and its inhabitants form an indivisible unit – and everywhere there is the same reddish colour, turning to black wherever there's been a bush fire. The herders frequently start fires to make a thin layer of short-lived grass grow under the scrub. The flames consume everything in their path, except for the *pisé* constructions which are protected by a natural barrier of undergrowth. Once the fires die down, the plain is covered in black stripes, similar to the ones on the inside walls of the dwellings.

Die einzigartigen schlanken *obu*-Hütten im Norden Kameruns sind für ihre kunstvollen Fassaden berühmt. In anderen Landesteilen stehen so genannte *saré*, mehrere Hütten in kleinen Einfriedungen.

In der Sahelzone verwischt der Harmattan die Landschaft und lässt von den mit Gestrüpp bedeckten Weideplätzen bis zu den Dorfbrunnen alles austrocknen. Die gemauerten Wände bestehen infolgedessen aus lehmiger Erde, die zuvor tüchtig geknetet wurde. Eine Lehmmischung bildet das Gewölbe, während das Dach aus Hirsehalmen besteht, die mit Pflanzenfasern umwickelt und zusammengehalten werden. Außer einer kleinen Tür gibt es keine Öffnungen – hier kommt es darauf an, die mörderisch heiße Sonne abzuhalten. Auf dem Speicher unter dem Strohdach werden die Vorräte an Hirse und Erdnüssen gelagert, die als Grundnahrungsmittel dienen. Leitern gibt es nicht, man muss sich schon selbst hochziehen, um an die Vorräte zu gelangen. Aus der Ferne verschmelzen die Dörfer mit der Vegetation – die Bewohner werden eins mit der Savanne – überall die gleiche Rotschattierung, die ins Schwarze übergeht, wenn es gebrannt hat. Denn Brandrodung ist eines der Hilfsmittel dieser Hirtenvölker, weil sie die zarten Gräser, die dann kurzzeitig unter dem abgebrannten Gestrüpp wachsen, für ihre Herden brauchen. Die Flammen vernichten alles Leben in der Landschaft, nur die Lehmhütten sind durch eine natürliche Sperre aus Astwerk geschützt. Wenn das Feuer erloschen ist, sieht die Savanne schwarzgefleckt aus. Diese Flecken finden sich auch an den Innenwänden der Hütten wieder.

Les cases-obus, élancées, caractérisées par leur façade travaillée et renforcée de nervures, sont uniques et célébrées dans le nord du Cameroun. Ailleurs dans le pays, les habitations, des *saré* selon l'appellation locale, évoquent de petites enceintes.

La zone est sahélienne, l'harmattan brouille le paysage, assèche tout, des pâturages broussailleux aux puits des villages. Ainsi, les murs en pierres cimentées sont formés de terre argileuse préalablement malaxée. Un assemblage de pain de terre structure la voûte. Le toit est une simple natte à base de tiges de mil réunies par un raphia. Pas d'ouverture sinon une petite porte, car l'enjeu, ici encore, est de se préserver d'un soleil assassin. Sous le chaume, un petit grenier abrite les réserves de mil et d'arachides qui constituent l'alimentation de base. Il n'y a pas d'échelle pour y accéder, on se hisse à la force des bras. De loin, les villages se confondent avec la végétation – la savane et ses habitants forment un tout –, partout la même teinte rousse qui vire au noir les jours d'incendie. Afin de faire pousser sous les broussailles une herbe tendre mais éphémère pour leurs troupeaux, les pasteurs pratiquent intensivement le brûlis. Les flammes attaquent tout sur leur passage, sauf les cases de pisé protégées par une barrière naturelle de branchages. Le feu éteint, la savane affiche ses marques noires. Ces teintes que l'on retrouve sur les murs intérieurs des cases.

❋ **ABOVE** The technique used makes the construction of the *obu* huts waterproof, as well as facilitating the climb to the top when repairs are needed during the rainy season. ❋ **OBEN** Die Schichttechnik der Lehmbauweise der *obu*-Hütten verstärkt einerseits die Dichte und erleichtert andererseits den Aufstieg bis zur Spitze, damit die Hütte nach der Regenzeit besser repariert werden kann. ❋ **CI-DESSUS** Les cases-obus sont fabriquées avec de la terre. La technique en empilement permet à la fois de renforcer l'étanchéité mais aussi facilite l'escalade jusqu'au sommet lors des réfections après la saison des pluies.

❋ **ABOVE** A *saré* in the north, nearer the mountains. Its main characteristic is that it expands or contracts in the course of its life. To build these *sarés*, the villagers use earth, a very little water, pieces of crumbling, twisted wood, stones and millet stalks. ❋ **OBEN** Weiter im Norden in der Nähe der Berge: eine *saré* genannte Ansammlung von Hütten, die im Laufe der Zeit größer wird oder schrumpft. Aus einem winzigen Wasservorrat, krummen, brüchigen Ästen, Steinen und Hirsehalmen bauen die Dorfbewohner ihre Hütten. ❋ **CI-DESSUS** Plus au nord, près des montagnes, un *saré* qui se caractérise parce qu'il prend de l'ampleur ou s'amenuise au cours d'une vie. Pour les construire, les villageois n'ont que très peu d'eau, du bois tordu et friable, des pierres et des tiges de mil.

❋ **ABOVE** The head of the family controls the room facing the entrance, while his wives and children occupy the others along with the kitchen houses. To protect themselves from the sun, people spend much of their time inside or in the shade nearby. The village comes to life at the end of the day. ❋ **OBEN** Der Familienvorstand wohnt in der Hütte direkt am Eingang, während seine Frauen und Kinder in anderen Hütten leben, wo auch die Küchen untergebracht sind. Als Schutz gegen die Sonne verbringen die Menschen den ganzen Tag in ihren Hütten oder im Schatten. Erst nach Sonnenuntergang wird das Dorf lebendig. ❋ **CI-DESSUS** Le chef de famille contrôle la case qui fait face à l'entrée, ses femmes et ses enfants disposent des autres avec les cuisines. Pour se protéger du soleil, on vit beaucoup à l'intérieur ou à l'ombre, dans la cour. Le village s'anime au coucher du soleil.

Emir's Palace
Kano

This is a place to be entered on tiptoe,
as if one were visiting Versailles in the time of Louis XIV.

Flashback to the 19th century: The centuries-old Hausa states are conquered and absorbed into the Fulani empire. From then on the Fulani reigned supreme, appointing emirs and, while developing great splendour, imposing a new, strictly islamic law.

Their new religious order spared no expense: the first European explorers to reach Kano in the early 20th century rhapsodized about the beauty of the arches in the audience chamber, the refinement of the decoration and the sophistication of the private apartments. Without any political mandate in modern Nigeria, to this day the emirs of the north have maintained autonomy in the transmission of cultural values and traditional ceremonials in the towns of Daura, Katsina, Kano and Zaria. So today these palaces are not museums. Inside, they have walls built in *tubali*, plastered and covered in mica – a shiny mineral that abounds in volcanic rock – to offset massive iron-bound doors. The deep black of the floors increases the gloom. Coloured geometrical motifs cover every inch of the ceilings and arches. Outside, there is a kind of citadel encircled by an eight-foot-high wall. The effect is of a great strongbox; although there is no treasure inside, it keeps intact the memory of a time when the Sahara caravans came here to trade in gold, ivory and slaves.

Rückblende ins 19. Jahrhundert: Die seit Jahrhunderten existierenden Hausastaaten werden von den Fulbe-Stämmen erobert und in deren Reich eingegliedert. Fortan herrschen in diesem Gebiet die Fulbe, die Emire einsetzen und bei gleichzeitiger großer Prachtentfaltung eine neue, strenge islamische Gesetzgebung durchsetzen.

Im 20. Jahrhundert staunen Forscher über die Schönheit der Bögen im Empfangssaal, die Feinheiten der Dekoration und die Eleganz der Privatgemächer. Auch im modernen Nigeria konnten sich die Emire im Norden des Landes ihre Autonomie bewahren. In den Städten Daura, Katsina, Kano und Zaria leben sie nach ihren kulturellen Wertvorstellungen und führen die traditionellen Zeremonien durch. Bei den Palästen handelt es sich also keineswegs um Museen. Im Inneren der Prunkbauten harmonieren die Wände aus *tubali*, die vergipst und mit Mica (einem glänzenden Mineral, das im Vulkangestein reichlich vorhanden ist) bestrichen wurden, mit den schweren Türen aus Brettern mit schmiedeeisernen Kanten. Die tiefschwarzen Böden verstärken noch die düstere Wirkung des Halbdunkels. An den Decken und Bögen entfalten sich bunte grafische Muster. Die Zitadelle selbst ist von einer zwei Meter dicken Mauer umgeben. Der Ort wirkt wie ein Tresor, der zwar keine Schätze in klingender Münze mehr bewahrt, dafür aber umso mehr historische Erinnerungen – an die Zeit, als die Karawanen aus der Sahara hier ihre Tauschgeschäfte mit Gold, Elfenbein und Sklaven abwickelten.

Flash-back au 19e siècle. Les états Haoussa qui existent depuis des temps immémoriaux sont conquis par les Fulbe et inclus dans leur empire. Dès lors, les Fulbe règnent sur ce territoire et les émirs instaurent une nouvelle lois islamique des plus strictes qui s'impose avec faste.

Les explorateurs européens du début du 20e siècle ne s'y trompent pas. Tous soulignent la beauté des arches dans la chambre d'audience, le raffinement de la décoration, la sophistication des appartements privés. Sans mandat politique dans le Nigeria moderne, les émirs du nord du pays conservent dans les villes de Daura, Katsina, Kano ou Zaria une autonomie dans la transmission des valeurs culturelles et le maintien des cérémonies traditionnelles. Les palais ne sont donc pas des musées. À l'intérieur, les murs édifiés en *tubali*, plâtrés et recouverts de mica (un minerai brillant abondant dans les roches éruptives), répondent aux portes massives en planches bordées de fer. Le noir profond des sols accentue la pénombre. Partout sur les plafonds et les arches s'enroulent des motifs géométriques colorés. Dehors, un mur de près de deux mètres limite la citadelle. L'endroit est un coffre-fort. S'il ne renferme plus de trésors en monnaies sonnantes et trébuchantes, il séquestre au moins une mémoire. Celle des temps où les caravanes sahariennes échangeaient ici de l'or, de l'ivoire et des esclaves.

✷ **ABOVE** The inner courtyard of the Kano palace of Emir H.H. Aminu Ado Bayero. The walls are covered in a clay rendering, painted by hand with circular motifs. The palace proper is hidden behind the walls of a small citadel. ✷ **OBEN** Der Innenhof des Palastes in Kano, im Besitz des Emirs H.H. Aminu Ado Bayero. Auf die Mauern wurde per Hand mit kreisenden Bewegungen ein Lehmputz aufgetragen. Der Palast liegt fast verborgen hinter den Mauern der kleinen Zitadelle. ✷ **CI-DESSUS** Cour intérieure du palais de Kano de l'émir H.H. Aminu Ado Bayero dont les murs sont recouverts d'un enduit d'argile peint à la main en mouvements circulaires. Le palais se dissimule derrière les murs de la petite citadelle.

PREVIOUS PAGES AND ABOVE Details of the ceilings of the emir's palace at Kano. The women's quarters, enlivened by greens, reds, and yellows. ❊
VORHERGEHENDE SEITEN UND OBEN Details der Decken im Palast des Emirs von Kano. Die Frauengemächer strahlen in Grün-, Rot- und Gelbtönen. ❊
PAGES PRECEDENTES ET CI-DESSUS À Kano, détails des plafonds du palais de l'émir. Les quartiers des femmes, animés de couleurs vertes, rouges et jaunes.

PAGES 586–587 The entrance to the palace at Zaria. ❋ SEITEN 586–587 Das Eingangstor zum Palast von Zaria. ❋ PAGES 586–587 La porte d'entrée du palais de Zaria.

SUSANNE WENGER OSHO9BO

For the last 50 years, this Austrian artist has been perpetuating the religious and philosophical foundations of the Yoruba region.

Fantastic animals – lions, cats, and grasshoppers – form a kind of honour guard to the beautiful Brazilian-baroque townhouse of Susanne Wenger.

For over half a century, this artist has been closely linked to the Yoruba people; with her, the sculptors and craftsmen of the city have founded a creative school, the Mbari Mbayo Club, which in the Igbo language means literally "when we see it, we're happy". The Yoruba culture, based on theatre, music, poetry and masquerade, celebrates harvests and the arrival of rain by sacred rituals that Wenger has reinterpreted in her house. "Nature is my only master," she likes to say. These works, whether they are sculptures, batiks or paintings, seem to grow around her home like rampant plants. A few miles away, beside the river, the sacred Yoruba forest is also an extension of her work. Here people come to pause reverently before the images and invoke the ancestral Yoruba ideal – that of patience and tranquillity in the face of a turbulent world. Susanne Wenger, confronted by Iya Nla, the deity who maintains order in the world at the same time as threatening its stability, has responded with a new form of sacred art.

Fantasietiere, Löwen, Katzen und Heuschrecken bewachen wie eine Leibgarde Susanne Wengers Haus im brasilianischen Barockstil.

Seit einem halben Jahrhundert fühlt sich die Künstlerin dem Volk der Yoruba eng verbunden. Gemeinsam mit Handwerkern und Bildhauern der Stadt hat sie eine kreative Schule gegründet, den Mbari Mbayo Club, was in der Igbosprache bedeutet: »Wenn wir es sehen, sind wir glücklich«. Die Kultur der Yoruba stützt sich auf das Theater, die Dichtung und die Maskerade. Die Künstlerin aus dem Westen interpretiert die heiligen Rituale zum Erntedank oder zum Beginn der Regenzeit auf ihre Art neu. »Ich erkenne nur die Natur als meine Meisterin an«, lautet das Credo der Dame des Hauses. Ihre Werke, seien es Skulpturen, Batikkunst oder Gemälde, sprießen wie Pflanzen in ihrem Heim. Einige Kilometer von der Künstlerresidenz entfernt setzt Susanne Wenger ihre Arbeit am Flussufer in dem so genannten »Heiligen Hain« fort. Andächtig verharrt man vor den Darstellungen, die ein altes Ideal der Yoruba beschwören: in einer turbulenten Welt, Ruhe und Gelassenheit zu bewahren. Die Österreicherin, die unter dem Schutz der mächtigen Urmutter Iya Nla steht, die für Ordnung in der Welt sorgt, indem sie ihre Stabilität bedroht, hat eine eigene Antwort gefunden: eine neue Sakralkunst.

En ville, des animaux fantastiques, lions, chats et sauterelles forment un garde-fou à une belle maison de style baroque brésilien, celle de Susanne Wenger.

Voilà plus d'un demi-siècle que cette artiste est étroitement liée au peuple Yoruba. Avec elle, les artisans et sculpteurs de la ville ont inventé une école de création, le Mbari Mbayo Club, littéralement en langue Igbo, «quand nous le voyons, nous sommes heureux». La culture Yoruba, fondée sur le théâtre, la poésie et la mascarade, célèbre les moissons et l'arrivée des pluies par des rituels sacrés réinterprétés dans sa maison par l'artiste occidentale. «Je n'ai pas d'autre Maître que la nature», a coutume de répéter la maîtresse des lieux. Ces œuvres, qu'elles soient sculptures, batik ou peinture, grandissent chez elle comme des plantes. À quelques kilomètres de la résidence, en bordure d'une rivière, la forêt sacrée prolonge le travail. On s'y recueille devant des représentations en invoquant l'idéal ancestral Yoruba: garder patience et tranquillité d'esprit dans un monde turbulent. Susanne Wenger, placée sous la toute puissance de la mère ancestrale, Iya Nla, laquelle assure l'ordre du monde tout en menaçant sa stabilité, a trouvé sa réponse: un nouvel art sacré.

❋ **FACING PAGE** Seen from the gate, fantastic animals symbolise a view of the universe as a single entity. **ABOVE** Inspired by the Brazilian baroque style, the house of Susanne Wenger contains the results of nearly 50 years' work on the confluence between sacred art and scenes of ordinary life. ❋ **LINKE SEITE** Die Fantasietiere am Eingang symbolisieren eine Annäherung an ein Universum, das als Gesamtheit betrachtet wird. **OBEN** Susanne Wengers Haus im brasilianischen Barockstil beherbergt ihr Werk aus 50 schöpferischen Jahren. In ihrer Kunst vermischen sich sakrale Elemente mit Szenen aus dem Alltag. ❋ **PAGE DE GAUCHE** Dès le portail, des animaux fantastiques symbolisent une approche de l'univers conçu comme un tout. **CI-DESSUS** D'inspiration baroque brésilien, la maison de Susanne Wenger abrite un travail de près de 50 ans à la confluence entre l'art sacré et les scènes de la vie quotidienne.

❋ **ABOVE** Oshogbo, the cradle of Yoruba art, has produced many gifted young artists. Some, like Twins Seven Seven, have won international fame. ❋ **OBEN** Oshogbo, die Wiege der Yoruba-Kunst, hat viele Künstler hervorgebracht. Einige wie der Künstler Twins Seven Seven sind international bekannt. ❋ **CI-DESSUS** Berceau de l'art Yoruba, Oshogbo est demeurée une pépinière d'artistes. Certains, comme Twins Seven Seven, ont atteint une renommée internationale.

❋ **ABOVE** With her totems and sculptures, Susanne Wenger brings the religious and philosophical founding principles of the Yoruba nation both into her own house, and into the sacred forest. ❋ **OBEN** Indem sie ihre Totems und Skulpturen erschafft, verewigt Susanne Wenger in ihrem Haus und in dem »Heiligen Hain« die religiösen und philosophischen Vorstellungen der Yoruba. ❋ **CI-DESSOUS** À travers la réalisation de totems et de sculptures, Susanne Wenger perpétue dans sa maison et la fôret sacrée les fondements religieux et philosophiques du pays Yoruba.

※ **FACING PAGE AND ABOVE** The nearby sacred forest contains enormous sculptures and sanctuaries dedicated to the various Yoruba gods, notably the famous sanctuary of Osun. ※ **LINKE SEITE UND OBEN** In dem nahe gelegenen »Heiligen Hain« stehen riesige Skulpturen und Heiligtümer, die den verschiedenen Göttern der Yoruba geweiht sind, darunter auch das Heiligtum der Göttin Osun. ※ **PAGE DE GAUCHE ET CI-DESSUS** La forêt sacrée voisine renferme d'énormes sculptures et des sanctuaires dédiés aux différents dieux Yoruba, dont le célèbre sanctuaire d'Osun.

Ganvié

Tamberma Houses

Scott House

ABEASE BOYS

Kassena

Spiritual Master

Tiemoko Soul

Abidjan

BENIN, TOGO, GHANA, BURKINA FASO, IVORY COAST

Ganvie
Lake NOKOUE

The raised lake houses of a township
only 20 kilometres from the nation's capital.

A swarm of pirogues loaded with children, food and jerry cans of water crosses the lagoon.

Their destination is a tangle of houses made from palm fronds, with roofs topped by a thick layer of straw, balanced on stilts standing in five feet of dull blue-green water. These rectangular huts are home to 45,000 people. Inside their houses, the surface of the water flickers through the interstices of the bamboo floors. Simple rattan furniture and basic household utensils are the only items to be seen. At the foot of each hut is its *acadja*, or cage made of branches, for raising crayfish and fish. The lake's annual yield used to be quite astounding, with a ton of fish per hectare, but now it has fallen off disastrously following the construction of a port at the sea-estuary, which has let salt water into the lake; and as a result Ganvié has lapsed into poverty of late. The Toffinous (watermen) originally came here as refugees from tribal wars and the slave-hunters sent by the king of Abomey. The word Ganvié itself means "the town of those who have found peace". For how much longer?

Ein Schwarm von Pirogen fährt durch die Lagune, schwer beladen mit Kindern, Lebensmitteln und Wasserkanistern. Und das Dorf?

Ein Wirrwarr von Häusern aus Palmblättern, gekrönt von dicken Strohdächern, stützt sich auf Pfähle, die in 1,50 Metern Höhe aus dem meergrünen Wasser ragen. In den rechteckigen Häusern wohnen 45000 Menschen. Durch die Spalten im Bambusboden kann man die Lagune sehen, und das Mobiliar besteht aus Rattanmöbeln und einigen wenigen Küchengerätschaften. Unter den Häusern liegen mit Astwerk abgesteckte Wasserfelder, so genannte *acadjas*, in denen Fische und Krebse gezüchtet werden. Zweimal im Jahr wird geerntet. Früher war die Ausbeute grandios (eine Tonne Fisch pro Hektar), aber seit an der Flussmündung ein Hafen gebaut wurde, sinkt der Ertrag. Das Meerwasser überschwemmt den See und wegen der Versalzung bleiben die Fische aus, sodass Ganvié in Armut versinkt. Einst waren die Toffinu (»Wassermenschen«) vor Stammeskriegen und den Sklavenjägern des Königs von Abomey hierher geflüchtet. Ganvié bedeutet »Gemeinschaft der friedlich Erretteten«. Wie lange wird das noch so sein?

Un essaim de pirogues chargées d'enfants, de nourriture et de bidons d'eau douce traverse la lagune. Le village?

Un enchevêtrement de maisons en nervures de palmiers, les toits coiffés d'une épaisse couche de paille, soutenues par des pilotis enfoncés dans 1,50 m d'eau glauque. Des cases rectangulaires abritant 45000 personnes. À l'intérieur, le sol en bambou à claire-voie s'ouvre par interstices sur la lagune. Des meubles en rotin et les ustensiles ménagers de base forment le mobilier. Au pied de ces cases, les *acadjas*, des bassins d'élevage faits de branchage, abritent des poissons et des écrevisses. La récolte a lieu deux fois par an. Autrefois miraculeuse (un hectare donnait une tonne de poisson), la production a fondu avec la construction d'un port à l'entrée de l'estuaire. Depuis que l'eau de mer envahit le lac et que les poissons disparaissent sous l'effet de la salinité, Ganvié s'enfonce dans la pauvreté. Les Toffinou (les «hommes de l'eau») s'étaient réfugiés ici pour échapper aux guerres tribales et aux chasseurs d'esclaves du roi d'Abomey. Ganvié signifie «la cité de ceux qui ont trouvé la paix». Pour combien de temps encore?

✳ **PREVIOUS PAGES AND ABOVE** Daily work is punctuated by the filling of earthenware water jugs called *canaris*. The village is criss-crossed with water-ways. Every house has its own landing stage and access ladder. ✳ **VORHERGEHENDE DOPPELSEITE UND OBEN** Das Alltagsleben wird vom Wasserholen mit großen Tontöpfen, den so genannten *canaris* bestimmt. Das Dorf ist von Wasserstraßen durchzogen. Jedes Haus hat einen Anlegeplatz, von dem eine Leiter zum Haus führt. ✳ **DOUBLE PAGE PRECEDENTE ET CI-DESSUS** L'activité quotidienne est rythmée par le remplissage d'eau douce des pots de terre appelés *canaris*. Le village est strié de voies d'eau. Chaque demeure à son ponton. Une échelle donne accès aux habitations.

❋ **ABOVE** This bar was rebuilt in 1983 for a visit by François Mitterrand. The complex is constructed of palm fronds and bamboo on wooden stilts or imperishable teak pilings. Each year they have to survive a period of violent storms. ❋ **OBEN** Die Bar, die 1983 anlässlich des Besuches des französischen Präsidenten François Mitterrand renoviert wurde. Die Hütten aus Palmblättern oder Bambus, die erhöht auf den Pfählen oder nicht faulenden Plattformen aus Teakholz stehen, sind jedes Jahr von neuem fürchterlichen Stürmen ausgesetzt. ❋ **CI-DESSUS** La fierté du village? Son bar refait à neuf pour la visite du président français François Mitterrand en 1983. Construites en feuille de palme ou en bambou, juchées sur des pilotis de branchage ou des poteaux de teck imputrescibles, les cases subissent chaque année des tempêtes terribles.

❋ **ABOVE** The residents of Ganvié live in a state of perpetual levitation, with the polluted waters of the lagoon making constant inroads upon them during the flood season. In this marsh country, the people feel protected from malevolent spirits. In fact, the germs which breed abundantly in these waters transmit typhus and tuberculosis, both of which are better under control on dry land than here. ❋ **OBEN** Die Menschen in Ganvié leben in einem permanenten Schwebezustand, denn ihre Unterkünfte werden von der Lagune und der bei Hochwasser entstehenden Umweltverschmutzung angegriffen. Die Bewohner der Sümpfe fühlen sich vor bösen Geistern geschützt. Dabei vermehren sich in diesen Gewässern die Keime rasend schnell und bringen Krankheiten wie Typhus und Tuberkulose mit sich, die auf dem Festland besser unter Kontrolle zu bringen wären. ❋ **CI-DESSUS** On vit en lévitation permanente dans ces cases rongées par la lagune et la pollution charriée pendant les crues. Dans ces marais, les habitants se sentent protégés des esprits malins. En vérité, les germes qui prolifèrent à vitesse foudroyante dans l'eau transmettent le typhus et la tuberculose, maladies mieux contrôlées à terre.

Tamberma Houses

Togo

Each of these little compounds sprinkled around the millet fields contains its quota of *tatas*, round interconnected huts.

The name is significant: *Tamberma*, a word slightly deformed in Tamari, the local language, means "good mason". In this valley, the houses resemble the fortified farms of the Somba peoples of northern Benin.

Made up of bedrooms, a kitchen, an attic and a stable, the round Tamberma houses are linked to each other by fortress-like walls made of mud reinforced with straw. The earth insulates against the hot blast of the *harmattan* wind, but also against noise and fire. Rough or smooth, this brand of architecture – with roofs resting on forked beams – is very close to that of the houses in northern Ghana too. A single opening gives access to the ground floor. Here, on a tamped, slightly concave floor, the women pound sorghum and millet into flour. The extension includes a stable, where the animals go for shelter during the wet season. A few steps lead to an intermediate floor; this houses the indoor kitchen, the antechamber to a terrace in whose upper part are grain stores with three different sections, and (finally) small sleeping rooms you have to crawl into. A hatch reminds us that when there were raids here, the attackers would be greeted with a hail of poisoned arrows. Today, they have the more peaceful function of indicating the sites of new houses. A ceremony is traditionally held for this purpose, and the young men of the village build their *tatas* on the spot where the arrow lands.

Der Name ist Programm: Nur wenig verändert bedeutet *Tamberma* in der Tamarisprache »guter Maurer«. Die Behausungen in diesem Tal ähneln befestigten Höfen, wie man sie von den Sombastämmen im Norden Benins kennt.

Die Häuser, bestehend aus Schlafzimmern, Küche, Speicher und Stall, sind durch Mauern aus Lehm und Stroh miteinander verbunden, deren Stärke einer Festung Ehre machen würde. Der feuerfeste Lehm isoliert gegen Lärm und den heißen Atem des Harmattan. Die Architektur dieser Häuser aus glattem oder schraffiertem Lehm mit ihren von gegabelten Trägerbalken gestützten Dächern erinnert auch an den Hausbau im nördlichen Ghana. Es gibt keine Fenster, nur eine Tür führt ins Erdgeschoss, wo die Frauen Sorghum und Hirse auf dem gestampften, leicht ausgehobenen Boden stapeln. Im hinteren Teil befindet sich der Stall, in dem sich das Vieh in der Regenzeit aufhält. Stufen führen ins Zwischengeschoss mit der Küche, die als Durchgang zur Terrasse dient. Im höheren Teil dieser Terrasse ist der Speicher untergebracht, der in drei Kammern unterteilt ist. Dorthin und in die auf gleicher Höhe liegenden kleinen Zimmer gelangt man, indem man sich mit Schwung hochzieht. Eine Falltür erinnert daran, dass Angreifer früher, zu Zeiten der Raubzüge, mit Giftpfeilen empfangen wurden. Die Pfeile dienen heute friedlicheren Zwecken, so wird damit etwa der Standort neuer Häuser bestimmt. Im Rahmen einer feierlichen Zeremonie bauen die jungen Männer des Dorfes ihre *tatas* dort, wo ihre Pfeile gelandet waren. Cupido hätte nicht besser zielen können.

Le nom est tout un programme: *Tamberma*, légèrement déformé en tamari, la langue locale, signifie «le bon maçon». Dans cette vallée, les habitations ressemblent à des fermes fortifiées semblables à celles des tribus Somba du nord du Bénin.

Composées de chambres à coucher, d'une cuisine, d'un grenier et d'une étable, ces cases rondes, reliées entre elles par des murs dignes d'une forteresse, sont faites de boue renforcée de paille. La terre isole du souffle chaud de l'harmattan, mais aussi du bruit, et résiste au feu. Lissée ou hachurée, cette architecture au toit reposant sur des poutres en fourches est également proche des maisons du nord du Ghana. Une seule ouverture donne accès au rez-de-chaussée. Ici, sur un sol damé et légèrement creusé, les femmes pilent le sorgho et le mil. Dans le prolongement, se trouve l'étable, refuge du bétail en saison humide. Quelques marches mènent à l'étage intermédiaire où est située la cuisine intérieure, antichambre d'une terrasse qui, en sa partie supérieure, abrite des greniers à trois compartiments et de petites chambres que l'on gagne en rampant. Une trappe rappelle que les assaillants, au temps des razzias, étaient accueillis à coup de flèches empoisonnées. Plus pacifiquement, ces mêmes flèches servent aujourd'hui à déterminer l'emplacement des maisons. Au cours d'une cérémonie, les fils du village édifient leur *tata* à l'endroit où la flèche s'est plantée. Cupidon n'aurait pas trouvé mieux!

✳ **ABOVE** The use of *banco* (ochre clay) fortified with straw, cow faeces and a decoction of *néré* grain as a binding agent makes the walls completely waterproof.
✳ **OBEN** Die Häuser verdanken ihre Dichtheit dem Baumaterial *banco* (ockerfarbener Lehm), gemischt mit Stroh und Kuhfladen sowie dem Bindemittel *néré* aus einem Absud von Samenkörnern. ✳ **CI-DESSUS** L'utilisation de *banco* (terre glaise ocre) additionné de paille, de bouse de vache et d'une décoction de graines *néré* qui sert de liant assure aux murs une étanchéité parfaite.

※ **ABOVE AND FOLLOWING PAGES** These houses are planned like bastions, with only one way in. In front of the main door, phallus-shaped mounds show the sites of graves. They are regularly sprinkled with millet beer and the blood of sacrificed animals. ※ **OBEN UND FOLGENDE DOPPELSEITE** Wie bei einer richtigen Festung gibt es nur einen einzigen Zugang zu den Häusern. Vor der Eingangstür markieren mehrere phallusartige Erdhügel die Lage der Gräber. Sie werden regelmäßig mit Hirsebier und dem Blut von Opfertieren begossen. ※ **CI-DESSUS ET DOUBLE PAGE SUIVANTE** Véritable bastion, ces maisons n'ont qu'une seule entrée. Devant la porte principale, plusieurs monticules de forme phallique désignent l'emplacement des tombes. Ils sont régulièrement arrosés de bière de millet et du sang des animaux sacrifiés.

※ **FACING PAGE AND ABOVE** A conical clay altar, with the remains of sacrifices and libations. Still loaded with necklaces of goats' skulls, goats' horns, and sticks, these altars – which are very numerous in the Tamberma country – are generally placed in front of the houses. ※ **LINKE SEITE UND OBEN** Auf dem kegelförmigen Altar aus Lehm liegen noch Reste von (Trank-)Opfern. Altäre, die wie dieser mit Ketten aus Zickleinköpfen und Ziegenbockhörnern sowie mit Stäben und Stöcken geschmückt sind, findet man im Land der Tamberma häufig direkt vor den Häusern. ※ **PAGE DE GAUCHE ET CI-DESSUS** Un autel de terre conique laisse apparaître des restes de sacrifices et de libations. Chargés encore de colliers de crânes de chevreaux, de cornes de boucs et de bâtons, ces autels très nombreux en pays Tamberma sont placés devant les maisons.

Scott House

Accra

A house with an eye on the past as well as the future, built by a British architect so enthralled by Ghana that he made his life there.

Some houses reflect the heart and temperament of the people who live in them. The Scott house is one of these; indeed it resembles an autobiographical account of its owner.

A lieutenant-colonel in the Royal West Africa Frontier Force during the Second World War, Kenneth Scott returned to Ghana in the late 1940s and remained there till his death in 1982. With his open-necked shirt and flowing mane of hair, Scott was a dashing president of the Accra Polo Club – but above all he was a founding member of the Ghana Institute of Architects and the archetypal post-colonial dandy. Most unusually for Accra in the 1960s and 1970s – because at that time nearly all the builders were in Lagos, Africa's New York – Kenneth Scott created an open house with no real doors, in homage to such modernist architects as Walter Gropius and Ludwig Mies van der Rohe. The angular and circular shapes he devised modulate the light and create spaces that appear to be wide open to the sky. This is the whole attraction of the building, which is both retro and futuristic, like an experimental project from the past. Kenneth Scott left his mark on many a public building in Accra, and he will long be remembered in Ghana – and what's more, his widow Thérèse Striggner Scott still lives in the house he built.

Es gibt Häuser, die die Seele und das Temperament ihrer Bewohner spiegeln. Scott House ist eins davon – es trägt regelrecht autobiographische Züge.

Kenneth Scott, der im Zweiten Weltkrieg als Oberstleutnant der Royal West Africa Frontier Force in Ghana diente, entdeckte das Land Ende der 1940er Jahre für sich und verließ es bis zu seinem Tod im Jahr 1982 nie wieder. Scott war der Inbegriff des postkolonialen Dandys: Offenes Hemd, leuchtende Mähne, Präsident des Accra Polo Clubs. Gleichzeitig gehörte er zu den Gründungsmitgliedern des Ghana Institute of Architects. Im Gegensatz zu dem, was in den 1960er, 1970er Jahren in Accra üblich war – damals zog es die Architekten, die etwas auf sich hielten, eher nach Lagos, ins »afrikanische New York« –, baute sich Kenneth Scott als Hommage an die modernen Architekten wie Walter Gropius und Ludwig Mies van der Rohe ein offenes Haus ohne richtige Tür. Eckige und runde Formen modulieren das Licht und schaffen Räume unter freiem Himmel. Die besondere Ausstrahlung dieses gleichermaßen nostalgisch und futuristisch wirkenden Hauses liegt in der Suggestion, man wohne in einem ehemals avantgardistischen Haus. An Kenneth Scott, der zahlreichen öffentlichen Gebäuden in Accra seinen Stempel aufdrückte, erinnert man sich in Ghana gern. Seine Witwe Thérèse Striggner Scott wohnt bis heute in dem Haus.

Certaines habitations reflètent l'âme et le tempérament de ceux qui les habitent. La Scott House fait partie de celles-là, tant elle se lit comme un récit autobiographique.

Lieutenant-colonel dans la Royal West Africa Frontier Force durant la Deuxième Guerre mondiale, Kenneth Scott retrouvait le Ghana à la fin des années 1940 pour ne plus quitter ce pays jusqu'à sa mort, en 1982. Chemise ouverte, crinière flamboyante, président de l'Accra Polo Club mais surtout membre fondateur du Ghana Institute of Architects, l'homme fut l'archétype du dandy post-colonial. Situation inédite à Accra dans les années 1960, 1970 – à l'époque, les bâtisseurs se pressaient plutôt à Lagos, considéré comme un New York africain –, Kenneth Scott a créé une maison ouverte, sans véritable porte, un hommage aux architectes modernistes tels que Walter Gropius et Ludwig Mies van der Rohe. Les formes angulaires et circulaires modulent la lumière et créent des espaces à ciel ouvert. C'est tout l'attrait de l'édifice, à la fois rétro et futuriste, qui donne l'impression de séjourner dans un projet expérimental du passé. Kenneth Scott, qui a marqué de son empreinte nombre de bâtiments publics d'Accra, n'est pas prêt d'être oublié au Ghana. D'ailleurs, sa veuve Thérèse Striggner Scott vit encore dans ces murs.

❋ **ABOVE** Faithful to Le Corbusier's dictum, "a house is a machine for living", the architect Kenneth Scott filled his house with recesses. Rather than pushing itself forward, the aesthetic of the place is quietly insinuated. Here, the outside concrete dining table and benches harmonize well with the surrounding décor. ❋ **OBEN** Getreu der Maxime von Le Corbusier »Das Haus ist eine Maschine zum Wohnen«, sorgte Kenneth Scott in seinem Haus für viele Rückzugsmöglichkeiten. Die Ästhetik des Gebäudes drängt sich nicht auf, sondern schleicht sich langsam ins Bewusstsein des Besuchers. Der Tisch und die Bänke aus Beton, an denen die Mahlzeiten im Freien eingenommen werden, passen gut in ihre Umgebung. ❋ **CI-DESSUS** Fidèle à Le Corbusier, «une maison est une machine à habiter», l'architecte Kenneth Scott a multiplié les espaces de repli. Ici, plutôt que de s'imposer, l'esthétique des lieux s'insinue doucement chez le visiteur. Pour les repas pris à l'extérieur, la table et les bancs en béton s'harmonisent avec le décor ambiant.

※ **ABOVE** The raised main building overlooks the garden from behind a set of slatted concrete blinds, which protect the rooms in the back of the house from the sun. **FACING PAGE BELOW** The single storey guest building behind the main house. **BELOW** A spacious outside loggia runs along the front of the salon, giving a complete view of the garden. ※ **OBEN** Das Hauptgebäude liegt etwas erhöht oberhalb des Gartens. Betonjalousien schützen die rückwärtigen Zimmer vor der Sonne. **LINKE SEITE UNTEN** Das Gästehaus hinter dem Hauptgebäude liegt auf gleicher Höhe wie der Garten. **UNTEN** Die weiträumige Loggia vor dem Salon bietet einen schönen Panoramablick auf den Garten. ※ **CI-DESSOUS** Surélevée, la maison principale domine le jardin avec un jeu de jalousies en béton qui protègent les pièces arrière du soleil. **PAGE DE GAUCHE EN BAS** La maison d'amis, édifiée à l'arrière de la maison principale, est construite en plain-pied. **CI-DESSOUS** La spacieuse loggia extérieure longe le salon, offrant ainsi une vue totale sur le jardin.

✳ **ABOVE** Seemingly part of the surrounding natural environment, the kitchen opens directly onto the garden. Here the accent is sober, contemporary and entirely minimalist. ✳ **OBEN** Als wäre sie Teil ihrer natürlichen Umgebung, geht die Küche direkt auf den Garten hinaus. In diesem Raum wirkt der Minimalismus streng, schnörkellos, nüchtern auf das Wesentliche konzentriert – ein Inbild dieses modernen Hauses. ✳ **CI-DESSUS** Comme absorbée par la nature environnante, la cuisine s'ouvre directement sur le jardin. Ici, le minimalisme est de rigueur, pas de fioritures, l'essentiel reste sobre, à l'image de cette habitation contemporaine.

✳ **ABOVE** The bathrooms are much more inward-looking, naked spaces in the spirit of Scott's ideal. Mosaics between the bathtub and the work surface, with tones of black and grey against a white background. ✳ **OBEN** Die Gestaltung der Bäder wirkt ruhiger. Der blanke Raum verbindet sich mit der Atmosphäre im Haus. Die Mosaiksteinchen zwischen der Badewanne und der Ablage spielen auf weißem Grund mit den Farben Schwarz und Grau. ✳ **CI-DESSUS** Les salles de bains sont plus introverties. L'espace, épuré au maximum, va de pair avec l'esprit des lieux. Le jeu des mosaïques entre la baignoire et le plan de travail s'égaie sur des tons de noir et gris sur fond blanc.

Kassena
Burkina Faso & Ghana

This frontier habitat is ruled by the twin concerns of functionality and aesthetic value.

The architecture of the Kassena country is the most beautiful Africa has to offer. The Kassena themselves are hunters and farmers, men and women who from time immemorial have applied their skills as potters to the building of fortified farmsteads.

Their compounds stand in fields of sorghum and millet, each with its grain stores, huts, stockyards and altars dedicated to ancestors. Walls meander between each building. These places are not so much turned in on themselves as fully geared for survival: local warfare and the slave trade made them what they are. The Kassena compounds were deliberately sited a certain distance from one another, so that when one fell into the enemy's hands, its survivors had somewhere safe to go. Originally covered in unadorned reddish clay, the walls of the houses are now painted black and white. Masonry work (*banco*) is the task of the men; the women take care of details and decoration. Kassena motifs are inspired by cosmic mythology; they can be geometrical or figurative, and they illustrate the obedience of this remarkable people to an original relationship between man and his environment. Some of the drawings depart from this pattern to represent imaginary consumer goods (TVs, cars). For the moment, in many rooms the interior furnishings are confined to shelves, chairs and beds made exclusively from clay.

Die Architektur der Kassena, so hört man, sei die schönste in ganz Afrika. Seit Menschengedenken setzen die Männer und Frauen dieses Volkes von Jägern und Feldbauern ihre Fähigkeiten als Töpfer auch beim Bau ihrer Gehöfte ein.

Die Bebauung, die aus den Hirsefeldern herausragt, besteht aus Hütten, Getreidespeichern, Altären zu Ehren der Ahnen und Einfriedungen für das Vieh. Zwischen den Häusern schlängeln sich niedrige Mauern. Diese Bauweise dient weniger der inneren Einkehr als dem Überleben. Stammeskriege und mehr noch die Jagd auf Sklaven haben die Siedlungsweise geprägt. Die Siedlungen der Kassena wurden in beträchtlicher Entfernung voneinander errichtet, damit die Überlebenden, wenn eine von ihnen in die Hände des Feindes fiel, sich in benachbarte Siedlungen flüchten konnten. Die Hausmauern, die ursprünglich mit rotbraunem Lehm bedeckt wurden, werden nun schwarz-weiß bemalt. Die Maurerarbeit mit *banco* ist den Männern vorbehalten, während die Frauen die Häuser fertig stellen und verzieren. Die sowohl geometrischen als auch gegenständlichen Motive sind der kosmischen Mythologie entlehnt und bebildern den Glauben dieses Volkes an eine tiefe Beziehung zwischen Mensch und Natur. Einige Darstellungen entfernen sich von dem traditionellen Schema und bilden imaginäre Konsumgüter wie Fernseher und Autos ab. Zur Zeit sind die Möbel in den meisten Hütten noch aus Lehm (Regale, Sitzgelegenheiten und Betten).

C'est dit: l'architecture de terre des Kassena est peut-être la plus belle d'Afrique. Peuple de chasseurs et d'agriculteurs, ces hommes et ces femmes appliquent depuis des temps immémoriaux leurs savoir-faire de potiers à la construction de fermes fortifiées.

Émergeant des champs de mil et de sorgo, les concessions mêlent les cases, les greniers à céréales, les autels des ancêtres et l'enclos à bétail. Des murets serpent entre chaque édifice. Repli sur soi? Question de survie plutôt. Les guerres tribales et, plus encore, la traite des Noirs, ont modelé l'habitat. Les habitations Kassèna étaient établies à bonne distance les unes des autres et lorsqu'ils voyaient qu'une concession était tombée aux mains de l'ennemi, les rescapés pouvaient s'enfuir. Couverts de glaise, à l'aspect rouge brun à l'origine, les murs des maisons sont repeints maintenant en noir et blanc. L'œuvre de maçonnerie (*banco*) est réservée aux hommes tandis que les finitions et les décorations reviennent aux femmes. Les motifs sont inspirés de la mythologie cosmique. Géométriques ou figuratifs, ils soulignent l'illustre obéissance de ce peuple à une relation originelle entre l'homme et son environnement. Quelques dessins s'éloignent du schéma pour représenter des biens de consommation imaginaires (télévision ou voiture). Pour le moment, le mobilier intérieur, dans bien des cases, est exclusivement en terre (étagères, sièges et lits).

❋ **FACING PAGE AND ABOVE** Each compound is fully autonomous, beside its mango and kapok groves. The roof terraces are used for drying millet. ❋ **LINKE SEITE UND OBEN** Hinter den Mango- und Kapokbäumen beginnt das autonome Gebiet der jeweiligen Siedlung. Auf den Terrassendächern wird die Hirse zum Trocknen ausgelegt. ❋ **PAGE DE GAUCHE ET CI-DESSUS** À la lisière des manguiers et des fromagers, chaque concession a son autonomie. Les toits-terrasses assurent le séchage du millet.

❋ **ABOVE** In the Kassena country, pots are passed down from mother to daughter. Their size and number is indicative of their owners' social status. ❋ **OBEN** Bei den Kassena geben die Mütter ihre Kenntnisse der Töpferkunst an die Töchter weiter. An der Zahl und Größe der Töpfe lässt sich der soziale Status ablesen. ❋ **CI-DESSUS** En pays Kassena, les poteries passent de mère en fille. Leur taille et leur nombre indiquent le statut social.

✻ **ABOVE** The motifs painted on the façades of the houses are the work of women; they usually represent the *zalenga*, a net in which calabashes are stored and the *wanzagese*, featuring pieces of crushed calabash. ✻ **OBEN** Die Frauen bemalen die Fassaden mit den Motiven des *zalenga*, einem Wurzelfasernetz, das die Kalebassen einer Frau zusammenhält und des *wanzagese*, das Scherben zerbrochener Kalebassen darstellt. ✻ **CI-DESSUS** Sur les façades des maisons, les motifs peints le plus souvent par les femmes Kasséna sont le *zalenga*, un filet végétal de rangement de calebasses, et le *wanzagese*, figurant des morceaux de calebasses brisées.

❋ **ABOVE** V-shaped compositions are a sign of welcome to visitors. **FOLLOWING PAGES** Kassena villages are laid out as small separate compounds, each run by its own family chief. ❋ **OBEN** Die gemalten V-Zeichen heißen Besucher willkommen. **FOLGENDE DOPPELSEITE** Die Kassena-Dörfer bestehen aus kleineren, voneinander getrennten Einfriedungen, in denen jeweils das Familienoberhaupt das Sagen hat. ❋ **CI-DESSOUS** Les compositions en V sont un signe de bienvenue aux visiteurs. **DOUBLE PAGE SUIVANTE** Les villages Kassena se présentent sous la forme de petites enceintes séparées les unes des autres, dont chaque maître est le chef de famille.

※ **ABOVE** In Ghana, a natural rendering made with earth, ashes, cowpats, tree resin and nut butter is used as insulation against the heat. ※ **OBEN** Als Schutz gegen die Hitze dient in Ghana ein natürlicher Rauputz aus einer Mischung aus Lehm, Asche, Kuhfladen, Baumharz und Schibutter. ※ **CI-DESSUS** Au Ghana, un crépi naturel fait d'un mélange de terre, de cendre, de bouse de vache, de résine d'arbre et de beurre de karité est censé isoler de la chaleur.

❋ **ABOVE** Still in Ghana, the geometrical motifs are inspired by cosmic mythology but also by scenes of daily life – with soldier figures like these. ❋ **OBEN** Die geometrischen Formen der Mauern leiten sich aus der kosmischen Mythologie her. Es gibt aber auch Alltagsszenen mit Soldatenfiguren. ❋ **CI-DESSOUS** Toujours au Ghana, les motifs géométriques de ces murs sont inspirés de la mythologie cosmique mais aussi de scènes de la vie quotidienne avec ces figures de soldats.

Spiritual Master
LOBI'S VILLAGE

The compound of the spiritual master Palenkité Noufe takes its visitors to the heart of Lobi magic.

His tomb, dug in the centre of the courtyard, stands in front of the house. The statuette of a man, with a pipe in his mouth and a hat on his head, shows what he looked like. Each day, new offerings fill his dish and his glass.

In accordance with the belief that the dead live on among the living, Palenkité Noufe has been buried in his former compound since 1998. His son has taken over his duties. At the door of his thatched house, the statue of a hippo stands guard. Traces of offerings of milk and millet cover its back. The sacred chamber is just beyond: this room, built with stones chosen personally by the Master, was formerly his place of work, where he carried out his priestly and commercial functions. In animist societies, the spiritual master has the task of interpreting the will of spirits, ancestors and gods. In times of misfortune, animals are sacrificed to propitiate the souls of the dead and obtain their help. The religion involves the adoration of sacred objects made of clay or wood, which are assembled on veritable domestic altars. On the right hand side of the threshold, the altar of the Lady of the River is carved in bas-relief. She is depicted standing with her legs apart, covered in shells from her forehead to her navel. To appease the spirits, this figure is regularly sprinkled with millet beer and the blood of sacrificed animals, and the earth walls are included in this ritual. The liquid, on its way to the great beyond, licks at the roof – which is made of ashes, cowpats and straw thoroughly mixed together.

Das mitten im Innenhof ausgehobene Grab liegt direkt vor seinem Haus. Die Statue eines Mannes mit einer Pfeife im Mund und einer Mütze auf dem Kopf beschwört seine Gestalt. Sein Teller und sein Glas werden täglich mit Opfergaben gefüllt.

Getreu der Vorstellung, dass die Toten mit den Lebenden zusammenwohnen, wurde Palenkité Noufe 1998 in seiner Konzession bestattet. Sein Sohn übernahm das Amt. Vor dem Haus hält ein Flusspferd Wache, dessen Rücken Spuren von Opfergaben – Hirse oder Milch – aufweist. Direkt dahinter liegt der Raum mit den heiligen Gegenständen – die Bausteine wurden vom Priester eigens ausgewählt. Im Schutz dieses Raumes übt er seine Tätigkeit aus. In animistischen Ländern übernimmt der Priester die Aufgabe, den Willen der Geister, Ahnen und Götter zu interpretieren. In schlechten Zeiten opfert man Tiere, um die Geister der Toten zu beschwichtigen und ihre Hilfe zu erlangen. Auf den Hausaltären werden heilige Gegenstände aus Lehm und Holz platziert. Rechts an der Schwelle des Hauses befindet sich der Altar der Flussgöttin, im Relief geschnitzt. Die aufrecht stehende weibliche Figur mit den gespreizten Beinen ist von der Stirn bis zum Nabel mit Muscheln verziert. Zur Besänftigung der Geister wird sie ebenso wie die Lehmmauern regelmäßig mit Hirsebier und Tierblut begossen. Auf dem Weg ins Jenseits benetzt die Flüssigkeit auch das Dach, das aus einer Mischung aus Asche, Stroh und Kuhfladen hergestellt wurde.

Sa tombe, creusée au milieu de la cour, est située devant sa maison. La statuette d'un homme, pipe à la bouche, casquette sur la tête, évoque sa silhouette. Chaque jour, des offrandes emplissent son assiette et son verre.

Selon la croyance qui veut que les morts cohabitent avec les vivants, Palenkité Noufe est enseveli dans sa concession depuis 1998. Son fils a pris la relève. Devant l'entrée de la maison au toit de chaume, un hippopotame monte la garde. Des traces d'offrandes, mil ou lait, couvrent son dos. La chambre des fétiches apparaît juste derrière. Édifiée à l'aide de pierres choisies par le Maître, elle abritait ses activités, à mi-chemin entre le sacerdoce et le commerce. En pays animiste, le féticheur se charge d'interpréter la volonté des esprits, des ancêtres et des dieux. Dans le malheur, on procède à des sacrifices d'animaux pour apaiser les esprits des morts et obtenir le secours des disparus. Le culte s'accompagne d'une adoration des fétiches d'argile ou de bois qui sont rassemblés sur de véritables autels domestiques. Au seuil de la maison, à droite, l'autel de la Dame du fleuve est sculpté en bas-relief. Debout, les jambes écartées, la forme féminine est ornée de coquillages du front jusqu'au nombril. Pour apaiser les esprits, la belle est régulièrement arrosée de bière de millet et du sang des animaux sacrifiés. Les murs de terre n'échappent pas à ce rite. Le liquide, en chemin vers l'au-delà, lèche le toit fait de cendre et de paille mélangée à de la bouse de vache.

❋ **FACING PAGE** The feminine form, stained with libations and adorned with shells, evokes the black Volta, a frontier river of great mythical and religious importance to the Lobi. **ABOVE** Four traditional Lobi domestic altars. ❋ **LINKE SEITE** Die weibliche Figur, die mit Spuren der Trankopfer bedeckt und mit Muscheln verziert ist, beschwört den Schwarzen Volta, den mythisch und religiös bedeutsamen Grenzfluss. **OBEN** Vier traditionelle Hausaltäre der Lobi. ❋ **PAGE DE GAUCHE** La forme féminine, couverte de traces de libations et ornée de coquillages, évoque la Volta Noire, fleuve frontalier à l'importance mythique et religieuse. **CI-DESSOUS** Quatre autels traditionnels domestiques Lobi.

❋ **ABOVE** The carved wooden ladder leads up to the roof, where the grain is dried. The clay jars used for storing grain are as useful to the spirits as they are to the living. ❋ **OBEN** Die aus Holz geschnitzte Leiter führt aufs Dach, wo das Getreide trocknet. In Krügen aus Lehm wird das Getreide gelagert – für die Lebenden und die Geister. ❋ **CI-DESSUS** L'échelle en bois sculpté mène au toit où sèchent les céréales. Les jarres d'argile utilisées pour stocker les céréales servent aux vivants comme aux esprits.

※ **ABOVE** To placate the spirits, boiled millet is tossed against the walls. Death isn't viewed as a tragic event in these parts, because people believe the dead do not entirely depart the world of the living. ※ **OBEN** Zur Besänftigung der Geister wird Hirsebrei auf die Mauern geschmiert. Der Tod wird hier nicht tragisch genommen, weil der Verstorbene weiter Anteil an der Welt der Lebenden hat. ※ **CI-DESSUS** Pour apaiser les esprits, on jette de la bouillie de mil sur les murs. La mort n'a pas de caractère tragique ici car le défunt ne disparaît pas entièrement du monde des vivants.

TIEMOKO SOUL

LOBI'S VILLAGE

The Lobi, a warrior people, built compounds they could defend, and that were well-provided with water, grain stores and stables.

As with the Kassena, and for the same reasons (to escape marauding slave traders), compounds in this part of Burkina Faso tend to be about a hundred yards apart. The *zaka* (family enclosure) brings together bedrooms, grain stores, terraces and kitchen area in an ensemble which can run to several rooms.

The Lobi have always been a fragmented group, with no system of general authority beyond each head of household; they traditionally bore the name of their home compound, and as hunters and warriors they put up a long resistance to the colonial French administration. Only recently did they renounce their central tenet as a people: "Never adopt a foreign way of life". Under the circumstances, it is small wonder that their houses are shaped as they are, turned in upon themselves. Lobi *zakas* have practically no entrances from the outside. In the old days, literally the only way in was through the roof terrace, using a Y-shaped ladder carved out of a tree trunk. Today there are doors, but the interiors of the huts are still plunged in a gloom that is scarcely relieved by light from a hatch in the ceiling. There is almost no furniture in these traditional huts: a small bench, perhaps, a mat for sleeping, a few personal items and the traditional pots and ewers for beer and food. The *zaka* is also a demonstration of the skills of the Lobi masons, who excel at both sculpture and pottery.

Aus den gleichen Gründen wie bei den Kassena (aus Furcht vor Sklavenhändlern) lagen die Besitzungen früher Hunderte von Metern auseinander. Die *zaka*, die Einfriedung einer Familienbehausung, verbindet mehrere Zimmer, Speicher, Terrassen und Küchen zu einem Ganzen.

Mehrere *zakas* können eine Einheit bilden. In dieser Form der Splittergesellschaft, in der es bis auf den Familienvater keine Führungsinstanzen gab, konnte das Volk von Jägern und Kriegern den Franzosen in der Kolonialzeit lange widerstehen. Erst vor kurzem gaben die Lobi ihre Devise »Folge niemals der Lebenseinstellung Fremder« auf. Deshalb verwundert es nicht, dass die Siedlungsweise so zurückgezogen wirkt. In einer *zaka* gibt es praktisch keine Tür- oder Fensteröffnungen. In früheren Zeiten konnte man die Häuser nur über die Dachterrassen betreten, indem man eine aus einem Baumstamm geschnitzte Y-förmige Leiter erklomm. Selbst seit Türen Einzug in diese Architektur hielten, liegen die Innenräume fast vollständig im Dunkeln – höchstens eine Falltür an der Decke lässt ein wenig Licht hinein. In den traditionellen Hütten gibt es nur wenige Möbelstücke: eine kleine Bank, eine Matte als Matratze, wenige persönliche Gegenstände sowie die herkömmlichen Töpfe und Krüge für Bier und Lebensmittel. Die *zaka* ist zudem ein gutes Beispiel für die Geschicklichkeit der Lobimaurer, die auch als Bildhauer und Töpfer arbeiten.

Comme chez les Kassena, et pour les mêmes raisons (échapper aux chasseurs d'esclaves), les possessions étaient autrefois distantes d'une centaine de mètres les unes des autres. La *zaka* (enclos familial) relie les chambres, les greniers, les terrasses et les cuisines en un ensemble qui peut former plusieurs pièces.

Société fragmentée, sans chefferie autre que celle du père de famille (les Lobi portent le nom de leur concession), cette population de guerriers et de chasseurs à longtemps résisté aux Français à l'époque coloniale et n'a que depuis peu renoncé à son dogme: «Ne jamais suivre la devise de l'étranger.» Dans ces conditions, comment s'étonner des formes d'un habitat replié sur lui-même? La *zaka*, est presque entièrement dépourvue d'ouvertures. Autrefois, on accédait même à l'intérieur des habitations par les toits terrasses en grimpant sur ces échelles en Y sculptées à même les troncs d'arbre. Si les portes ont fait leur apparition, les intérieurs sont toujours plongés dans une obscurité à peine corrigée par une trappe au plafond. Les meubles sont rares dans ces cases traditionnelles: un petit banc, une natte en guise de matelas, de petits objets personnels, et les traditionnels pots et jarres destinés à la bière et aux aliments. La *zaka* est aussi une démonstration de l'habileté des maçons Lobi, à la fois sculpteurs et potiers.

⁜ **ABOVE** In the courtyard, only the chickens are allowed out to scratch around among the children. The other domestic animals are kept securely in pens, chewing the cud all day. This place of collective life is also used for the spirit-cult, with altars in front of each house. ⁜ **OBEN** Im Hof ist es nur dem Federvieh erlaubt, dem geflochtenen Hühnerstall zu entfliehen und zwischen den Kindern herumzulaufen. Das übrige Vieh käut im Stall wieder. An diesem Ort des Zusammenlebens hat auch der Geisterkult seinen Platz – die Altäre stehen direkt vor dem Haus. ⁜ **CI-DESSUS** Dans la cour, seule la volaille peut s'échapper du poulailler tressé et gambader au milieu des enfants. Le bétail, lui, rumine dans son enclos. Ce lieu de vie collective est aussi réservé au culte des esprits puisque des autels se dressent devant les maisons.

✳ **ABOVE** The roof of this house is accessible using a Y-shaped ladder, leaned against a wall built of five layers of earth. This space is used as a grain store, to dry and stock cereals.
✳ **OBEN** Auf das Dach gelangt man über eine Y-förmige Leiter, die an der Mauer aus fünf Lehmschichten Halt findet. Die Dachterrasse dient als Speicher, wo das Getreide getrocknet und gelagert wird. ✳ **CI-DESSUS** On accède au toit de cette maison à l'aide d'une échelle en forme de Y qui prend appui sur un mur formé de cinq couches de terre. Cet espace est utilisé comme un grenier, pour sécher et stocker les céréales.

ABiDJan
IVOry coast

Built with a sense of poetry and respect for local tradition, these houses are more to be apprehended than read.

We should try to create habitats that are true to local forms, and above all, not palaces. In the strength of this conviction, the architect Frédéric Thomas has developed his own unusual approach with three villas built in and around Abidjan.

The one feature they all have in common is a shell of rough clay bricks made by hand, on site. This laudable idea sprang from a practical wish to adapt to the hot and humid local climate. Thus all the Thomas houses are positioned to catch the prevailing wind and thus are as ventilated as it is possible to be, at all times. The plate glass windows may heat up the interiors, but they also keep them dry in conjunction with the draughts sweeping through. The result is that the only areas that need to be electrically air-conditioned are the bedrooms – everywhere else the heavy air is stirred by fans. Apart from their materials, the aesthetic harmony of the Thomas houses is invariably generated by their apertures. The light varies as the days go by, thanks to the bay windows and arrow-slits which cast the beams of the setting sun on the walls inside. "Today people are bold enough to confront real challenges," says the architect. Nothing clashes in his work; there are very few objects imported from Europe. One result of this rigour has been that his designs were noticed recently by some chance Japanese visitors – and now he is busy building houses in the Far East.

Eine Behausung von lokalem Zuschnitt, kein Palast jedenfalls. Der Architekt Frédéric Thomas durfte seinen Überzeugungen entsprechend drei Villen in Abidjan und Umgebung individuell gestalten.

So bekamen alle drei den gleichen »Panzer« verordnet, eine Hülle aus ungebrannten Ziegeln, die direkt auf der jeweiligen Baustelle in Handarbeit hergestellt wurden. Eine schöne Idee, die jedoch vor allem der Anpassung an das warme, feuchte Klima dient. Die Häuser sind so ausgerichtet, dass sie ständig vom Wind belüftet werden. Durch die Fenster heizen sich die Räume zwar auf, trocknen jedoch gleichzeitig besser, da ständig eine Brise hindurchweht. Aus diesem Grund sind auch nur die Schlafzimmer klimatisiert, während in den anderen Räumen Ventilatoren die stickige Luft umwälzen. Neben dem Baumaterial spielen insbesondere die Fenster eine große Rolle für die harmonische Wirkung der Häuser. Im Lauf des Tages verändert sich die Stimmung je nach Lichteinfall durch die großen Fenster und die »Schießscharten«, die bei Sonnenuntergang die Mauern beleuchten. »Inzwischen sind die Leute offener für innovative Ideen«, glaubt der Architekt. Protz und Kitsch sucht man hier jedenfalls vergebens. An Material und Möbeln wurde kaum etwas aus Europa importiert. Interessanterweise fand die Arbeit des Architekten große Zustimmung bei Japanern auf der Durchreise durch Abidjan, weshalb er inzwischen auch in Asien sehr gefragt ist.

Un habitat fidèle aux formes locales, surtout pas un palais. Fort de ses convictions, l'architecte Frédéric Thomas a développé son approche singulière à travers trois villas situées à Abidjan et dans les environs.

Elles ont en commun la même carapace, une enveloppe de briques de terre crue pressées à la main sur le chantier. L'idée est belle, mais correspond surtout à une volonté de s'adapter à un climat chaud et humide. Orientées dans le sens du vent, les maisons sont ventilées en permanence. Si les verrières provoquent un réchauffement, elles assèchent également les intérieurs balayés par les brises. Du coup, seules les chambres sont climatisées, et partout ailleurs les ventilateurs tranchent l'air épais comme du manioc. Outre les matériaux, l'harmonie des maisons est générée par les ouvertures. La lumière varie au fil des heures de la journée grâce aux baies et à des meurtrières qui illuminent certains murs au soleil couchant. «Les gens sont mûrs pour de l'audace et des défis», estime l'architecte. Point de clinquant, en effet. Très peu d'objets ou de matériaux importés d'Europe. Par ricochet, ce travail a séduit des Japonais de passage à Abidjan et, du coup, l'architecte essaime maintenant sur le continent asiatique.

❊ **FACING PAGE** Apart from its materials, the harmony of this building derives from its openings to the outside. The light varies according to the time of day, thanks to the well of sunshine that illuminates the house. **RIGHT** Under this piece of pottery from Mali, the motifs of the floor are inspired by the dance tradition of the former Zaïre. **BELOW** The armchairs and sofas in the salon were designed by Jean-Pierre Thomas, the architect's brother, who lives in Abidjan. ❊ **LINKE SEITE** Neben dem Baumaterial sorgen die Fenster in diesem Haus für eine harmonische Atmosphäre. Je nach Tageszeit herrscht eine andere Stimmung, geprägt durch den Lichteinfall ins Haus. **RECHTS** Tontöpfe aus Mali auf einem Boden, dessen Muster von Tanzschritten aus dem früheren Zaire inspiriert ist. **UNTEN** Die Sessel und Kanapees im Salon wurden nach Entwürfen von Jean-Pierre Thomas angefertigt. Der Designer, ein Bruder des Architekten, lebt in Abidjan. ❊ **PAGE DE GAUCHE** Outre les matériaux, l'harmonie de cette maison est donnée par les ouvertures. La lumière varie à toute heure de la journée grâce au puit de soleil qui illumine la maison. **À DROITE** Sous la poterie du Mali, les motifs du sol sont inspirés de pas de danse typiques de l'ex-Zaïre. **CI-DESSOUS** Dans le salon, les fauteuils et les canapés ont été dessinés par Jean-Pierre Thomas, designer établi à Abidjan et frère de l'architecte.

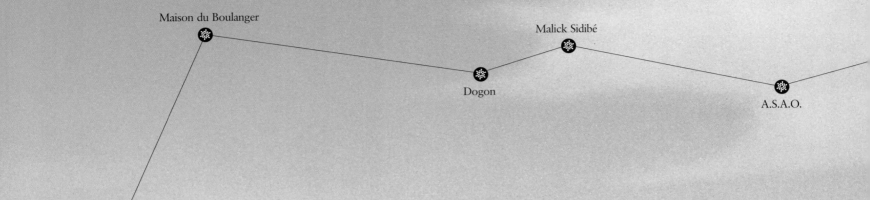

Maison du Boulanger

Malick Sidibé

Dogon

A.S.A.O.

Not Vital

NIGER, MALI, SENEGAL, MAURITANIA

Marie-José Crespin

Oualata

Soninke People

Nomads

NOt Vital

Agadez

A sculptor living among the Tuaregs,
in whose work the animal and mineral elements are made one.

Not Vital – half man, half animal is the title of a documentary film about the Swiss sculptor – and indeed, nature and culture are combined in the work of this artist.

Not Vital draws his inspiration from the air of his mountain birthplace, though he lives between America, Switzerland and Italy. A lover of wide open spaces, he has also built himself a house in Niger, fulfilling his dream of an architecture truly capable of melting into the landscape. The result is perfectly adapted to Agadez, where the dunes of the Ténéré meet the mountains of Air, and represents a new departure in the artist's work. From the walls of his house you can see a city of perfectly-preserved Sudanese buildings, with walls of ochre banco (mud) and a mosque built in 1515 studded with wooden piles. The signs of wealth are clearly visible in the facades of the old parts of town, especially on the house of the chief of the bakers, with its meticulously carved and coloured walls. It is a city that appears suspended in time, peopled by blue-robed Tuaregs.

Not Vital – Half Man, Half Animal lautet der Titel eines Dokumentarfilms über den Schweizer Künstler. Not Vital, geprägt durch die Bergwelt seiner Heimat, lässt in seinen Werken Natur und Kultur aufeinandertreffen.

Der Künstler, der in den Vereinigten Staaten, der Schweiz und Italien lebt, liebt weite Landschaften und hat sich mit seinem Haus in Niger einen Traum verwirklicht: eine Architektur, die mit der Landschaft verschmilzt. Der Bau passt wunderbar nach Agadez, das die Dünen der Ténéré mit den Air-Bergen verbindet. Dieses Haus eröffnet Not Vital einen neuen Weg in seiner Arbeit. Es bietet ihm die Möglichkeit, die Verwandlungen des Lebens in einem einzigen Augenblick einzufangen. Von den Mauern seines Hauses blickt man auf eine perfekt erhaltene sudanesische Architektur mit ockerfarbenen Lehmbauten und eine auf Holzpfählen errichtete Moschee aus dem Jahr 1515. In den alten Stadtvierteln zeugen die fein ziselierten und kolorierten Wände vom Reichtum der Stadt. Agadez lebt, losgelöst von der Zeit, im Rhythmus der blauen Gewänder der Tuareg, die im Wind schlagen.

Not Vital – Mi homme, mi animal, c'est le titre d'un film consacré au sculpteur suisse. Nature et culture se rejoignent dans l'œuvre de cet artiste inspiré par l'air de ses montagnes natales.

Not Vital habite entre l'Amérique, la Suisse et l'Italie. Amoureux des grands espaces, il réalise au Niger une maison qui incarne son rêve: une architecture capable de se fondre dans le paysage. La construction s'adapte parfaitement à Agadez qui marie les dunes du Ténéré et les montagnes de l'Aïr. Cette maison ouvre une nouvelle voie dans le travail de Not Vital, elle lui permet de capter l'instant à travers les métamorphoses de l'être. Des murs de sa maison, on contemple une architecture soudanaise parfaitement conservée avec des maisons en banco de couleur ocre et sa mosquée hérissée de pieux en bois construite en 1515. Les signes de richesse s'étalent sur les façades des vieux quartiers, particulièrement du côté de la maison du «chef des boulangers» aux murs finement ciselés et colorés. La ville vit suspendue dans le temps au rythme des robes bleues des Touaregs qui claquent dans le vent.

※ **PAGE 614** The house is in the very heart of the town, with terraces decorated by Not Vital with the horns of cattle. In this society, where everything finds a use of some kind, these are among the only things that are destroyed. While watching people burning the horns that are such an integral part of his sculptures, Not Vital had the idea of integrating them into his architecture too. **ABOVE** Not Vital has created a world of his own, in which the land assumes a primary dimension. **BELOW** The sculptor's bedroom, with its warm earth tones. **FACING PAGE** A Sudanese construction, with walls of ochre mud. ※ **SEITE 614** Das Haus im Herzen der Stadt hat mehrere Terrassen, auf denen der Künstler Tierhörner platziert hat. In dieser Gesellschaft findet alles außer Horn eine Verwendung. Beim Anblick verbrennender Hörner kam Not Vital die Idee, diese, die sonst integraler Bestandteil seiner Skulpturen sind, in die Architektur einzubeziehen. **OBEN** Hier schuf Not Vital seine ganz eigene Welt, in der dem Land eine ursprüngliche Dimension zukommt. **UNTEN** Warme Erdtöne dominieren das Schlafzimmer des Bildhauers. Eine schmale Doppeltreppe führt auf eine Terrasse. **RECHTE SEITE** Die sudanesische Bauweise mit ihren ockerfarbenen Lehmwänden. ※ **PAGE 614** En plein cœur de la ville, la maison est dotée de terrasses où l'artiste a implanté des cornes de bétail. Dans cette société ou tout sert, les cornes sont les seules a être détruites. En voyant brûler les cornes qui font sinon partie intégrante de ses sculptures, Not Vital a eu l'idée de les intégrer à l'architecture. **CI-DESSUS** Not Vital recrée ici son univers où la terre prend sa dimension première. **CI-DESSOUS** La chambre du sculpteur est bordée des tons chauds de la terre. Un double escalier très étroit donne accès à une terrasse. **PAGE DE DROITE** Une construction soudanaise avec ses murs en banco de couleur ocre.

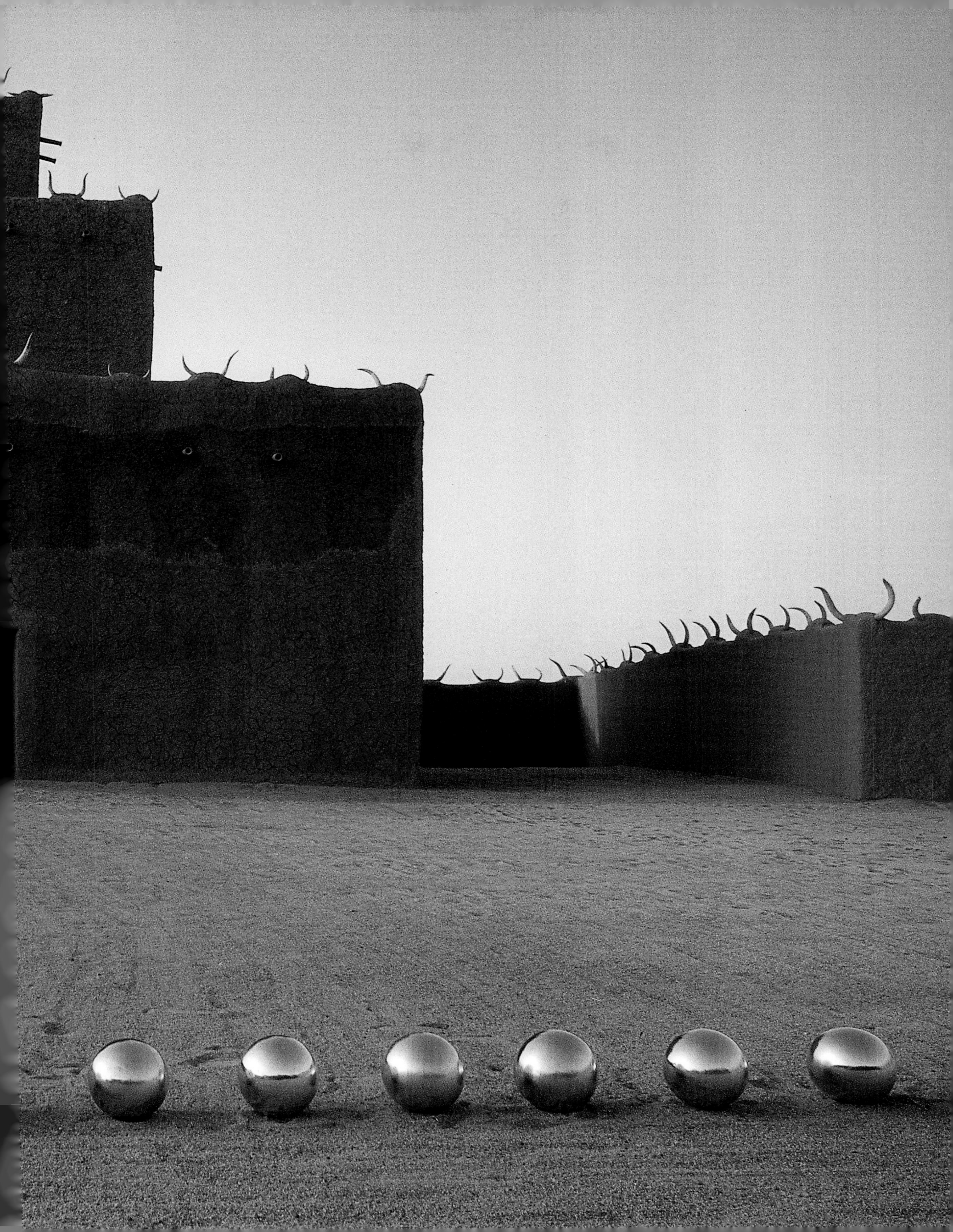

❊ **PRECEEDING PAGES** Horns on the walls: a ghostly but somehow protective presence. A sculpture in the courtyard entitled *Camel*, consisting of thirteen silver balls containing the mortal remains of an entire camel. The house is on three levels, seemingly protected by the cattle horns set into the walls surrounding it. **FACING PAGE** An oversized candlestick made of a cow's horn, an ingenious lighting system. ❊ **VORHERGEHENDE DOPPELSEITE** Gespenstisch wirken die Hörner, die wie Wachtposten auf den Mauern stehen. Im Hof ist die Skulptur »Camel« auf-gebaut. Die 13 Silberkugeln enthalten die sterblichen Reste eines ganzen Kamels. Das Haus erstreckt sich über drei Stockwerke, bewacht von den Tierhörnern auf den Umfassungs-mauern. **LINKE SEITE** Ein übergroßer Kerzenleuchter aus Tierhorn, ein findiges Beleuchtungssystem. ❊ **PAGE DE GAUCHE** Un chandelier surdimensionné en corne de bétail, système ingénieux d'éclairage. **DOUBLE PAGE PRÉCÉDENTE** Présence fantomatique de la faune, ces cornes postées comme des sentinelles sur les murs. Dans la cour est exposée la sculpture «Camel». 13 boules en argent contenant les restes d'un chameau entier. La maison s'élève sur trois niveaux, gardée par des cornes de bétail que l'on retrouve sur les murs d'enceinte.

❋ **ABOVE AND FACING PAGE** Not Vital's own creative work is in perfect harmony with the traditional paintings and austere Tuareg beds. ❋ **OBEN UND LINKE SEITE** Not Vitals freie Kreativität harmoniert gut mit den traditionellen Gemälden und den spartanischen Betten der Tuareg. ❋ **CI-DESSOUS ET PAGE DE GAUCHE** La créativité débridée de l'artiste et le recours aux peintures traditionnelles s'harmonisent avec le mobilier spartiate: lits touaregs.

MAISON DU BOULANGER
AGADEZ

A traditional Tuareg house, where bread for the town has been made for many centuries.

In this holy city of Islam, there is no changing of water into wine. But the baker continues to make countless loaves in his traditional oven.

Here at the edge of the desert, not far from the sultan's palace from which the Imam or *cadi* oversees the spiritual life of the 159 tribes of the region, there is a palpable sense of religious sanctity. The Tuaregs who have imposed their character on Agadez have adapted the Muslim religion to their nomadic existence. Their piety and respect for the Koran run deep, but with them they have also preserved their ancestral beliefs, in which dialogue with the spirit world plays an important part. Thus, in order to heal wounds or ward off ill luck, their mud walls are decorated with talismanic motifs. On the outside of the baker's house, a dome typical of Sudanese architecture responds just as faithfully to the projecting beams and to the openings which, like fantastic corridors, lead to rooms where Tuareg and religious motifs blend comfortably with chests and niches. The contrast of bright light and deep shadow is everywhere, as is the pervasive odour of baking bread. Taste it, and you will be transfigured.

In dieser heiligen Stadt des Islam verwandelt man kein Wasser in Wein. Und doch zog einst der Bäcker aus seinem traditionellen Ofen unzählige Brötchen.

Am Rande der Wüste, nicht weit vom Palast des Sultans, wo der Imam oder *cadi* über das spirituelle Leben von 159 Stämmen der Region wacht, ist man erfüllt von religiösem Geist. Die Tuareg haben Agadez geprägt und die muslimische Religion an ihr Nomadenleben angepasst. Obwohl sie dem Koran treu und respektvoll gegenüberstehen, bewahren sie doch den eng mit der Geisterwelt verbundenen Glauben ihrer Vorfahren. So haben die Dekorationen auf den Wänden der Lehmhäuser die Funktion von Talismännern. Sie sollen Glück bringen bzw. Unglück abwenden und Krankheiten heilen. Das Maison du boulanger entspricht auch von außen der sudanesischen Architektur, mit der typischen Kuppel, den vorspringenden Balken, den Türöffnungen, die zu den Räumen führen, in deren Nischen Tuareg-Symbole und religiöse Motive der Muslime sich vermengen. Der starke Kontrast zwischen Hell und Dunkel ist allgegenwärtig so wie einst wohl der Duft frisch gebackenen Brotes. Eine Kostprobe ist eine geradezu transzendente Erfahrung.

Dans cette ville sainte, Islam oblige, on ne transforme pas l'eau en vin. Mais le boulanger, lui, tirait à l'époque de son four traditionnel une infinité de petits pains.

À la lisière du désert, non loin du palais du sultan où siège l'imam, le *cadi* qui contrôle les 159 tribus de la région, la référence sacrée s'impose dans les esprits. Les Touaregs qui façonnent Agadez ont adapté la religion musulmane à leur vie nomade. Fidèles et respectueux du Coran, ils conservent néanmoins leurs croyances ancestrales si attachées à un dialogue avec le monde des esprits. Ainsi, afin de guérir des blessures ou d'éloigner le malheur, les murs en terre de banco, semblables à des talismans, sont décorés de motifs destinés à attirer la chance. À l'extérieur de la maison du boulanger, le dôme typique de l'architecture soudanaise, répond tout aussi fidèlement aux poutres saillantes, aux ouvertures qui, tels des passages fantastiques, mènent à des pièces où s'entrecroisent motifs touaregs, signes religieux et niches voisinant avec des coffres-forts. Le contraste entre ombre et lumière est très présent ainsi que l'odeur du pain fabriqué jadis en ces lieux au rythme des tambours. En soi, une expérience transcendante.

626 Maison du Boulanger Niger

✳ **FACING PAGE** The baker stacks his utensils in an earthen niche etched with Islamic motifs. **RIGHT** The passages running along the building are screened with geometrical openwork patterns. **BELOW** The ochre mud walls of the main reception room are decorated with traditional local motifs. The ceiling is a composition of tree branches.
✳ **LINKE SEITE** Die Arbeitsutensilien des Bäckers in einer mit islamischen Motiven verzierten Nische. **RECHTS** Die um das Gebäude führenden Gänge sind mit geometrischen Mustern durchbrochen. **UNTEN** Der große Salon aus ockerfarbenem Lehm ist mit regionalen Motiven geschmückt. Die Decke besteht aus Holzstämmen. ✳ **PAGE DE GAUCHE** Le boulanger entreposait ses outils dans une niche aux motifs islamiques ciselés dans la terre. **A DROITE** Les coursives ont été créées le long de la bâtisse avec un jeu ajouré travaillé en formes géométriques. **CI-DESSOUS** Le grand salon en terre de banco de couleur ocre est décoré de motifs d'inspiration locale. Le plafond a été façonné avec des branches d'arbres.

DOGON
Bandiagara Fault

This place has fascinated travellers ever since its discovery, though its deepest meaning still baffles western logic.

Rising from the plains to a height of 800 feet, the Bandiagara fault is the most astonishing geological site in West Africa. The habitat is worthy of similar interest, to say the least.

In a zone some 200 kilometres long, the *banco* villages of ochre clay start where the cave-dwellings end. The latter were occupied by the Telem people up till the 15th century, when the Dogon arrived to build their houses and granaries at the foot and on top of the cliffs and convert the caves into tomb-sites. Today the Dogon too are still seen as somewhat mysterious. According to the ethnologists that throng the area, Dogon abodes, whether made of clay or stone, are symbolic representations of the human body. This world outside the world, which we do not understand, can impregnate a place where the dead, accused of acting against the order of the world we know, are present in every alley that twists among the huts and in every conical granary with its millet-straw thatch. At the fetish man's cave are numerous tombs; using carbon-14 techniques, researchers have established that the oldest are eight centuries old. From these eyries cut directly into the russet cliff face, the community can be seen in its authentic reality, united in the light of its cooking fires. In the far distance, the flickering lights of a Peul encampment remind us of more distant wanderings.

Der 250 Meter hohe Felsen von Bandiagara zählt zu den eindrucksvollsten geologischen Sehenswürdigkeiten in Westafrika. Die Behausungen in dieser Region sind ebenso sehenswert wie die Landschaft.

Bis 200 Kilometer weit erstrecken sich die Dörfer, gebaut aus *banco*, ockerfarbenem Lehm, am Fuß der Begräbnishöhlen in der Klippe. Bis zum 15. Jahrhundert lebte hier das Volk der Tellem, das von den Dogon vertrieben wurde, die am Fuß und oben auf der Felsenklippe Häuser und Speicher bauten, während die Höhlen den Toten vorbehalten waren. Bis heute wahren die Dogon ihre geheimnisvollen Bräuche. Den Ethnologen zufolge, die sich in dieser Region förmlich drängeln, sehen die Dogon in ihrer Behausung aus Lehm oder Stein ein Symbol des menschlichen Körpers. Diese jenseitige Welt ist für den westlichen Verstand schwer nachvollziehbar. In dieser Vorstellung sind die Toten, die beschuldigt werden, sich gegen die Weltordnung aufzulehnen, immer anwesend. Die kegelförmigen Speicher in den gewundenen Gassen sind mit Hirsestroh gedeckt. Neben der Höhle der Hohepriester liegen zahlreiche Höhlengräber (mit Hilfe der C_{14}-Datierung konnten Wissenschaftler das Alter der Gräber bestimmen – die ältesten sind 800 Jahre alt). Von diesen Höhlen aus, die in den rötlichen Fels geschlagen wurden, hat man einen guten Blick auf die zusammengeschweißte Gemeinschaft im Licht der Küchenherde. Aus der Ferne erinnern die Feuer eines Peul-Lagers an die ruhelosen Irrfahrten in dieser Gegend.

S'élevant sur la plaine à hauteur de 250 mètres, la faille de Bandiagara est le site géologique le plus impressionnant d'Afrique occidentale. Les habitations qui s'y trouvent sont, et c'est le moins que l'on puisse dire, à la mesure de cet intérêt.

Sur près de 200 kilomètres, les villages en *banco* (terre glaise ocre) s'enchaînent au pied de refuges troglodytes habités jusqu'au 15e siècle par le peuple Telem. Les Dogons ont débarqué dans la région à cette époque, édifiant maisons et greniers en bas et autour des falaises, tandis que les grottes, en hauteur, devenaient des lieux de sépulture. Aujourd'hui, les Dogons conservent leur part de mystère. D'après les ethnologues qui se pressent ici, leur habitat, qu'il soit en terre ou en pierre, est une représentation symbolique du corps humain. Ce monde hors du monde qui échappe à la raison occidentale, imprègne un espace où les morts, accusés d'intenter à l'ordre du monde, sont partout présents, des ruelles tortueuses aux greniers coniques coiffés de paille de mil. Du côté de la grotte des féticheurs, c'est un grand fouillis de tombeaux (à l'aide du carbone 14, les chercheurs ont daté à huit siècles les plus anciens). Depuis ces nids d'aigles creusés à même la façade rougeâtre, la communauté apparaît dans sa vérité, soudée à la lueur des foyers. Au loin, les feux d'un campement Peul rappellent une errance lointaine.

❋ **ABOVE AND FACING PAGE** The *banco* (ochre clay) grain silos, thatched with millet straw, contain the food reserves of the Dogon. ❋ **OBEN UND RECHTE SEITE** In den Silos aus *banco* (ockerfarbenem Lehm), die mit Hirsestroh gedeckt sind, lagern die Dogon ihre Vorräte. ❋ **CI-DESSOUS ET PAGE DE DROITE** Les silos en *banco* (terre glaise ocre), coiffés de paille de mil, abritent les réserves des Dogons

✳ **ABOVE** The priest is a central figure in Dogon society, which believes that a dead man's soul can leave his body and become a threat to cosmic order. The shaman's role is to drive away spirits such as these and re-establish "peace". **PAGES 638–641** Scenes from daily life at Mopti and Djenné. ✳ **OBEN** Der Hohepriester spielt im Leben der Dogon eine bedeutende Rolle. Dieses Volk glaubt, dass sich der Geist nach dem Tod vom Körper löst und die kosmische Ordnung bedroht. Der Priester muss den Geist vertreiben und den »Frieden« wiederherstellen. **SEITEN 638–641** Alltagsszenen in Mopti und Djenné. ✳ **CI-DESSUS** Le féticheur est un personnage central de la société Dogon qui croit que l'esprit d'un mort quitte son corps et menace l'ordre cosmique. Son rôle est de chasser cet esprit afin de rétablir la «paix». **PAGES 638–641** Scènes de la vie quotidienne à Mopti et Djenné.

MALICK SIDIBE
Bamako

The world famous photographer Malick Sidibé has been working in the same Bamako studio for more than 40 years.

The Malick Studio in Bamako is a shrine for lovers of photography the world over. Now an African institution, Malick Sidibé owes his celebrity to his *Bamako by Night*, published in the 1960s.

At that time, he hung out in local nightclubs with his camera and gradually built up a portrait of a generation learning to love English pop music and sixties fashions, at the same time as it was tasting political independence for the first time. The years have passed, but Mali's national fascination with photography has endured. Now over 60, Malick Sidibé is busy training a new wave of younger photographers. The models still turn up at his studio looking their best, and in the streets outside photography is alive and well in many portrait studios and brightly-painted shops. Bamako, the capital of Mali, is Africa's darkroom; its reputation has grown apace with the development of its photography biennale. Where does all this interest originate? "In colonial times it was formally forbidden to take photographs outside," says the founder of the *Revue Noire*, Pascal Martin Saint Léon. "So all the photographers went back to their studios and worked exclusively with portraits." Anyone coming to Bamako will be amazed at the sheer celebrity of Mali's three leading practitioners of the art – Malick Sidibé, of course, but also Seydou Keita and Madou Traoré.

Zum Studio Malick nach Bamako pilgern Fotoamateure aus der ganzen Welt. Malick Sidibé, eine Institution auf dem Kontinent, verdankt seinen Ruhm den *Bamako by Night*-Fotos aus den 1960er Jahren.

Mit umgehängtem Fotoapparat strich er damals durch die Nachtlokale und zeichnete das Porträt einer Jugend, die gerade englische Popmusik, die Mode der Sixties und ihre eigene Unabhängigkeit entdeckte. Seitdem ist die Zeit auch an der von rotem Laterit geprägten Hauptstadt Malis nicht spurlos vorübergegangen, aber das allgemeine Interesse an der Fotografie ist nach wie vor sehr lebendig. Malick Sidibé, der Generationen von Fotografen geprägt hat, ist heute über 60, aber noch immer sitzen die Modelle herausgeputzt in seinem Studio. Draußen auf der Straße blüht das Geschäft mit der Fotografie in vielen Porträtstudios und kleinen bunten Läden. Seit eine Fotobiennale ins Leben gerufen wurde, ist das Ansehen Bamakos gestiegen. Wieso ist das Interesse so groß? »In der Kolonialzeit waren Außenaufnahmen offiziell verboten«, erklärt Pascal Martin Saint Léon, der Gründer der Revue Noire. »Deshalb haben sich viele Fotografen in ihre Studios zurückgezogen und die Kunst des Porträts gepflegt.« Die Popularität der drei großen malischen Fotografen Malick Sidibé, Seydou Keita und Madou Traoré ist in der Tat erstaunlich.

Le studio Malick, à Bamako, est un lieu de pèlerinage pour les amateurs de photographie du monde entier. Devenu une institution sur le continent, Malick Sidibé doit sa célébrité à son *Bamako by Night* des années 1960.

Appareil en bandoulière, il a traîné dans les boîtes de nuit et brossé le portrait d'une jeunesse qui découvrait la musique pop anglaise et la mode des sixties en même temps que l'indépendance. Les années ont passé dans la capitale du Mali imprégnée de latérite rouge, mais l'intérêt pour la photographie ne s'est jamais démenti. Aujourd'hui sexagénaire, Malick Sidibé forme les nouvelles générations de photographes. Dans son studio, les modèles portent toujours beau pour leur séance photo. À l'extérieur, dans les rues, la photographie foisonne à travers des studios de portraits et des petites boutiques colorées. Chambre noire de l'Afrique, la réputation de Bamako s'est amplifiée avec l'organisation d'une biennale de la photo. D'où vient un pareil intérêt? «Pendant la colonisation, il était formellement interdit de prendre des images en extérieur», précise le fondateur de la Revue Noire, Pascal Martin Saint Léon. «Du coup, les photographes se sont repliés dans leur studio pour travailler essentiellement le portrait.» En voyage à Bamako, le visiteur est en effet surpris par la renommée des trois grands photographes du Mali: Malick Sidibé, donc, mais aussi Seydou Keita et Madou Traoré.

※ **PREVIOUS PAGES, FACING PAGE AND ABOVE** Malick Sidibé records the affluent side of urban life (scooters, transistor radios, cigarettes, young people at parties in Bamako) as well as the ritual ceremonies of hunters from his own village in the bush. Apart from holding the presidency of the Mali Photographers' Group (GNPPM), he is known for his skill at repairing cameras. ※ **VORHERGEHENDE DOPPELSEITE, LINKE SEITE UND OBEN** Malick Sidibé setzt die »Reichtümer« des Stadtlebens in Szene: Mopeds, Radios, Zigaretten und die Feste der Jugendlichen in Bamako. Gleichzeitig bildet er aber auch die rituellen Jagdzeremonien in seinem Dorf im Busch ab. Als Präsident der Vereinigung malischer Fotografen, der GNPPM, ist er zudem für die sachgerechte Reparatur von Fotoapparaten bekannt. ※ **DOUBLE PAGE PRECEDENTE, PAGE DE GAUCHE ET CI-DESSUS** Malick Sidibé met en scène des «richesses» de la vie urbaine (mobylettes, transistors, cigarettes, fêtes des jeunes de Bamako), mais aussi les cérémonies rituelles des chasseurs dans son village de la brousse. Président du Groupement des Photographes maliens, le GNPPM, il est aussi connu pour ses qualités de réparateur d'appareils photographiques.

ATELIER
SOUS VERRE

TRANSPORT EN COMMUN

QUI
ETAIT de PASSAGE

?

GOREE
3250

GALERIE

ATELIER
ENFANTS

A.S.A.O.
GOREE ISLAND

A mid-19th century house where the melancholy past has been set aside to celebrate the art of the present.

This studio-house on an island off Dakar has the dual function of a guesthouse and a gallery for exhibitions. Its soft ochre walls try to make you forget the cruelty of an earlier time.

The place is like its owner, a businesswoman who has done many different things in her life; having begun as a costume designer for a great film maker, she went on to become a producer for another and today divides her time between Gorée and Paris, running a company which trades with Africa. On the island, it's Amy, a young Senegalese, who takes care of the three guest rooms. "This house is full of life – you really feel good here," says Valérie. The presence of Moussa Sakho's studio adds poetry and atmosphere, with young people assembling every Wednesday for art classes. As a small foundation, the guesthouse passes on its revenues to an association that helps the Gorée dispensary; it is also dedicated to helping French children in difficulty. Valérie was originally attracted to Senegal by its clothing and printed fabrics. Today her shop in the Marais quarter of Paris is filled with everyday art, in the form of tablecloths, cushions, plastic fans, basketwork trays and mahogany dishes.

Das Haus mit Atelier auf hoher See vor Dakar dient gleichzeitig als Ausstellungsort und als kleines Gästehaus. Beim Anblick der zart ockerfarbenen Wände könnte die grausame Vergangenheit der Insel, die ihre Wirkung bis in die heutige Zeit entfaltet, leicht in Vergessenheit geraten.

Das Haus entspricht seiner Besitzerin, einer Geschäftsfrau, die bereits die unterschiedlichsten Berufe ausgeübt hat. Sie arbeitete als Kostümbildnerin für einen berühmten Kinoregisseur, produzierte Filme und leitet zur Zeit, zwischen Paris und Gorée pendelnd, ein Unternehmen, das fairen Handel mit Afrika treibt. Auf der Insel selbst kümmert sich Amy, eine junge Senegalesin, um die drei Gästezimmer. »In der lebhaften Atmosphäre dieses Hauses fühlt man sich schnell wohl«, sinniert Valérie. Die Nähe zum Atelier des Künstlers Moussa Sakho bringt Poesie ins Haus, zumal er jeden Mittwoch die junge Generation der Insel das Malen lehrt. In Form einer kleineren Stiftung werden die Gewinne des Gästehauses an eine Gesellschaft weitergegeben, die einerseits das Gesundheitsamt unterstützt und andererseits französischen Kindern in Not unter die Arme greift. Ursprünglich waren es die Kleidung und bedruckte Stoffe, die Valérie in den Senegal brachten. Seitdem präsentiert sie in ihrem Pariser Geschäft im Marais auch kunsthandwerkliche Alltagsgegenstände wie Plastikfächer, geflochtene Tabletts, Mahagoni-Teller, Matten und Kissen.

Cette maison-atelier au large de Dakar sert à la fois de chambre d'hôtes et de lieu d'exposition. Ses murs ocre et tendres tentent de faire oublier la cruauté d'un passé bien présent encore.

L'habitation est à l'image de sa propriétaire, une femme d'affaires qui croise les genres, un temps costumière pour un grand cinéaste, productrice à un autre et aujourd'hui, entre Gorée et Paris, à la tête d'une société qui fait du commerce avec l'Afrique sans omettre de lui tendre la main. Sur l'île, c'est Amy, une jeune Sénégalaise, qui veille sur les trois chambres d'hôtes. «On se sent bien dans cette maison très vivante», médite Valérie. La présence de l'atelier de Moussa Sakho ajoute de la poésie et de l'ambiance: les jeunes aiment s'y retrouver chaque mercredi pour des cours de peinture. Petite fondation, la chambre d'hôtes redistribue ses revenus à une association qui vient en aide au dispensaire de Gorée mais est aussi consacrée à l'accueil d'enfants français en difficulté. À l'origine, Valérie fut attirée au Sénégal par les vêtements et les pagnes imprimés. Sa boutique parisienne du Marais s'ouvre désormais à l'art du quotidien sous la forme d'éventails en plastique, de plateaux de vannerie, d'assiettes en acajou, de nappes et de coussins.

❊ **FACING PAGE** Portait of Moussa Sakho, whose garden studio enlivens Valérie's establishment. **LEFT AND ABOVE** Fifteen minutes by by boat from Dakar, the house welcomes both guests and exhibitions. ❊ **LINKE SEITE** Porträt Moussa Sakhos, dessen Atelier im Garten des Hauses liegt. **LINKS UND OBEN** Eine Fähre bringt die Hotelgäste innerhalb einer Viertelstunde von Dakar zu Valéries Haus, in dem auch Ausstellungen gezeigt werden. ❊ **PAGE DE GAUCHE** Portrait de Moussa Sakho dont l'atelier, situé dans le jardin de la maison anime celle-ci. **A GAUCHE ET CI-DESSUS** À un quart d'heure en chaloupe de Dakar, cette maison accueille à la fois des hôtes et des expositions.

❋ **BELOW** Hidden by its screen of greenery, the house lives cheek by jowl with nature, inside and out. **FACING PAGE** Portraits on glass are a prominent feature of the simply renovated kitchen, offsetting the green and grey colour scheme and the plump-pea patterns on the walls. ❋ **UNTEN** Das innen und außen üppig geschmückte Haus liegt beinahe verborgen in der tropischen Pflanzenwelt. **RECHTE SEITE** Porträts in der Technik der Hinterglasmalerei prägen die unaufwändig renovierte Küche und betonen die grün-weiß getüpfelten Wände mit dem Erbsenmuster, das die üppige Vegetation vor der Tür aufgreift. ❋ **CI-DESSOUS** Dissimulée par un écrin de verdure, la maison se vit en intérieur comme en extérieur. **PAGE DE DROITE** Les portraits sous-verre dominent une cuisine simplement rénovée et mettent en valeur ce parti pris de vert et blanc accentué par les motifs de gros pois qui couvrent les murs, rappelant ainsi la végétation environnante.

❋ **FACING PAGE** A yellow room, designed for a child. The wooden mezzanine lends a Swiss Family Robinson air, with its salvaged furniture painted yellow like the sunshine. **ABOVE** Here and there, objects made by the island's craftsmen. A few painted wooden boats have pride of place on the old kitchen side-board, which has been refreshed with a coat of yellow-gold paint. ❋ **LINKE SEITE** Gelb ist die dominierende Farbe im Kinderzimmer. Das Mezzanin aus Holz erinnert stark an eine Hütte à la Robinson. Die sonnengelb gestrichenen schlichten Möbel wurden wieder aufgearbeitet. **OBEN** Hier und da scheint das Kunsthandwerk der Insulaner auf. Auf einer mit Gelb aufgefrischten Kommode in der Küche steht eine Sammlung bemalter Holzboote. ❋ **PAGE DE GAUCHE** Dans la chambre d'enfant, le jaune domine. La mezzanine en bois donne un aspect très cabane de Robinson avec ces meubles de récupération simplement peints couleur de soleil. **CI DESSUS** Ici et là, les objets rappellent le travail des artisans de l'île. Quelques bateaux de bois peint se profilent sur une vieille commode de cuisine rafraîchie de jaune d'or.

Marie-Jose Crespin

Goree Island

A houseful of treasures: a jewellery designer's extraordinary collection of antiques on Gorée.

This 18th century colonial house on the ramparts of Gorée was formerly the residence of a slave trader. Fronting the sea, hidden by a tangle of bonzai baobabs, bougainvilleas and mangoes, it seems to have forgotten everything: in the spacious rooms protected from the heat of the sun by pierced shutters, no trace remains of the tragic past.

On the contrary, the décor here is a joyful celebration of cross-cultural art, a riot of sculptures and African masks. The cement tile floors, the furniture fashioned from various tropical woods and the bright fabrics everywhere testify to an *art de vivre* bursting at the seams with gaiety and colour. The terrace serves as a living room, overlooking an enchanted garden dotted with 1930s *iroko* French chairs. Inside the house, the collection of ethnic objects brings together pieces from Black Africa, North Africa, Asia Minor and south America, with a few touches of modernity supplied here and there by contemporary objects. With its furniture, its lacquered doors and its patchwork of earthenware tiles, the kitchen seems locked in the 1950s. Actually it was at that time that the father of Marie-José Crespin bought the house; Marie-José played here as a child. And the house has been steadily enriched ever since, with the priceless gifts of mixture and variety.

In früheren Zeiten diente das im 18. Jahrhundert erbaute Kolonialhaus an der Stadtmauer Sklavenhändlern als Wohnhaus. Die Erinnerung ist in den Mauern des Hauses gespeichert, das mit Blick aufs Meer in einem Dschungel von Bonsai-Affenbrotbäumen, Bougainvillea und Mangobäumen steht.

In den großen Zimmern mit durchbrochenen Klappläden zum Schutz gegen die Sonne erinnert dagegen nichts mehr an die tragische Vergangenheit. Die Inneneinrichtung preist im Gegenteil, wie zur Ehrenrettung der Geschichte, die Kultur der Rassenmischung durch die ausgestellten afrikanischen Skulpturen und Masken. Eine Lebenskunst voller Fröhlichkeit und Farbe drückt sich in den gekachelten Böden, Möbeln aus exotischen Hölzern und leuchtend bunten Stoffen aus. Wie ein zusätzliches Zimmer ragt die Terrasse in den Garten hinaus – die französischen 1930er-Jahre-Stühle aus Irokoholz sind schlicht bezaubernd. Im Haus selbst wurden in einer Sammlung ethnischer Kostbarkeiten Objekte aus Schwarzafrika, Nordafrika, Kleinasien und Südamerika kombiniert. Auch die zeitgenössische Kunst ist mit mehreren Werken vertreten. Die Küche, eingerichtet mit lackierten Türen, Emailfliesen und altmodischen Möbeln, scheint in den 1950er Jahren stehen geblieben zu sein. In jener Zeit hat Marie-José Crespins Vater das Haus auch gekauft. Die Dame des Hauses hat schon als Kind hier gespielt – seitdem ist das Haus um vieles reicher geworden, vor allem aber wird hier der kulturellen und ethnischen Vielfalt Raum gegeben.

Sur les remparts de Gorée, cette maison coloniale du 18e siècle servait autrefois d'habitation aux commerçants de la pire espèce: les négriers. Face à la mer, dissimulée par une jungle de baobabs-bonzaïs, de bougainvilliers et de manguiers, les murs ont désormais la mémoire qui flanche.

Dans les grandes pièces abritées du soleil par des persiennes ajourées, aucune trace ne subsiste de ce passé tragique. Au contraire, bras d'honneur à l'histoire, la décoration célèbre une culture métissée à travers ses sculptures et ses masques africains. Sols en carreaux de ciment, meubles en bois exotiques et tissus lumineux témoignent d'un art de vivre plein de gaieté et de couleurs. Véritable pièce à vivre, la terrasse qui surplombe le jardin enchante d'emblée avec ses chaises françaises des années 1930 en bois d'iroko. À l'intérieur de la maison, la collection d'objets ethniques marie des pièces d'Afrique noire, d'Afrique du Nord, d'Asie mineure et d'Amérique du Sud. Quelques créations contemporaines posées ici et là modernisent l'ensemble. Avec son mobilier, ses portes laquées et ses carreaux de faïence en patchworks, la cuisine semble figée dans les années 1950. C'est en effet à cette époque que le père de Marie-José Crespin s'est porté acquéreur des lieux. Enfant, la maîtresse de maison y gambadait. Depuis, la maison s'est enrichie d'un des biens les plus précieux: le métissage.

✳ **ABOVE** In the owner's study, objects found in Dakar, Mopti, Marrakesh and Lagos. The Mauritanian table was originally a baggage frame used for camels. ✳ **OBEN** Im Büro bewahrt die Dame des Hauses Objekte aus Dakar, Mopti, Marrakesch und Lagos auf. Der mauretanische Tisch war früher ein »Gepäckbock« für Dromedare. ✳ **CI-DESSUS** Dans le bureau de la propriétaire, des objets trouvés à Dakar, Mopti, Marrakech ou Lagos. La table mauritanienne est à l'origine un «porte-bagages» que l'on pose sur le dos des dromadaires.

NOMADS
Mauritania

For the desert conditions in which they live,
the nomads have never found anything to compare with their *khaimas* (Moorish tents).

The Sahara – a place of gravelly plains, superheated rocks and sand dunes. The men who live here have to face the most extreme conditions. Their camp is invariably the focus of a loose brotherhood. Each member of the group has his *khaima*, a tent of rectangular canvas.

Its structure consists of two V-shaped masts, joined at the top by a wooden crosspiece. The whole assembly is held down by ropes and small pegs driven in at each corner of the fabric. On the sides, geometrical motifs proclaim the identity of the occupants, while inside, piles of carpets insulate against the sand. In one corner, a kind of baggage frame contains books, clothes, and food. By definition, the *khaima* is expected to follow the rhythm of the seasons, or more precisely those of the rains, along a north-south nomadic axis which determines the migration of camels and livestock. The nomads travel with their families, of course, but the notion of hospitality is anchored deep in their tradition. Any traveller who happens on an encampment is systematically invited to take tea – three cups, no less – according to the ancient ritual. Frequently he receives gifts made by the nomads themselves; and if night falls, he will certainly be invited to sleep on a mat under the canvas.

Sahara. Steinige Ebenen, glühend heiße Felsen und Sanddünen. Die Menschen leben unter extremen Bedingungen. In den Lagern leben häufig erweiterte Großfamilien, von denen jede ihr eigenes *khaïma*, ein rechteckiges Zelt aus Tuch hat.

Zwei sich verjüngende Zeltmasten bilden ein umgekehrtes V und werden in der Spitze mit einem Stück Holz zusammengehalten. Vier kleine Zeltpflöcke in den Ecken sowie Seile sichern die Konstruktion. Geometrische Muster auf den Zeltwänden verweisen auf die Stammeszugehörigkeit. Auf der Erde werden Teppiche zum Schutz gegen den Sand ausgebreitet. In einer Ecke steht etwas erhöht auf einem »Gepäckbock« eine Truhe mit Büchern, Kleidung und Lebensmitteln. Das *khaïma* passt sich dem Rhythmus der Jahreszeiten an, besser gesagt den Regenzeiten. So zieht sich, bedingt durch die Wanderungen der Dromedar- und Viehherden, eine Nord-Süd-Achse des Nomadentums durch das Land. Die Gastfreundschaft ist in der Tradition der Nomaden fest verankert. Reisende, die zufällig ein Lager entdecken, werden stets zum Tee eingeladen, der dem Brauch gemäß dreimal aufgegossen wird. Häufig werden ihnen auch kunsthandwerkliche Objekte angeboten. Wenn es in der Wüste dämmert, werden sie eingeladen, auf einer Matte zu schlafen. Für die Dauer einer Nacht kann man sich dann von der modernen Welt verabschieden.

Sahara. Plaines caillouteuses, rochers surchauffés et dunes de sable. L'homme vit ici dans des conditions extrêmes. Son campement abrite le plus souvent une fratrie élargie. À chacun sa *khaïna*, cette tente de toile en rectangle.

Deux mâts en V renversés, effilés et réunis au sommet par une pièce en bois. Des petits piquets plantés aux quatre coins et des cordages maintiennent l'ensemble. Sur les parois, des motifs géométriques indiquent l'identité tribale. Voilà pour la «charpente». Sur le sol, les tapis étalés isolent du sable. Dans un coin, une sorte de porte-bagages surélève le coffre qui contient les livres, les vêtements et la nourriture. Par définition, la *khaïna* est appelée à suivre le rythme des saisons, ou plus exactement celle des pluies, en un axe de nomadisation nord-sud qui détermine les migrations des troupeaux de dromadaires et de bétail. On vit en famille, certes, mais la notion d'hospitalité est ancrée au plus profond de la tradition nomade. Le voyageur qui découvre par hasard un campement est systématiquement invité à savourer un thé, en trois fois selon le rituel. Souvent, on lui propose des objets artisanaux. Si la nuit tombe sur le désert, il est invité à dormir sur une natte. Alors, l'espace d'une nuit, il dit adieu au monde moderne.

✳ **BELOW** In the orange-tinted desert, the white canvas *khaimas* follow the rhythm of the rains, migrating alongside their owners' livestock. **FACING PAGE** The baggage frame with its coloured legs protects cushions, clothes and food from the driving sand. **FOLLOWING PAGES** The canvas sides of the tent are decorated with multicolored geometrical patterns that repeat the tribal motif sewn into the top of the tent. ✳ **UNTEN** In der orangefarbenen Wüste folgen die Nomaden mit ihrer *khaïma* aus weißem Tuch dem Rhythmus der Regenzeiten, damit das Vieh genügend zu Fressen bekommt. **RECHTE SEITE** Der »Gepäckbock« mit den bunten Beinen schützt Kissen, Kleidung und Lebensmittel vor Sand. **FOLGENDE DOPPELSEITE** Bunte geometrische Zeichen zieren die Zeltwand. Sie nehmen das auf die Zeltspitze genähte Stammesmuster wieder auf. ✳ **CI-DESSOUS** Dans le désert orange, les *khaïma* en toile blanche suivent le rythme de la pluie pour les migrations du bétail. **PAGE DE DROITE** Le porte-bagages aux pieds colorés protège du sable les coussins, les vêtements, mais aussi la nourriture. **DOUBLE PAGE SUIVANTE** La paroi de toile est décorée de signes géométriques multicolores qui rappellent le motif tribal cousu au sommet de la tente.

✳ **ABOVE** Drought, industrialization and various forms of modernization in their country have brought the nomads closer to the main roads. Dwellings that serve as shops and store-houses have been set up close to the tents. ✳ **OBEN** Wegen der Trockenheit sowie der Industrialisierung und anderen Ausprägungen der Modernisierung des Landes zieht es viele Nomaden in die Nähe der Straßen. Die Bretterbuden, die als Läden und Lagerstätten dienen, werden neben den Zelten errichtet. ✳ **CI-DESSUS** La sécheresse, l'industrialisation et les diverses formes de modernisation du pays ont fait affluer de nombreux nomades près des routes. Les cabanes, qui servent à la fois de boutiques et de lieux de stockage, ont été installées à proximité des tentes.

OUALATA

Mauritania

This city, which formerly lay at a junction of the old caravan routes, still has a secret language of its own.

From the Middle Ages to the end of the 18th century, Oualata lived contentedly from the caravans of Black Africa bringing gold from Bambuk and salt from Idjil, as well as those of Morocco laden with pottery, scents and jewellery.

Oualata, at "the edge of eternity", was only rivalled by Timbuktu. Today, in its sand-choked alleys, there are few traces of the heroic past, when sages came to study and were given free bed and board by the townspeople. There's little left, indeed, except the arabesques, restored to contemporary taste in the 1980s by one of the town's notables. Finger-painted on walls rendered with red clay (a mixture of sand and lime), these frescoes cover façades, door frames and window frames. Since the Koran forbade the representation of human beings, their decorative conventions describe the various parts of the body by way of symbols. Very present in courtyards, they are also to be found in the interiors of two-storey Sudanese style houses. Typically, the buildings consist of long, parallel rooms or else single, much larger spaces with a central pillar supporting the beams. There are recesses, too, close to the sleeping mats, where owners display their books and oil lamps. These symbolize the greatest treasures of Oualata today, namely light and knowledge.

Vom Mittelalter bis ins 18. Jahrhundert führte Oualata ein begünstigtes Dasein, denn hier machten die Karawanen aus Schwarzafrika Station, die Gold aus den Bambouk-Bergen und Salz vom Kedia d'Idjil mitführten. Die Karawanen aus Marokko dagegen waren mit Tonwaren, Parfüm und Schmuck beladen.

Oualata, »das Gestade der Ewigkeit«, hatte nur einen einzigen Rivalen: Timbuktu. Von diesen Zeiten der Blüte, als Gelehrte noch freie Kost und Logis hatten, um in Ruhe studieren zu können, ist in den Gassen, die von der gefräßigen Wüste mit Sand zugeschüttet werden, nicht mehr viel zu sehen. Übrig geblieben sind höchstens die Arabesken, die ein Notabler der Stadt im Zeitgeschmack der 1980er Jahre hat instand setzen lassen. Die Fingermalerei (in einer Mischung aus Sand und Kalk) auf den mit rotem Lehm verputzten Wänden ziert die Fassaden sowie die Tür- und Fensterumrahmungen. Da der Koran die Darstellung von Menschen verbot, illustrierte diese ornamentale Kunst die verschiedenen Körperteile symbolisch. Die verschwenderischen Muster in den Innenhöfen finden sich auch im Innern der ein- bis zweistöckigen Häuser im sudanesischen Stil. Am Eingang liegen oft längliche, parallel angeordnete Zimmer, an die sich ein großer Raum mit einem stützenden Mittelpfeiler anschließt. In den Nischen über den Schlafmatten stellen die Bewohner Bücher oder Öllampen zur Schau. Das Licht und das überlieferte Wissen sind die einzigen Schätze, die Oualata geblieben sind.

Du Moyen-Âge à la fin du 18e siècle, Oualata vivait heureuse en accueillant les caravanes d'Afrique noire chargées d'or du Bambouk, de sel d'Idjil, ou celles du Maroc bourrées de poteries, de parfums et de bijoux.

Oualata, «le rivage de l'éternité», n'avait que Tombouctou pour rivale. Aujourd'hui, dans les ruelles ensablées par un désert vorace, peu de traces sont encore visibles de ces temps héroïques où les érudits, hébergés et nourris gratuitement, pouvaient y étudier librement. Ne subsistent guère que ces arabesques remises au goût du jour par un notable de la ville au début des années 1980. Peintes au doigt sur des murs enduits d'argile rouge (un mélange de sable et de chaux), ces fresques posées à plat ornent les façades, les tours de portes et de fenêtres. Le Coran interdisant la représentation des êtres humains, cet art décoratif décrit de manière symbolique des parties du corps. Très présents dans les cours, les motifs se déploient également dans les intérieurs des maisons à étage de style soudanien. Au seuil des demeures, on découvre tantôt des pièces longues et parallèles, tantôt une salle plus vaste dont le pilier central supporte la charpente. Dans les niches, à proximité des nattes pour dormir, les propriétaires mettent en valeur des livres ou des lampes à huile. Les seuls trésors de Oualata: la lumière et la connaissance.

✳ **FACING PAGE AND ABOVE** Oualata's rose patterns are known all over the world, but the town's interiors are almost entirely devoid of furniture. The study of the Koranic texts appears to be its people's only source of wealth. ✳ **LINKE SEITE UND OBEN** Die Bilder der Rosettenornamentik von Oualata gingen um die Welt, doch in den Häusern stehen nur wenige Möbel. Das Studium der Koransuren ist scheinbar der einzige Reichtum der Einwohner. ✳ **PAGE DE GAUCHE ET CI-DESSUS** Si les images des rosaces d'Oualata ont fait le tour du monde, les intérieurs sont presque dénués de mobilier. L'étude des textes coraniques semble être la seule richesse des habitants.

✳ **ABOVE** The motif of the "mother's thigh" is to be found in every house. This symbol of fertility, representing a part of the human thigh, is repeated in an infinite variety of ways. ✳ **OBEN** In allen Häusern findet sich das Motiv »Mutter mit Schenkeln«, ein Fruchtbarkeitssymbol, das einen Teil des Schenkels in vielen künstlerischen Variationen darbietet. ✳ **CI-DESSOUS** Dans chaque maison, on retrouve le motif de la «mère aux cuisses», symbole de fécondité représentant une partie de la cuisse répétée en combinaisons infinies.

※ **ABOVE** Frescoes like these can be seen on door frames, façades and window frames all over Oualata. Here they have been finger-painted on the red clay walls of this little girl's house. ※ **OBEN** Das kleine Mädchen hat mit Fingermalerei die roten Lehmwände des Hauses verziert. Überall in Oualata sind die Fassaden und die Tür- und Fensterumrahmungen opulent geschmückt. ※ **CI-DESSUS** Peintes au doigt sur les murs d'argile rouge de la maison de cette petite fille, les fresques ornent ici comme partout dans Oualata les façades, les tours de portes et de fenêtres.

❋ **PRECEDING DOUBLE PAGE** Oualata's mural decorations bear witness to the town's prosperity in the times when caravans regularly passed through. **ABOVE** Oualata, which lies away from the roads, has remained a town of cults and cultures in which scholars still dedicate their lives to reading the Koran. ❋ **VORHERGEHENDE DOPPELSEITE** Die Wandmalereien bezeugen den Wohlstand der Stadt Oualata zur Zeit der Karawanen. **OBEN** Oualata, das abseits der Straßen liegt, ist eine Stadt des Kultes und der Kultur geblieben, in der bis heute gelehrte Männer ihr Leben dem Koranstudium weihen. ❋ **DOUBLE PAGE PRECEDENTE** Les décors muraux sont les témoins de la prospérité d'Oualata à l'époque des caravanes. **CI-DESSUS** À l'écart des routes, Oualata reste une ville de culte et de culture où des hommes consacrent leur existence à l'étude des textes coraniques.

✳ **ABOVE** This child's home is typical of Oualata, with long, parallel rooms and a larger main room with a central pillar to hold up the beams. In the evening, lanterns are placed in the niches. ✳ **OBEN** Das Kind auf der Schwelle betrachtet die charakteristische Inneneinrichtung eines Hauses in Oualata, das aus kleinen länglichen, parallel angeordneten Zimmern und einem größeren Raum mit einem zentralen Stützpfeiler besteht. Abends leuchten die Laternen in den Nischen. ✳ **CI-DESSUS** Au seuil de sa demeure, cet enfant contemple un intérieur typique de Oualata fait de petites pièces longues et parallèles et d'une salle plus vaste dont le pilier central supporte la charpente. Le soir les niches s'emplissent de lanternes.

SONINKE PEOPLE
SELIBABI REGION

The interior of these houses is characterized by a play of geometrical lines and beautiful figurative effects.

The entrance is decorated with flat stones in zigzag patterns. Niches set into the walls serve as shelves, but one scarcely notices them, so stunning are the colours all around. Beyond the wooden doors with their padlocks, decorative motifs literally invade the interior.

Red, brown, blue, grey or yellow, the painters of these rooms have created their composite décor with skills passed down through many generations. The original motifs of this region to the north of the town of Sélibabi were painted in mud with natural oxides. Today the women use more robust commercial paints. Naturally enough, their work has spiritual significance, emphasising the original relationship between man and his environment. Astonishingly, only one room in the house is brightened in this way with geometrical designs, and that space is the women's province as well as the focus of daily life, since all the cooking and other domestic tasks are carried out there. Photos, advertisements for cigarettes (Mauritanians smoke like chimneys) and plastic "made in China" cooking utensils serve as decorative elements. Also from the Middle Kingdom are the dishes reserved for ceremonial occasions, which hang on the walls above the woven mats.

Am Eingang bilden flache im Zickzack angeordnete Steine ein Wabenmuster. Die Mauernischen dienen als Regale, beeindrucken aber vor allem durch ihr Farbenspiel. Hinter den Holztüren mit Vorhängeschloss überziehen unzählige farbige Muster das Hausinnere.

Die überlieferte Malerei in den Farben Rot, Braun, Blau, Grau und Gelb schafft ein Interieur nach altem Vorbild. Früher wurden im Norden der Stadt Sélibabi Erdfarben mit natürlichen Oxiden verwandt. Heute bevorzugen die Frauen haltbare Industriefarben. Die spirituelle Bedeutung der Ornamentik weist auf eine ursprüngliche Verbindung zwischen den Menschen und ihrer Umwelt hin. Erstaunlicherweise gibt es aber nur einen Raum, in dem dieses Spiel mit geometrischen Formen zum Tragen kommt, nämlich dort, wo die Frauen ihren alltäglichen Aufgaben nachkommen. Sie sind für Küche und Haushalt zuständig. Die Plakate mit Zigarettenwerbung (der Anteil der Raucher in diesem Land ist unglaublich hoch) unter den Fotos sowie Küchenutensilien aus buntem Plastik »Made in China« dienen ebenfalls der Dekoration. Weiter oben zieren die für Zeremonien reservierten Teller, die ebenfalls aus dem Reich der Mitte stammen, die Wände über den Webmatten. Das hat etwas vom »Global Village«, oder?

L'entrée est ornée de décors de pierres plates en zigzag formant des alvéoles. Des niches, créées à même le mur, servent d'étagères, mais c'est à peine si on les remarque, tant le regard est attiré par le jeu des couleurs. Derrière les portes en bois fermées par un cadenas, des motifs envahissent l'intérieur.

Rouges, brunes, bleues, grises ou jaunes, les peintures créent le décor en un savoir-faire ancestral. À l'origine, dans cette région située au nord de la ville de Sélibabi, les motifs étaient peints à la boue avec des oxydes naturels. Aujourd'hui, les femmes emploient des peintures du commerce qui résistent mieux à l'usure du temps. Naturellement, ces ornements ont une signification spirituelle, soulignant l'obéissance à une relation originelle entre l'homme et son environnement. Étonnamment, seule une pièce de la maison est ainsi animée par ce jeu de lignes géométriques: l'espace dévolu aux femmes, celui de la vie quotidienne aussi puisque la cuisine et les taches ménagères leur sont réservées. Sous des photos, des publicités pour des marques de cigarettes (le pourcentage de fumeurs est hallucinant dans ce pays) et des ustensiles de cuisine en plastique coloré «made in China» servent également d'éléments de décoration. En hauteur, toujours en provenance de l'Empire du Milieu, les plats réservés aux cérémonies couvrent les murs au-dessus de nattes tissées. Vous avez dit Global Village?

✳ **ABOVE** Soninke villagers gather to talk at the end of the day. **FACING PAGE** The entrance to an ochre-clay house. ✳ **OBEN** Die Dorfbewohner vom Volk der Soninke treffen sich abends zum Plausch. **RECHTE SEITE** Der Eingang eines ockerfarbenen Lehmhauses. ✳ **CI-DESSUS** Les villageois Soninké se retrouvent en fin de journée pour discuter. **PAGE DE DROITE** Entrée d'une maison en terre ocre.

❋ **FACING PAGE** Behind the wooden doors with their padlocks, the colour seems to flow away in wavelets. **ABOVE** A cameo of ochres and browns covers this shared room with its harmoniously blended squares, triangles and diamond shapes. The absence of any kind of furniture emphasizes the sheer vigour of the wall paintings. ❋ **LINKE SEITE** Hinter den mit Vorhängeschlössern versehenen Holztüren überlagern sich die Farben im Wellenmuster. **OBEN** Die ockerfarbene und braune Malerei im Gemeinschaftsraum harmoniert mit den quadratischen, dreieckigen und rautenförmigen Mustern an den Wänden. Die Wirkung der Wandmalerei wird noch dadurch verstärkt, dass die Räume nicht möbliert sind. ❋ **PAGE DE GAUCHE** Derrière les portes en bois fermées par un cadenas, les couleurs se chevauchent en vaguelettes. **CI-DESSUS** Camaïeu d'ocre et de bruns dans cette pièce commune où, à même les murs, les formes carrées, triangulaires ou en losanges s'épousent harmonieusement. L'absence de mobilier renforce encore la vigueur de ces peintures murales.

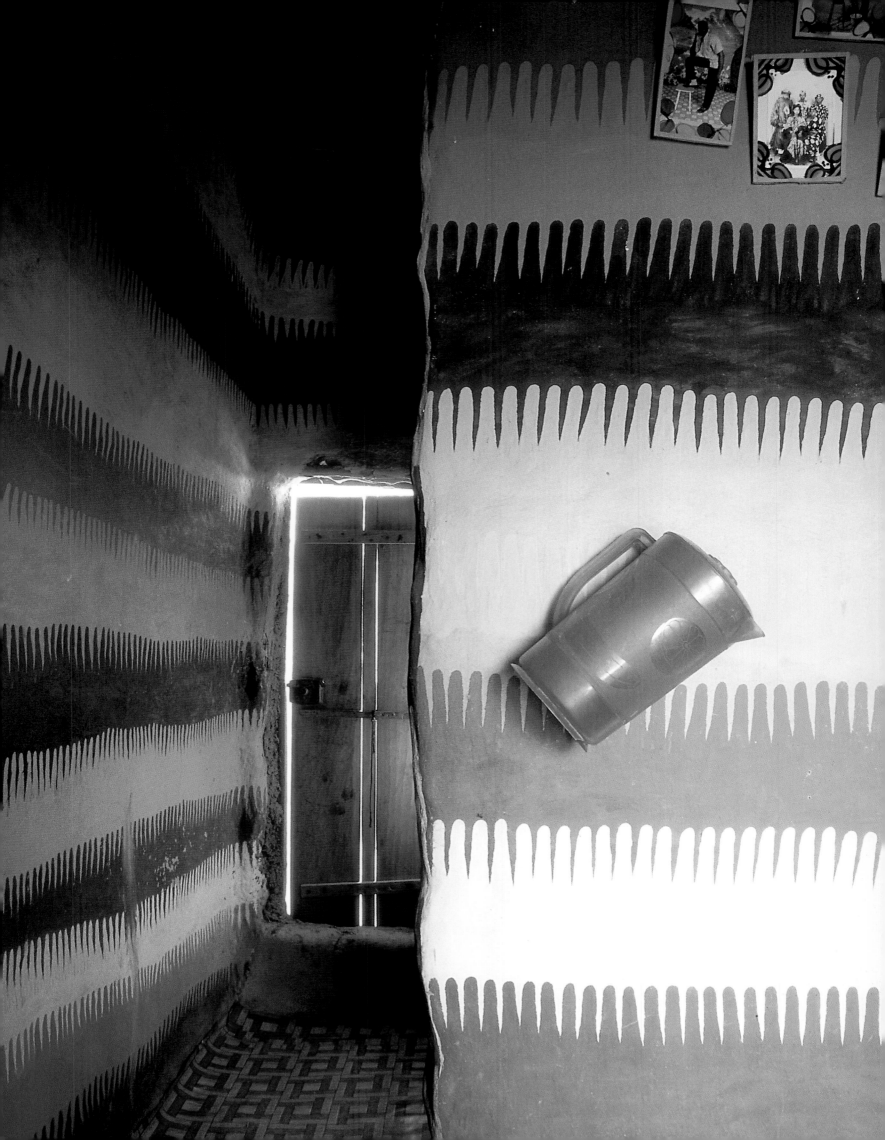

Souvenir de Mano Gandega Lan '20

ACKNOWLEDGEMENTS

The photographer would like to thank everyone who let her into their homes and their lives, and all those along the way who have given their time, advice and encouragement. Many thanks to all the friends who offered hospitality to her during her many travels through Africa. Without this support the book would have been impossible.

MANY THANKS TO:

Aboudramane, Asdine Alaia, Romi Amancha, Alexandra d'Arnoux, Marie Aimée, George Arquier, Ghislaine Bavoillot, Marie-Claude Beaux, Catherine Beracassat, John Erik Berganus, Claire Bergeaud, Roussel Bernard, Jean Pascal Billaud, Françoise Blanc, Marie-Claire Blanckaerdt, Anna Bonde, Ann Bony, Christian Bouillet, Gösta Classon, Marita Coustet, Antoine and Marie Odile Debary, Jean Detière, Françoise Dorget, Rosemarie and Alan Dufour, Jérôme Dumoulin, Men Durieux, Renate Gallois Montbrun, Jean Louis Geizer, Jean Pierre Godeaut, Christine Grange-Bary, Jean Jartier, Hélène Joubert, Yves Jacques Kabasso, Matheo Kries, Patricia Laigneau, Jancy Lamom, Juan Lazzaro, Bruno de Laubadère, Étienne le Roy, Romi Loch-Davis, Aline Luque, André Magnin, Christiane Marquesi, Jean Hubert Martin, Steven R. Mendelson, Marion Meyer, Donald Namekomg, Mai Olivier, Karen Petrossian, Pierre Peyrol, Hélène Pour, Andrée Putman, Michel Reilhac, Mirella Ricciardi, Nicole Richy, Ute Rohrbeck, Sunil Sehti, Marie Paul Serre, Philippe Sculliet, Luc Svetchine, Hervé Tchakaloff, Frédérique Thomas, Rixa von Treuenfels, Alexander von Vegesack, Martin Veith, Christoph von Weyhe, Bernard Wuermser.

IN MOROCCO THANKS TO:

Belkahia, Abdellatif Ait Benabdallah, Charles Chauliaguet, Feisal Cherradi, Françoise Dorget, Fabrice and Marcia Dubois La Chartre, Xavier Guerrand-Hermès, Amine Kabbaj, Joël Martial, Eli Moujhal, Carla and Franca Sozzani, Quentin Wilbaux.

IN TUNISIA THANKS TO:

Jellal Ben Abdallah, Tarak and M'na Benmilled, Ahmed Djellouli, Nicolas Feuillate, Ali Ben Khalifaa, Ali Ben Khazifa, Christophe Kicherer, Mme Jacques Lanxade, Yves Marbrier, Jean-Pierre and Zeineb Marcie-Riviere, Leila Mencharie, Pierre Pes, Sadar and Zaina Sfar, Toni Facelli Sensi, Fatma and Kilani Ben Slimane.

IN EGYPT THANKS TO:

Nagib Abdallah, Zeina Aboukheir, Loulia Damerji, Nagiba Demergé, Alain Fouquet, Titi Grace, Mustafa al Gundi, Maryse Helal, Amr Khalil, Christian Louboutin, Amina and Raouf Mishriki, Mounir and Leila Neamautalla, Jaqueline and Farouk Yunes, Vincent Grimaud and Danilles Wosny.

IN KENYA AND TANZANIA THANKS TO:

Dr. Abungu, Rick and Bryony Anderson, Colette Belle, Bruno Brighetti, Yago Casado, Nani Croze, Dorothee and Michael Cunningham-Reid, Alan Donovan, Oria and Iain Douglas-Hamilton, Frédérique Scholl and Viviana Gonzales, Ariel Gramatidis, Mahmud Janmohamed, Ramesh N. Jobaputra, Anthony Kigondu, Sharma Lanina, Shufaa Lukoo, Mr Makweki, John Mohamed, Katharina Schnezer and Hermann Stucki, Emerson Skeens, Anita and Bernard Spoerri, Armando Tanzini, Anna and Tonio Trezebinski, Bongi Zulu, J.P. Zwager.

IN THE SEYCHELLES AND MAURITIUS THANKS TO:

Corinne Asselin, Jean Barbier, Donna Bernard, Joseph Chassagne, Thierry Chokaloff, Yann Conacaud, Jacques Cuiten, Salim Currimjee, Patrice Binet Descamps, Jacques Duret, Rashio Ghanty, Catherine Gris, Edwige and François de Grivel, François Henquet, Marie-Ann Hodoul, Arnaud Lagesse, Henriette Lagesse, Martine Lagesse, Jean François Koenig, Gerard Maillot, Jacqui de Maroussem, Peter and Ros Metcalf, Jaqueline Oireaux, Marie Pierre Potier, Silvie Reol, Deborah Roubane, Pierre and Dorothea Roubanne, Pascale Vallet, Alain Marcel Vauthier, Bernard le Venneur.

IN SOUTH AFRICA THANKS TO:

Kim Appelby, G.N. Bacon, Barbara Bailey, Beezy Bailey, Tracy Bamber, Willie Bester, Kathrine Blondeau, John and Cheryl Burgess, Sumien Brink, Norman and Janette Catherine, Christa and Michael Clark, John Clark, Adrienne Cohen, Brigitte Cross, Mike Donkin and Coenie Visser, Ian Douglas, Paul Duncan, Marmel Dutoit, Darryl and Coral Evans, Ekim Falconer, Marianne Fassler, Geordi and Boyd Fergusson, Lynne Fraser, Christophe Gallut, Gianna Ghersi, Monica Graaff, Monika Graeff, Jonathan Green and Marina Pretorius, Louise Hennigs, Nathalie Jacobson, Sue Jackson, Ian Johnson, Craig Kaplan, Joseph Kerhman, Terence Joseph Kerham, Anthony Kigondu, Barbara King, Malcolm Kluk, Julia Krone, Jean-Marc Lederman, Jenny and Desmond Loch-Davies, Pierre Lombart, Tracy Rushmere and Peter Maltbie, Trish Marshall, Annemarie Meintjies, A.C. van der Menne, Anja van der Merewe, Esther Mahlangu, Liz Morris, Hannes Myburgh, V.E. Mwabeni, Mankayi Ncediswa, Daku Sampi Nggobe, Yvonne Ntabeni, Vicky Ntozini, Cathy O'Clery, Anton Oosthuizen, Kate Otten, Sandy Ovenstone, Craig Port, Carla Pretorius, Silvio Rech and Lesley Carstens, Reyno, Peter Rich, Lew Rood, Shahn and Alice Rowe, Mandy St. Clair, Richard Santer, Bernardo James Smith, Charles Smith, Olivier Souchon, Gillian Stoeltzman, J.G.J. du Toit, Nonkosi Tshingana, Jeanie Warren, Ralph Weiden, Grant White, Ted Williams, Greg Wright.

In Benin, Togo, Ghana, Burkina Faso thanks to:

Georges Adeagbo, Sana Allou, Ghislain F. do Behanzin, Jean-Pierre Clain, Anicet Dakpogan, Iamett-Damien, Youle Dapour, Gabin Djimasse, Micheline Egoumlety, Dominique Hazoume, Romuald Hazoume, Sabine Hentzsch, Andre Joly, Baba Keita, Konnonj, Joseph Kpobly, Bayeti Ndah, Palenkite Noufe, Nat Nunoo-Amarteifio, Abougé Inoussé Ouele, Hermann Ouele, Kabauga Ouele, Kink Ouele, Kawe Pala, Madeleine Père, Allou Sana, Nabo Sana, Thérèse Striggner Scott, David Tetteh, Cyprien Tokoudagba, Tiemoko Youl.

In Cameroon and Nigeria thanks to:

Philippe Adrian, Hadjia Abba Ado, Musa Adolor, H.H. Aminu Ado Bayero, Henri Bulisi, Kamga David, Nike Davies-Okundaye, Michael P. Evans, Musa Hambolou, Chief Muraina Oyelami, Jean-Michel Rousset, Raymond Siaka, Remy Siaka, Takam Toukam, Philippe Gilles Petit de la Villeon, Germain Vigliano, Susanne Wenger, Abu Zaria.

In Ivory Coast thanks to:

Elisée Brou, Pauline, Jean Luc, Sarah, and Vincent Duponchelle, Macline Hien, Monique le Houelleur, Hughe and Muriel le Houelleur, Yousouf and Monique Kone, Yves Lambellin, George Retord.

In Niger and Mali thanks to:

Salia Male Dolo Amahiguere, Barcelo, Papa Moussa Ousman Cisse, Yves de la Croix, Asama Dara, Daodo Diabite, Boubakar Diaby, Alpha Yaya Diana, Omar Diko, Adam Douyou, the family Haidara, Jean François Lanteri, Malick Sidibé, Samuel Sidibé, Aminata Traore, Not Vital.

In Senegal and Mauritania thanks to:

Baubau Samare Agoinit, Philippe Alquier, Diallo Bine Amadou, Mme Coulibaby, Marie-José Crespin, Tidiane Diagana, Bruno Dufour, Babcar Fall, Mr Horma, Jacques Piccard, Moussa Sakho, Amy Saw, Valerie Schlumberger, Dirk Thies, Jean Claude Thoret, Jean Paul Thorré, Mucky and Dieter Wachter.

Special thanks to:

Michèle Champenois who helped me to recall all those many adventures for the introduction.

The publisher and the editor would like to thank Doran Ross, Los Angeles, for his skilled support, and Jean Marc Patras, Paris, for providing the transparencies of the works by Chéri Samba. They would also like to thank the Musée de l'Impression sur Étoffes, Mulhouse, France, and the Collection of The Newark Museum, Newark, New Jersey.

ADDRESSES

ACCOMODATION (HOUSES, GUEST ROOMS, HOTELS)

MOROCCO

DAR EL HANNA (*page 46*)
Information and reservations:
fon: +212 (67) 59 60 27 / fon: +33 (6) 646 430 82
e-mail: j.martial@wanadoo.fr

EGYPT

ADRERE AMELLAL (*page 112*)
Siwa Oasis
Egypt
fon: +20 (2) 736 78 79 / 738 13 27
fax: +20 (2) 735 54 89
e-mail: info@eqi.com.eg

AL MOUDIRA (*page 158*)
Luxor
Egypt
fon: +20 (12) 392 83 32 / 325 13 07
fax: +20 (12) 322 05 28
e-mail: moudirahotel@yahoo.com
www.moudira.com

KENYA

ALAN DONOVAN (*page 188*)
Guest House
Information and reservations:
fon: +254 45 202 32 / +254 721 518 389
e-mail: ahalan@africaonline.co.ke
www.africanheritage.net
www.seekenya.com

In France:
Jean-Paul Merlin
As'Art
3, passage du grand cerf
75002 Paris
fon: +33 (1) 448 890 40
fax: +33 (1) 448 890 41
e-mail: asart@wanadoo.fr

THE GIRAFFE MANOR (*page 202*)
P.O. Box 15004
Langata, Nairobi
Kenya
fon: +254 (20) 89 10 78
fax: +254 (20) 89 09 49
e-mail: giraffem@kenyaweb.com
www.giraffemanor.com

SIROCCO HOUSE (*page 210*)
Guest House
P.O. Box 54667
Nairobi
Information and reservations:
Oria Douglas-Hamilton
fon: +254 (2) 33 48 68
e-mail: oria@iconnet.co.ks

DODO'S TOWER (*page 216*)
P.O. Box 24397
Nairobi
Kenya
fon: +254 (20) 57 46 89
fax: +254 (20) 57 73 81
e-mail: mellifera@swiftkenya.com

HIPPO POINT (*page 228*)
P.O. Box 1852
Naivasha
Kenya
fon: +254 (311) 301 24 / 200 98
fax: +254 (311) 212 95
e-mail: hippo-pt@africaonline.co.ke
www.hippopointkenya.com

KATHARINA SCHMEZER & HERMANN STUCKI (*page 244*)
Information and reservations:
fon: +41 (78) 717 04 75
e-mail: lamu-house@uelischmezer.ch

TANZANIA

NGORONGORO CRATER LODGE (*page 276*)
Information and reservations:
Conservation Corporation Africa
www.ccafrica.com

EMERSON & GREEN (*page 288*)
236 Hurumzi Street
P.O. Box 3417
Stone Town
Zanzibar
Tanzania
fon: +255 (24) 223 01 71
fax: +255 (24) 223 10 38
e-mail: emegre@zanzibar.org
www.zanzibar.org

MNEMBA ISLAND LODGE (*page 296*)
Information and reservations:
Conservation Corporation Africa
www.ccafrica.com

BOTSWANA

MOMBO CAMP (*page 330*)
JAO CAMP (*page 340*)
Information and reservations:
Wilderness Safaris
fon: +27 (11) 807 18 00
fax: +27 (11) 807 21 00
e-mail: enquiry@wilderness.co.za
www.wilderness-safaris.com

MCGUINNESS, JUSTIN: Tunisia Handbook, Bath 2002
(*Footprint Handbooks*)
MCINTYRE, CHRIS: Botswana, Chalfont St Peter, 2003
(*The Bradt Travel Guide*)
MILLER, ALO UND NIKOLAUS: Réunion, Köln 2002,
(*DuMont Reise-Taschenbuch*)

NANTET, BERNARD: Mauritanie, Paris 2001
(*Objectif Aventure, Guide Arthaud*)

OBERG, HEIDRUN: Seychellen. Mauritius. Komoren. Réunion.
Malediven, München/Wien/Zürich 1995 (*Reiseführer Natur, BLV*)

PASSOT, BERNARD: Le Bénin, Paris 1996
Photo-guide des animaux d'Afrique, Lausanne 2001
Pistes du sud tunisien, Calvisson 2000 (*Guide Jacques Gandini*)
Pistes du Maroc, Tome 1: Haut et Moyen Atlas,
Calvisson 2000 (*Guide Jacques Gandini*)
Pistes du Maroc, Tome 2: Le Sud, du Tafilalet à l'Atlantique,
Calvisson 2001 (*Guide Jacques Gandini*)
Pistes du Maroc, Tome 3: De l'Oued Draa à la Seguiet el Hamra,
Calvisson 2002 (*Guide Jacques Gandini*)
Pistes du Maroc, Tome 4: Le Maroc oriental, Calvisson 2003
(*Guide Jacques Gandini*)

QUACK, ULRICH: Mauritius. Réunion, Dormagen 2002
(*Iwanowski's Reisebuchverlag*)

REMY, MYLÈNE: La Côte-d'Ivoire aujourd'hui, Paris 2002
REMY, MYLÈNE: Le Sénégal aujourd'hui, Paris 2000
RICHMOND, SIMON, MURRAY, JON: Cape Town,
Melbourne 2002 (*Lonely Planet*)
RICHMOND, SIMON: South Africa, Lesotho & Swaziland,
Melbourne 2002 (*Lonely Planet*)
ROTTER, PETER: Bergsteigen – Safari – Trekking. Kilimanjaro.
Tanzania, München 2001

SCHETAR-KÖTHE, DANIELA: Tunesien. Land und Leute,
München 1996 (*Polyglott*)
SEMSEK, HANS GÜNTER: Ägypten und Sinai. Pharaonische
Tempel und islamische Tradition, Köln 2001 (*DuMont Kunstreiseführer*)
SOREAU, FRÉDÉRIC: Maroc. Le Grand Sud, Paris 2003 (*Aujourd'hui*)
SWANEY, DEANNA: Namibia, Melbourne 2002 (*Lonely Planet*)

TONDOK, SIGRID UND WIL U. A.: Ägypten individuell,
Bielefeld 2001 (*Reise Know-How*)
Tunisie, Paris 2003 (*Guides Bleus, Hachette*)
Tunisie, Paris 2003 (*Objectif Aventure, Guide Arthaud*)

WATERKAMP, RAINER UND WISNIEWSKI, WINFRIED:
Ostafrika. Kenia, Tanzania, Uganda. Tiere und Pflanzen
entdecken, Stuttgart 1999 (*Kosmos Naturreiseführer*)
WILLETT, DAVID: Tunisia, Melbourne 2001 (*Lonely Planet*)

ILLUSTRATED BOOKS

BALDIZZONE, TIZIANA ET GIANNI: Magiciens de la pluie, Paris 2002
BALFOUR, DARYL AND SHARNA: Simply Safari, New York 2001
BEARD, PETER H.: The End of the Game, London 2000
BECKWITH, CAROL, FISHER, ANGELA: African Ceremonies, New York 1999
BECKWITH, CAROL, FISHER, ANGELA: Unbekanntes Afrika:
Völker und Kulturen zwischen Hochland, Wüste und Ozean, Köln 2000
BERNUS, EDMOND, DUROU, JEAN-MARC: Touaregs. Un Peuple du
désert, Paris 1996
BERTINETTI, MARCELLO: In the Eye of Horus. A Photographer's
Flight Over Egypt, Vercelli 2001
BETTAÏEB, MOHAMMED-SALAH, JABEUR, SALAH, HAMZA, ALYA:
La Tunisie vue du ciel, Aix-en-Provence 1996
BURNS, NATASHA (*Text*), BEDDOW, TIM (*Fotos*): Safari Style.
Wohnideen aus Afrika, Köln 1998

CASTÉRA, JEAN-MARC, PEURIOT, FRANÇOISE, PLOQUIN,
PHILIPPE: Arabesque. Arts décoratifs au Maroc, Courbevoie 1998
COLBORNE, DESMOND (*Text*), DOS SANTOS, SØLVI (*Photos*):
South Africa. Private Worlds, London 1999
COURTNEY-CLARKE, MARGARET: Ndebele. The Art of an African Tribe,
New York 1986
COURTNEY-CLARKE, MARGARET: African Canvas, New York 1990
CRESSOLE, MICHEL: Sur les traces de l'Afrique fantôme, Paris 1990

DANTO BARRY, RAHIM: Portes d'Afrique, Paris 1999
DESJEUX, CATHERINE ET BERNARD: Afriques. Tout partout partager,
Brinon-sur-Sauldre 2001

FISHER, ANGELA: Africa Adorned, London 1987
FONTAINE, JACQUES, GRESSER, PIERRE, FAUQUÉ, NICOLAS
(*photos*): Tunisie. Carrefour des civilisations, Courbevoie/Paris 2000
FRANCK, MARTINE, SOULÉ, BÉATRICE, VOYEUX, MARTINE:
Ousmane Sow, Le soleil en face, Neuilly-sur-Seine 1999
FRASER, CRAIG (*Photos*): Shack Chic. Innovation in the Shack Lands
of South Africa, London 2002

GAEDE, PETER-MATHIAS: Ein Tag im Leben von Afrika, Köln 2002
GEORGE, UWE: Sahara. Expeditionen durch Raum und Zeit, Hamburg
2001

HUET, MICHEL (*Photos*), SAVARY, CLAUDE (*textes*):
Danses d'Afrique, Paris 1994

KRAUSE, AXEL (*Fotos*), SEMSEK, HANS-GÜNTER (*Text*): Ägypten,
Würzburg 2002

LA GUÉRIVIÈRE, JEAN DE: Exploration de l'Afrique noire, Paris 2002
LAINÉ, DANIEL: Rois d'Afrique, Paris 2001
LAUBER, WOLFGANG: Architektur der Dogon. Traditioneller Lehmbau
und Kunst in Mali, München 1998
LAVAUX, CATHERINE: Réunion du battant des lames au sommet,
Paris 1998

BIBLIOGRAPHY

LE GABON DE FERNAND GRÉBERT, 1913–1932, Musée d'etnographie de Genève, Paris 2003

LERAT, JEAN-MARIE: Chez bonne idée. Images du petit commerce en Afrique de l'Ouest, Paris 1990

LOSSKARN, ELKE (*Fotos*), LOSSKARN, DIETER (*Text*): Südafrika, Luzern 2000

LOVATT-SMITH, LISA: Moroccan Interiors, Köln 2003

MARI, CARLO: Auf der Spur des Wassers, München 2000

MARI, CARLO: Safari, München 2003

MARTIN, MICHAEL, ALTMANN, ANDREAS: Unterwegs in Afrika, München 2002

MARTIN, MICHAEL, JAUSLY, DORIS, MAERITZ, KAY, MICUS, STEPHAN: Die Wüsten Afrikas, London 1998

MONLAÙ, LAURENT: Le voyage en Afrique, Paris 2003

MOURAD, KHIREDDINE (*textes*), KERBRAT, MARIE-PIERRE: Arts et traditions du Maroc, Paris 1998

NICKERSON, JACKIE: Afrika. Leben mit der Erde, München 2002

POLIDORI, ROBERT, BACCHIELLI, LIDIANO, DI VITA, ANTONINO, DI VITA-EVRARD, GINETTE: La Libye antique. Cités perdues de l'Empire romain, Paris 1998

RAUZIER, MARIE-PASCALE, TRÉAL, CÉCILE ET RUIZ, JEAN-MICEL (*photos*): Couleur du Maroc, Paris 1999

READER, JOHN, LEWIS, MICHAEL: Africa, Washington, D.C. 2001

RENAUDEAU, MICHEL: Dogon, Paris 2001

RENAUDEAU, MICHEL: Tableaux Dogon, Paris 2002

RICCIARDI, MIRELLA: African Visions. The Diary of an African Photographer, New York 2002

RICCIARDI, MIRELLA: Vanishing Africa, London 1977

RIEFENSTAHL, LENI: Africa, Köln 2002

Sahara. L'Adrar de Mauritanie, Paris 2002

SAINT LÉON, PASCAL MARTIN (*ed.*): Anthologie de la photographie africaine et de l'océan Indien, Paris 1998

SÈBE, ALAIN, SÈBE, BERNY: Sahara: Unbekannte Wüste vom Atlantik bis zum Nil, Stuttgart 2002

SLIM, HEDI (*textes*), FAUQUÉ, NICOLAS (*photos*): La Tunisie antique. De Hannibal à Saint Augustin, Paris 2001

STOELTIE, BARBARA AND RENÉ: Living in Morocco, Köln 2003

TOURNADRE, MICHEL: La Mauritanie, Paris 1996

TRIKI, HAMED, DOVOFAT, ALAIN: Medersa de Marrakech, Aix-en-Provence 1999

TROTHA, DÉSIRÉE V.: Wo sich Himmel und Erde berühren. Tuareg in der Weite der Wüste, München 2003

WENDL, TOBIAS (*Hg.*): Afrikanische Reklamekunst, Wuppertal 2002

WEYER, HELFRIED: Ägypten. Wüste, Nil und Sinai, Steinfurt 2002

WUERFEL, JOE (*Photos*), BEARD, PETER (*Interview*): Sensual Africa, Zurich/New York 2000

Literary BOOKS

ACHEBE, CHINUA:
Things Fall Apart, London 2002
Okonkwo oder Das Alte stürzt, Frankfurt 2002
Le monde s'effondre, Paris 1973

ACHEBE, CHINUA:
Arrow of God, New York 2000
Der Pfeil Gottes, Wuppertal 2003
La flèche de Dieu, Paris 1978

ADAMSON, JOY:
Born Free. A Lioness of Two Worlds, New York 2000
Frei Geboren. Die Geschichte der Löwin Elsa, München 2002

AIDOO, AMA ATA:
Our Sister Killjoy, or, Reflections from a Black Eyed Squint, London 1999
The Dilemma of a Ghost, London 1997

ALLIN, MICHAEL:
Zarafa, London 1999
Zarafa, München 2002
La girafe de Charles X, Paris 2000

ANGELOU, MAYA:
All God's Children Need Travelling Shoes, London 2002

ARMAH, AYI KWEI:
The Beautiful Ones Are Not Yet Born, London 1988
Die Schönen sind noch nicht geboren, Düsseldorf 1984

ARMAH, AYI KWEI:
The Healers: a Historical Novel, Oxford 1993

BÂ, AMADOU HAMPÂTÉ:
The Fortunes of Wangrin, Bloomington 1999
L'étrange destin de Wangrin, Paris 1982

BÂ, MARIAMA:
So Long a Letter, Oxford 2000
Ein so langer Brief: ein afrikanisches Frauenschicksal, München 2002
Une si longue lettre, Paris 2001

BÂ, MARIAMA:
The Scarlet Song, London 1995
Un chant écarlate, Dakar 1998
Der scharlachrote Gesang, Frankfurt 1996

BADIAN, SEYDOU:
Caught in the Storm, Boulder 1998
Sous l'orage, Paris 2000

BADIAN, SEYDOU:
Le sang des masques, Paris 1976

BARLEY, NIGEL:
A Plague of Caterpillars: a Return to the African Bush, London 1989
Die Raupenplage, Stuttgart 1998
Le retour de l'anthropologue, Paris 2002

BARLEY, NIGEL:
The Coast, London 1991

BECKER, FRIEDRICH (*Hg.*):
Afrikanische Märchen, Frankfurt 1988

BELLOW, SAUL:
Henderson the Rain King, London 1996
Der Regenkönig, Bergisch Gladbach 2000
Le Faiseur de pluie, Paris 1961

BEN HAMED CHARHADI, DRISS:
A Life Full of Holes, Edinburgh 1999
Ein Leben voller Fallgruben, Zürich 1992

BEN JELLOUN, TAHAR:
This Blinding Absence of Light, New York 2002
Das Schweigen des Lichts, Berlin 2001
Cette aveuglante absence de lumière, Paris 2002

BEN JELLOUN, TAHAR:
The Sacred Night, Baltimore 2000
Die Nacht der Unschuld, Reinbek bei Hamburg 1991
La nuit sacrée, Paris 1987

BEN JELLOUN, TAHAR:
The Sand Child, Baltimore 2000
Sohn ihres Vaters, Berlin 1986
L'enfant de sable, Paris 1995

BLIXEN, TANIA:
Out of Africa, Frankfurt 2001 (*Penguin Books*)
Jenseits von Afrika, Reinbek bei Hamburg 1999
La ferme africaine, Paris 1978

BOWLES, PAUL:
Let It Come Down, Frankfurt 2000 (*Penguin Books*)
So mag er fallen, München 1990
Après toi le déluge, Paris 1994

BOWLES, PAUL:
The Sheltering Sky, Frankfurt 2000 (*Penguin Books*)
Himmel über der Wüste, Wien 1998
Un thé au Sahara, Paris 1980

BOYLE, T. C.:
Water Music, London 1998
Wassermusik, Reinbek bei Hamburg 1990
Water Music, Paris 1998

BREYTENBACH, BREYTEN:
The True Confessions of an Albino Terrorist, London 1984
Wahre Bekenntnisse eines Albino-Terroristen, Köln 1984

BRINK, ANDRÉ:
The Other Side of Silence, London 2002

CAILLIÉ, RENÉ:
Voyage à Tombouctou, Paris 1996

CARBERRY, JUANITA:
Child of Happy Valley, London 1999
Letzte Tage in Kenia. Meine Kindheit in Afrika, Berlin 2001

CHATWIN, BRUCE:
The Viceroy of Ouidah, London 1998
Der Vizekönig von Ouidah, München 2003

CHOUKRI, MOHAMED:
For Bread Alone, London 1993
Das nackte Brot, Frankfurt 1990
Le Pain nu, Paris 1997

CHRAÏBI, DRISS:
Mother Comes of Age, Washington, D.C. 1984

Die Zivilisation, Mutter!, Zürich 1989
La civilisation, ma Mère!, Paris 1988

CHRISTIE, AGATHA:
Destination Unknown, London 2003
Der unheimliche Weg, Bern 1994
Destination inconnue, Paris 1999

CHRISTIE, AGATHA:
Death on the Nile, New York 2000
Der Tod auf dem Nil, Bern 2001
Mort sur le Nil, Paris 2003

COETZEE, J. M.:
Disgrace, New York/London 2000
Schande, Frankfurt 2001
Disgrâce, Paris 2001

COLLEN, LINDSEY:
Die Wellen von Mauritius, Reinbek bei Hamburg 1998

CONDÉ, MARYSE:
Segu, New York 1996
Segu, München 1990
Ségou, Paris 1996

COUDERC, FRÉDÉRIC:
Prince ébène, Paris 2003

DADIÉ, BERNARD B.:
Climbié, Paris 1956
Climbié, London 1984

DANGAREMBGA, TSITSI:
Nervous Conditions, London 1988
Der Preis der Freiheit, Reinbek bei Hamburg 1993
À fleur de peau, Paris 1993

DEFOE, DANIEL:
Robinson Crusoe, London 2001
Robinson Crusoe, Düsseldorf 2003
Robinson Crusoé, Paris 1997

DIAWARA, MANTHIA:
In Search of Africa, Cambridge 1998
En quête d'Afrique, Paris 2001

DIBBA, EBOU:
Chaff on the Wind, London 1986

DIRIE, WARIS:
Desert Dawn, London 2002
Nomadentochter, München 2002
L'aube du désert, Paris 2002

DOUGLAS-HAMILTON, IAIN AND ORIA:
Among the Elephants, New York 1988
Unter Elefanten, Bergisch Gladbach 1989

DUGARD, MARTIN:
Into Africa: the Epic Adventures of Stanley and Livingstone, London 2003

DURRELL, GERALD:
The Bafut Beagles, Harmondsworth 1986
Die Spürhunde des großen Fon: auf Kleintierfang in Kamerun, Wien 1957

DURRELL, GERALD:
A Zoo in My Luggage, Bath 1994
Ein Koffer voller Tiere: Ich fange meinen eigenen Zoo, Frankfurt 1992

BIBLIOGRAPHY

DURRELL, LAWRENCE:
    The Alexandria Quartet, London 2001
    Das Alexandria-Quartett, Reinbek bei Hamburg 1977
    Le quatuor d'Alexandrie, Paris 1992

EDBERG, ROLF:
    The Dream of Kilimanjaro, London 1979
EQUIANO, OLAUDAH:
    The Life of Olaudah Equiano or Gustavus Vassa, the African,
    Mineola, New York 1999
    Die Merkwürdige Lebensgeschichte des Sklaven Olaudah
    Equiano, von ihm selbst veröffentlicht im Jahre 1789,
    Frankfurt 1990

FANON, FRANTZ:
    Wretched of the Earth, Frankfurt 2001 (*Penguin Books*)
    Die Verdammten dieser Erde, Frankfurt 1981
    Les Damnés de la Terre, Paris 2002
FORESTER, CECIL SCOTT:
    The African Queen, Harmondsworth 1980
    Die „African Queen", Berlin 1999
FORSYTH, FREDERICK:
    The Dogs of War, London 1996
    Die Hunde des Krieges, München 2001
FOX, JAMES:
    White Mischief, New York 1998
    Weißes Verhängnis. Die letzten Tage in Kenya, Zürich 1988
FRANK, KATHERINE:
    A Voyager Out: The Life of Mary Kingsley, New York 1991
FULLER, ALEXANDRA:
    Don't Let's Go to the Dogs Tonight, London 2003

GALLMANN, KUKI:
    African Nights, Frankfurt 1995 (*Penguin Books*)
    Afrikanische Nächte, München 1999
GALLMANN, KUKI:
    I Dreamed of Africa, London 2000
    Ich träumte von Afrika, München 2000
    Je rêvais de l'Afrique, Paris 2000
GARY, ROMAIN:
    The Roots of Heaven, London 1973
    Les racines du ciel, Paris 2002
    Die Wurzeln des Himmels, München 1985
GERCKE, STEFANIE:
    Ich kehre zurück nach Afrika, München 2002
GOLDING, WILLIAM:
    An Egyptian Journal, London 1989
    Ein ägyptisches Tagebuch. Reisen, um glücklich zu sein,
    München 1987
GORDIMER, NADINE:
    July's People, Frankfurt 2001 (*Penguin Books*)
    Julys Leute, Frankfurt 1991
    Ceux de July, Paris 1992
GOWDY, BARBARA:
    The White Bone, London 2000

    Der weiße Knochen, München 2000
    Un lieu sûr, Arles 2000

HEMINGWAY, ERNEST:
    Green Hills of Africa, London 1996
    Die grünen Hügel Afrikas, Reinbek bei Hamburg 1999
    Les vertes collines d'Afrique, Paris 1949
HOFMANN, CORINNE:
    Die weiße Massai, München 2000
    La Massaï blanche, Paris 2000
HOVE, CHENJERAI:
    Ancestors, London 1996
    Ahnenträume, München 2000
    Ancêtres, Arles 2002
HUXLEY, ELSPETH:
    The Flame Trees of Thika. Memories of an African Childhood,
    London 1998
    Die Flammenbäume von Thika. Erinnerungen an eine Kindheit in Afrika,
    Bergisch Gladbach 1988

JACQ, CHRISTIAN:
    Im Bann des Pharaos, Bern/München/Wien 2002
    L'affaire Toutankhamon, Paris 1992
JORIS, LIEVE:
    Mali Blues, Melbourne 1998
    Mali Blues. Ein afrikanisches Tagebuch, München 2000
    Mali Blues. Je chanterai pour toi, Arles 2002
JOUBERT, BEVERLY ET DERECK:
    Grands chasseurs sous la lune. Les lions du Savuti, Paris 2000

KANE, CHEIKH HAMIDOU:
    Ambiguous Adventure, Oxford 1989
    L'aventure ambiguë, Paris 1998
    Der Zwiespalt des Samba Diallo: Erzählung aus Senegal, Frankfurt 1980
KANT, IMMANUEL, HENSCHEID, ECKHARD:
    Der Neger (Negerl), Frankfurt 1985
KAYE, MARY MARGARET:
    Trade Wind, Bath 1984
    Tod in Sansibar, München 1990
    Zanzibar, Paris 1982
KESSEL, JOSEPH:
    Le lion, Paris 1966
KORNHERR, HANNELORE:
    Sehnsucht nach Kenia. Ein afrikanisches Reisetagebuch, Berlin 2002
KOUROUMA, AHMADOU:
    Waiting for the Vote of the Wild Animals, Charlottesville 2001
    En attendant le vote des bêtes sauvages, Paris 2000

LAING, B. KOJO:
    Search Sweet Country, London 1987
    Die Sonnensucher, München 1995
LAYE, CAMARA:
    The African Child, London 1989
    L'enfant noir, Paris 1994
    Einer aus Karussa, Zürich 1954

LAYE, CAMARA:
The Radiance of the King, New York 2001
Le regard du roi, Paris 1986
Der Blick des Königs, Berlin 1983
LESSING, DORIS:
The Grass is Singing, London 1994
Afrikanische Tragödie, Frankfurt 1995
LOTI, PIERRE:
Morocco, New York 2002
Im Zeichen der Sahara, München 2000
Au Maroc, Saint-Cyr-sur-Loire 1990

MAALOUF, AMIN:
Leo Africanus, New York 1988
Leo Africanus: Der Sklave des Papstes, Frankfurt 2000
Léon l'Africain, Paris 1988
MAHFOUZ, NAGUIB:
Arabian Nights and Days, London/New York 1995
Die Nacht der Tausend Nächte, Zürich 2000
Les mille et une nuits, Arles 2001
MAHFOUZ, NAGUIB:
The Cairo Trilogy. Palace Walk, Palace of Desire, Sugar Street, New York 2001
La trilogie, Paris 1993
MANDELA, NELSON:
Long Walk to Freedom, London 1995
Der lange Weg zur Freiheit, Frankfurt 1997
Un long chemin vers la liberté, Paris 1997
MANKELL, HENNING:
Der Chronist der Winde, München 2002
The White Lioness: A Mystery, Frankfurt 2003 (Penguin Books)
Die weiße Löwin, München 1998
MARKHAM, BERYL:
West with the Night, London 2001
Westwärts mit der Nacht. Mein Leben als Fliegerin in Afrika, München 2001
Vers l'ouest avec la nuit, Paris 1995
MARTELLI, GEORGE:
Livingstone's River. A History of the Zambezi Expedition, 1858–1864, London 1970
MATTHIESSEN, PETER:
Silences africains, Paris 1994
MEMMI, ALBERT:
The Pillar of Salt, Boston 1992
Die Salzsäule. Biographischer Roman, Hamburg 1995
La statue de sel, Paris 1993
MÉNARD, JEAN-FRANÇOIS:
La ville du désert et de l'eau, Paris 1997
MERNISSI, FATIMA:
Scheherazade Goes West. Different Cultures, Different Harems, New York 2001
Harem. Westliche Phantasien, östliche Wirklichkeit, Freiburg 2000
Le harem et l'occident, Paris 2001
MERNISSI, FATIMA:
Dreams of Trespass: Tales of a Harem Girlhood, Massachusetts 1995

Der Harem in uns. Die Furcht vor dem anderen und die Sehnsucht der Frauen, Freiburg 2000
Rêves de femmes: Une enfance au harem, Paris 1996
MOIRET, JOSEPH MARIE:
Memoirs of Napoleon's Egyptian Expedition 1798–1801, London 2001

NAIPAUL, V. S.:
A Bend in the River, London 2002
An der Biegung des großen Flusses, München 2002
À la courbe du fleuve, Paris 1982
NAIPAUL, V.S.:
Finding the Centre: Two Narratives, London 1985
NAIPAUL, V. S.:
North of South. An African Journey, Frankfurt 1997 (Penguin Books)
Au nord du Sud. Un voyage africain, Monaco 1992
NAZER, MENDE, LEWIS, DAMIEN:
Sklavin, München 2002

OGOBARA DOLO, SEKOU:
La mère des masques. Un Dogon raconte, Paris 2002
OKRI, BEN:
The Famished Road, London 1991
Die hungrige Straße Köln, 1994
OUOLOGUEM, YAMBO:
Bound to Violence, London 1986
Le devoir de violence, Paris 2003
Das Gebot der Gewalt, München 1969

PATON, ALAN:
Cry, the Beloved Country. A Story of Comfort in Desolation, London 1998
Denn sie sollen getröstet werden, Frankfurt 1988
Pleure, ô pays bien aimé, Paris 1992

RICARD, ALAIN:
Voyages de découvertes en Afrique. Anthologie 1790–1890, Paris 2000
RICHBURG, KEITH B.:
Out of America. A Black Man Confronts Africa, San Diego, California 1998
Jenseits von Amerika. Eine Konfrontation mit Afrika, dem Land meiner Vorfahren, Berlin 2000
ROSS, MARK C.:
Dangerous Beauty. Life and Death in Africa. True Stories from a Safari Guide, New York 2001
Afrika. Das letzte Abenteuer. Die Geschichte eines Safariführers, Berlin 2000
RUETE, EMILY:
Memoirs of an Arabian Princess from Zanzibar. An Autobiography, Zanzibar 1998
Leben im Sultanspalast. Memoiren aus dem 19. Jahrhundert, Berlin 2000
Mémoires d'une princesse arabe, Paris 1991

SAX LEDGER, FIONA:
Mr Bigstuff and the Goddess of Charm. Parties, Cars, Love and Ambition South of the Sahara, London 2000
SCHOLL-LATOUR, PETER:
Afrikanische Totenklage. Der Ausverkauf des Schwarzen Kontinents, München 2003

BiBLiOGraPHY

SHAKESPEARE, WILLIAM:
Antony and Cleopatra, Frankfurt 1994 (*Penguin Books*)
Antonius und Cleopatra, Ditzingen 1992
Antoine et Cléopâtre, Paris 1999

SEMBENE, OUSMANE:
God's Bits of Wood, London 1995
Gottes Holzstücke, Frankfurt 1988
Les bouts de bois de dieu, Paris 1994

SEMBÈNE, OUSMANE:
Xala, London 1987
Xala: die Rache des Bettlers, Wuppertal 1997
Xala, Paris 1995

SIENKIEWICZ, HENRYK:
Desert and Wilderness, Warsaw 1991

SISÒKÒ, FA-DIGI:
The Epic of Son-Jara: a West African Tradition, Bloomington, Indiana 1992

SOUZA, CARL DE:
Les jours Kaya, Paris 2000

STANLEY, HENRY MORTON:
How I Found Livingstone, Mineola 2002
Wie ich Livingstone fand, Stuttgart 1995
Comment j'ai retrouvé Livingstone, Arles 1994

STRATHERN, OONA:
Traveller's Literary Companion to Africa, Brighton 1994

TIMM, UWE:
Morenga, New York 2003
Morenga, München 2000

TUTUOLA, AMOS:
My Life in the Bush of Ghosts, New York 1994
Mein Leben im Busch der Geister, Berlin 1991
Ma vie dans la brousse des fantômes, Paris 1993

TUTUOLA, AMOS: Palm Wine Drinkard, London 1994
Der Palmweintrinker, Zürich 1994
L'ivrogne dans la brousse, Paris 1990

VERA, YVONNE:
Butterfly Burning, New York 2000
Schmetterling in Flammen, München 2001

VOLK, MORITZ (*Hg.*):
Afrika, meine Liebe. Ein Lesebuch, München 2002

WOOD, BARBARA:
Green City in the Sun, London 2001
Rote Sonne, schwarzes Land, Frankfurt 2000

WRIGHT, RICHARD:
Black Power: a Record of Reactions in a Land of Pathos, New York 1995
Schwarze Macht: zur afrikanischen Revolution, Hamburg 1956
Puissance noire, Paris 1955

ZWEIG, STEFANIE:
Nirgendwo in Afrika, München 2002
Une enfance africaine. Roman autobiographique, Monaco 2002

INDEX

imprint

© 2008 TASCHEN GmbH
Hohenzollernring 53, D-50672 Köln
www.taschen.com

Original edition:
© 2003 TASCHEN GmbH

To stay informed about upcoming TASCHEN titles,
please request our magazine at www.taschen.com/magazine
or write to TASCHEN, Hohenzollernring 53, D-50672 Cologne, Germany,
contact@taschen.com, Fax: +49-221-254919.
We will be happy to send you a free copy of our magazine
which is filled with information about all of our books.

EDITED BY
Angelika Taschen, Cologne

DESIGN
Sense/Net, Andy Disl and Birgit Reber, Cologne

PRODUCTION
Ute Wachendorf, Cologne

PROJECT COORDINATION AND TEXT EDITED BY
Christiane Blass, Susanne Klinkhamels, Cologne

EDITORIAL COORDINATION BY
Julia Krumhauer, Cologne

ENGLISH TRANSLATION
Anthony Roberts, Lupiac

GERMAN TRANSLATION
Anne Brauner, Cologne

Printed in China
ISBN 978–3–8365–0870–4